D0007074

John

Kenneth

Galbraith **&** His

Critics

OTHER BOOKS BY CHARLES HESSION

Co-author with S. M. Miller and C. Stoddarts
THE DYNAMICS OF THE AMERICAN ECONOMY
(Knopf) 1956

Co-author with H. Sardy, ASCENT TO AFFLUENCE:
A History of American Economic Development
(Allyn and Bacon, Inc.) 1970

Co-author with W. Adams, THE STRUCTURE OF
AMERICAN INDUSTRY (Macmillan) 1971

John Kenneth Galbraith & His Critics

CHARLES H. HESSION

Department of Economics

Brooklyn College

Introduction by PROFESSOR ROBERT LEKACHMAN

NEW AMERICAN LIBRARY
TIMES MIRROR

New York

724340

To MARIE—

For Everything

Copyright © 1972 by Charles H. Hession

Introduction Copyright © 1972 by Robert Lekachman

All rights reserved. No part of this work may be reproduced or transmitted in any form by any means now conceived or to be conceived, electronic or mechanical, including photocopying and recording, or by any information storage or retrieval system, without permission in writing from the publisher.

Library of Congress Catalog Card Number: 78-176428

Published by The New American Library, Inc.,

1301 Avenue of the Americas, New York, New York 10019

Published simultaneously in Canada

by George J. McLeod, Ltd., Toronto

Distributed by W. W. Norton & Company, Inc.,

55 Fifth Avenue, New York, New York 10003

First Printing 1972

PRINTED IN THE UNITED STATES OF AMERICA

Preface

In 1972 John Kenneth Galbraith will be president of the American Economic Association, having been elected to that honorific post during the preceding year by his peers in the guild of professional economists. Aside from that fact, this would appear to be an opportune time to review and evaluate his major work on economics. The dust of controversy surrounding some of his books has settled a bit, permitting us to see them in better perspective. Furthermore, with the passage of time since their publication there has been a growing recognition of their significance and importance for the understanding of contemporary American society. As one evidence of this we may note that the authoritative Professor Paul Samuelson recently stated that "the objective scholar must assert that economics will never be quite the same as in the days before the Galbraithian trilogy."[1] From the context of this statement, we know that the reference is to *American Capitalism, The Affluent Society,* and *The New Industrial State.* These books are closely examined in the following pages.

I have written this book mainly for the nonprofessional reader. I hope that it will promote a better understanding of Galbraithian economics and that, in addition, it will enable such a person to see his ideas from an angle other than that of their persuasive author. In this connection, it has been pointed out that there is perhaps a dangerous asymmetry involved in Galbraith's work. "Mr. Galbraith has written for the general public. He has been answered by his fellow economists in learned journals, particularly in the far from lively pages of the *American Economic Review* whose public is surely smaller than the *Women's Wear Daily.* . . . Mr. Galbraith's audience, being innocent of its existence [i.e., of the professional criticism], accepts for want of an accessible alternative his side of the issue."[2]

Whether one accepts the implications of this statement or not, there is much to be gained from reading the stimulating dialogue between Galbraith and his critics on the

[1] P. A. Samuelson, *Economics: An Introductory Course* (8th ed., New York: McGraw-Hill, 1970), p. 488.
[2] R. Lekachman, "Economics for Everybody?", *Commentary,* January 1956, p. 79.

important themes of his books. The issues he considers—countervailing power and its effects, economic affluence and the quality of life in modern society, the functioning of the "industrial state"—are questions of deep national concern.

In order to make the intellectual exchange between Galbraith and his critics as clear as possible, I have summarized the principal books under consideration and placed them in their historical context. This volume, therefore, is fairly self-contained and comprehensive; it should not be necessary for the reader to study the Galbraithian texts themselves in order to comprehend the analyses of his critics. Where applicable, I have added my own critical comment and evaluation of the conflicting points of view.

In writing this book, I have been able to draw upon the experience of more than a decade and a half in using Galbraith's books in my classes in economics and social science at Brooklyn College. I have treated some of his ideas in two earlier publications.[3]

I have been fortunate to have had the manuscript read by Professors Robert Lekachman and S. M. Miller; the finished product, however, is solely my responsibility. I might note that Professor Galbraith gave me an initial opportunity to interview him when the book was in the planning stages, but otherwise completely ignored my efforts, benevolently leaving himself and his books at the mercy of my critical dissection.

I should explain that while Galbraith has often shown considerable interest in the critical reaction to his books upon their publication, he has generally tended to discount the value of critics. In one place he writes, ". . . In social matters critics are an interim phenomenon. Given a little time, circumstances will prove you either right or wrong. . . ."[4] Without seeking to contradict his dictum, we consider in this book both the verdict of his contemporary critics and the reception that historical circumstances have thus far accorded his ideas.

C. H. HESSION

Brooklyn, N.Y.
June 1971

[3] I refer to C. H. Hession, S. M. Miller, and C. Stoddart, *The Dynamics of the American Economy* (New York: A. A. Knopf, 1956), and C. H. Hession and H. Sardy, *Ascent to Affluence: A History of American Economic Development* (Boston: Allyn and Bacon, 1969).

[4] J. K. Galbraith, *The Affluent Society* (2nd ed. revised, Boston: Houghton Mifflin, 1969), p. xxvi.

Contents

Introduction

ROBERT LEKACHMAN
State University of New York at Stony Brook

Economics deals with jobs and money, topics of an interest to humankind only slightly inferior to food and sex. Nevertheless, most economics is written with all the verve of a manual of dentistry, accounting, or sanitary engineering. No doubt this animadversion means no more than the tendency of economists in the company of other technical specialists to perform essentially for each other. Any guild judges its members' merits according to appropriately esoteric canons, certainly not by the applause of the ignorant multitude. In fact, it is in order to deter the meddling of the great unwashed that certified experts carefully erect their barriers of specialized terminology. Behind them professionals can relax and play their fashionable intellectual games, which in economics feature mathematics in increasing doses. The more highly developed is the social science, the more arcane is the tongue in which its mysteries are communicated. Sociology is less incomprehensible than economics. Political science is still readier of general access, and anybody can read history, a subject of accordingly lower prestige. I hasten to add that the other social sciences are rapidly gaining on economics. Soon they will be unintelligible too.

For an individual scholar, the conventional path to the professional summit is dotted with appropriate academic appointments, frequently cited journal articles (in the right places), and severe monographs. After appropriate seasoning, their author is anointed president of the MLA, ASA, APSA, AHA, or whatever. For a year he then speaks as his brethren's official voice and acts as the symbol of their calling.

These well-known attributes of academic gamesmanship come to mind because the hero of Professor Hession's judicious evaluation is so conspicuous a violator of his trade union's code. Although years ago he wrote technical articles

ix

in such prestigious places as the *American Economic Review,* his reputation is founded not upon them but upon three major works, *American Capitalism, The Affluent Society,* and *The New Industrial State,* which were deliberately aimed at large audiences of noneconomists. He has shamelessly surrounded these *opera* with such *jeux d'esprit* as *The Great Crash,* a mordant re-creation of 1929 and after; *The Scotch,* the very model of a lighthearted autobiography; and *Ambassador's Journal,* an acerbic record of an Indian tour of duty during the Kennedy years. Worse still, he has written a novel, commented upon Indian art and American public architecture, and otherwise conducted himself as a man of letters, cultural critic, and student of society. The man is a disgrace to his profession.

In the presence of these shortcomings, it is accordingly heartwarming to note that the 1972 president of the American Economic Association (AEA) will be none other than that same adroit gadfly, John Kenneth Galbraith. The honor does credit to AEA members even if it cannot accurately be claimed that most economists have been converted to countervailing power, social imbalance, dependence effects, or the central roles of the technostructure and the educational and scientific estate. Indeed, Professor Hession carefully charts the frequently hostile professional response to each of these notions. At the least, economists have identified in their new leader a force and influence which they cannot ignore.

As even casual readers and severe critics of Galbraith usually attest, the man writes a lovely English prose—witty, supple, eloquent, and edged with that sheen of malice which the fallen sons of Adam always find attractive when it is directed at targets other than themselves. Even economists are accessible to aesthetic pleasures. Nevertheless, Galbraith's mastery of the linguistic arts only partly explains his professional honors and popular triumphs. People listen to Galbraith because he talks about important subjects in imaginative and iconoclastic terms. Two of these subjects, power and culture, have steadily engaged his mind, as seldom have they interested most economists.

Quite the contrary. Since the days of Adam Smith, economists have conducted a love affair with competition. Competitive markets can be depended upon to allocate resources efficiently, reward ambitious workers, and respond accurately to shifting consumer tastes. Somewhat artlessly, John Stuart Mill in 1848 alleged that "only through the principle of competition has political economy any pretension to the character of a science." Although no self-respecting, living price theorist would accept so sweeping a statement, economists *do,* nearly two centuries after the *Wealth of Nations,* deploy much better explanations of competitive than of noncompetitive markets. Rather naturally, they concentrate upon cautious extension of comfortable boundaries in preference to dangerous explorations of uncharted analytical waters.

For men and women who enjoy a quiet life, there is a comforting corollary. Once one assumes that the economy is generally competitive, the necessity to analyze the location and concentration of economic power vanishes. A given entrepreneur may have the black soul of a monopolist, but he is too weak and small and his competitors far too numerous, to allow him to impose his will upon the community. The fierce rivalry which he cannot avoid yields him profit only when he reduces his prices, improves his product, and, by no intention of his own, benefits his customers. The economist can safely leave power to the political scientists who have their own defanging methods available, a story for another day.

Not even college freshmen believe this tale. Unaided common sense informs the students, their siblings, and their parents that America is a land dominated by the large and the powerful. Public utilities are universally local or national monopolies. Credit cards and credit-rating bureaus remind one and all that financial slips (or computer errors) will be broadcast to the 50 states and branch offices abroad. Annually *Fortune* celebrates the nation's 500 industrial goliaths. Recently it added a second team, 500 slightly smaller corporations. When they buy a car or an appliance, consumers are invited to sign what lawyers call contracts of adhesion, documents which purchasers can take or leave but seldom amend. A prospective tenant discovers when he rents an apartment (if he can locate such a thing) that the lease, still another contract of adhesion, has been drawn up by the local real estate board for the benefits of its membership—landlords. During a botulism scare during the summer of 1971, it emerged that a single company apparently made all the vichyssoise that a thirsty nation drank, under numerous labels.

In many ways, giant corporations exercise the power of private governments, subject to fewer checks than are applied to legislatures and presidents by courts and each other. General Motors could not behave like a Seventh Avenue garment manufacturer even if it wished to. The corporation's market weight is so enormous that even relatively minor pricing, styling, research and development, expansion, and location decisions send tremors through the economy. To rewrite the late Charles Wilson, what's good for General Motors may or may not be good for the country, but what GM does makes one hell of a difference to the rest of us.

At this juncture the lacunae in conventional market analysis are embarrassingly large. Received price theory simply fails adequately to explain the conduct of the concentrated industries which dominate the American economy. It is one of Galbraith's achievements that he has grappled fruitfully with this vital topic. *American Capitalism* floated the agreeable hypothesis that, at least when inflation did not facilitate collusion between manufacturers and unions, or wholesalers and retailers, concentrations of economic power generated their own checks. Countervailing power sometimes was exercised by militant trade unions which curtailed management power over industrial discipline and individual rewards. Large-caliber retailers like Sears and Macy's bargained hard and successfully to extract some of the oligopolistic profits from their suppliers, on the believable threat that otherwise they would start making the tires, the TV sets, or the cornflakes for themselves. In the absence of adequate private countervailance, the government, as it did during the New Deal, can prop up the market's weaker parties.

More recently, Galbraith's analysis of power has taken a different twist. *The New Industrial State* concentrates upon the internal management of the major corporation. A major role is played by the "technostructure," a collective noun for the army of engineers, accountants, lawyers, economists, personnel specialists, media manipulators, and other experts whose talents are pooled in the committee conduct of corporate affairs. In the new prominence of the experts, Galbraith sees reason for hope. For one thing, the experts soften old-fashioned, ruthless profit maximization by attention to growth, security, and even standards of professional workmanship. Still more important is the relationship between the technostructure and the educational and scientific estate, the "rapidly growing body of educators and research scientists," who are "directly nurtured by the industrial system." Although Galbraith is well aware of the danger that the technostructure may influence the educators and scientists rather more than the other way around, he asserts that the "educational and scientific estate requires only a strongly creative political hand to become a decisive instrument of political power." At the least, then, the intriguing possibility exists that cooperation between a technostructure increasingly dependent upon the university and an increasingly self-conscious (and self-confident) educational and scientific estate, will improve corporate conduct and redefine corporate goals.

One needn't fully endorse this analysis in order to emphasize two of its merits. Galbraith may have teased his profession into paying some systematic attention to wealth and power. A Galbraithian can appropriately challenge critics to produce their own version of how the economy operates and the mighty behave. If competition here has the effect its votaries have long assumed, then mighty leaps toward intellectual clarity should be in prospect.

Galbraith has served his public and his colleagues well in another way. During recent gloomy economic weather, he has with only a few (but an increasing number of) allies, preserved some shreds of public credibility for economic policy. I have in mind the remarkable combination of persistent inflation, high unemployment, and soggy rhetoric which Nixon Game Plans I, II, and III have conferred upon an unready nation. Economists can only sob when the Secretary of the Treasury and the Chairman of the Council of Economic Advisers inform Congress and the nation that nothing much can be done about unemployment until inflation, which has, by their account, only ceased to accelerate, is brought under control.

Republicans are as likely as Democrats to be God's creatures. If the current administration's economic officials appear slightly dim of wit, it is because free market ideology conceals reality and interferes with the application of needed remedies. Howling in the wilderness, Galbraith has uttered good sense and good economics. Major corporations, large trade unions, and the leading professional associations do exercise substantial control over prices, fees, and wages. They raise all three even when sales and jobs are scarce. The appropriate way to handle private power is through public regulation.

Because Galbraith faces the issue of size and power, he can advocate compulsory wage and price controls as the missing centerpiece of effective national economic policy. Two and a half years should suffice as demonstration of the inadequacy of the conventional blend of fiscal and monetary policy in a concentrated economy. Even so cautious and conservative a figure as Federal Reserve Chairman

Arthur F. Burns has conceded the desirability of a wage-price review board, though he has stopped far short of compulsory controls.

Economists last basked in public acclaim in 1964 and early 1965, a period when the Kennedy-Johnson tax cut was achieving its predicted effects: Economic growth accelerated, unemployment obediently shrank, and prices remained practically stable. Since mid-1965 the pragmatic American public has had little reason to applaud economists, least of all since January 1969. Official economists who urge their countrymen to put up with high unemployment for a while longer not only display unpleasing insensitivity to human suffering but something akin to intellectual insolvency. Good as it may be for the soul, confession is unlikely to enhance the sinner's public reputation.

Galbraith and those of like mind are a standing reminder that economics need not be as dismal as the Nixon administration insists. Sounder policy—effective controls, increased social and environmental expenditure, lower interest rates—is available. All that is lacking is the will and the wit.[1]

In Galbraith's vision of society, power and culture are closely entwined. Thus the mounting crisis in the division of resources between private consumption and public use, the theme of *The Affluent Society,* derives in part from the reluctance of corporate leaders and conservative politicians to enlist government compassionately and creatively to increase communal amenity and protect the weak. By old and bad business tradition, government is a machine which cranks out shipbuilding subsidies, oil import tickets, depletion allowances, accelerated depreciation, and guarantees to shaky defense contractors. For the rest, "free" enterprisers should be allowed to cultivate their profitable gardens, whatever the incidental public harms or environmental damages. The economist's external diseconomies are of no concern to the businessmen who profit from fouling the air that other people breathe and the streams in which they might swim.

This allocative crisis has a cultural component. Americans, who by comparison to the citizens of other advanced

---

[1] President Nixon's belated conversion on August 15, 1971, and after to an incomes policy reflects, I fear, more political apprehension than intellectual enlightenment. It remains to be seen whether belated intelligence will rectify past error.

societies are lightly taxed, seem perpetually upon or over the verge of tax rebellion. Galbraith's plausible but depressing interpretation of the great American aversion to taxes centers upon the commercialization of the private sector. A vast marketing and advertising mechanism bombards every American in his home, en route to his job, and at his work with the insistent message—buy, buy, buy. Even as a man's real income grows, his unsatisfied wants expand still more rapidly. Taxes simply narrow his opportunity to fill his yearnings.

He is the more afflicted because no parallel machinery of propaganda instructs him in the virtues of the public goods that his taxes purchase. Who advertises public education? Medical research? Rat control? Enforcement of sanitary standards in food processing plants? Out of self-interest as well as ideological faith, free enterprisers habitually ridicule government as corrupt, inefficient, unimaginative, bureaucratic, or all four simultaneously.

This distortion has a fateful consequence. The implicit preference system of the public is severely distorted. People feel no richer in the presence of rising real income not only because their expectations rise more sharply, but also because of the sleazy environment in which both work and the pursuit of private pleasure must take place. The implicit demand for a seemly environment can only with great difficulty be gratified by a society which has devoted its talents to exalting commercial culture at the expense of general amenity.

The ultimate triumph of private enterprise is its capacity to shape consumer markets according to the convenience of the major suppliers. Although producers mercifully do sometimes slip, the number of Edsels is small. For the most part, the customers, at least until recently, have obediently responded to the commands of the corporate ringmasters. Yet as even the brighter animal-tamers are beginning to recognize, too much attention to private profit and too little heed to the environment are eventually harmful even to the affluent and the powerful who cannot escape a common human need to breathe.

I have said enough to demonstrate that among economists Galbraith is an original. He believes in neither the empirical importance of market competition, nor that orthodox doctrine of consumer demand which asserts that consumer preferences, sprung miraculously from heaven, determine the pattern of sales and output. By the lights of many economists, not much is left of their subject after market organization is explained politically and socially, and consumer behavior is interpreted culturally.

One might defiantly retort that if what Galbraith does is not economics, then so much the worse for economists. A better response is available. The best economists have broken the bounds of received technique and expanded the ambit of economic speculation, after the various fashions of Keynes, Mill, Marx, and Smith. For the moment, I feel a certain confidence that mainstream economics, after a prolonged flirtation with models, abstraction, pure theory, and mathematic apparatus, is returning slowly to the older themes of political economy.

Recent political and public emphasis upon pollution and the natural environment challenges economists to pursue their inquiries far beyond safe, technical comparisons of the best variety of effluent charges or the relative merits of taxes and bounties. A genuine public impulse to preserve (or restore) a civilized environment demands a Galbraithian switch of priorities, a massive reallocation of resources from comparatively trivial private consumption to urgent public improvement.

In short, Galbraith is relevant and most of official economics increasingly irrelevant to the major public issues of the 1970s: the vexing collision between full employment and price stability, dangerous concentrations of wealth and power, cultural overemphasis upon private production and private consumption, starvation of the public services, and private affluence in the midst of public squalor.

If economics in the years to come is to be again as socially useful as occasionally in the past it has been, then economists will need to redefine their subject comfortably to house such topics. No man alive has done more to this end than John Kenneth Galbraith. Professor Hession deserves our gratitude for his illuminating an invaluable map of Galbraith's country.

1 The Making
of a Social Critic

"THE IMPORTANCE OF BEING
GALBRAITH"*

In a cover story devoted to John Kenneth Galbraith, *Time* magazine recently referred to him as "the most quotable—and possibly influential—critic of United States society." It went on to state, "He has become an all-purpose critic in the United States and beyond . . . [and yet] to some, he is just an all-purpose bore."[1] Regardless of the opinion that may be held concerning Galbraith and his works, there can be little disagreement about the omnipresence of this very conspicuous, six-foot-eight-inch Harvard University professor. As best-selling author, social critic, confidant of Presidents, and former ambassador to India, he has been very much in the American public eye (and ear).

Professor Galbraith has been an indefatigable scholar, public servant, and political activist in the last quarter-century. By one estimate, that of his secretary, between 1959 and 1968 he produced no fewer than 8 nonfiction works, a novel, 32 magazine articles, 54 book reviews, 35 letters to the editor, 8 introductions to books, numerous lectures, and major speeches for Lyndon Johnson and Edward, Robert, and John F. Kennedy. Earlier he had advised and written speeches for Adlai Stevenson. More recently, he has been national chairman of Americans for Democratic Action. In an allegedly one-dimensional society, he has been a multidimensional man with an extraordinary influence on the thinking of his time.

Opinions of his work, both in his profession of economics

* Acknowledgment is due David Halberstam, whose article in *Harper's*, November 1967, pp. 47 ff., bears this title.
[1] "The Great Mogul," *Time*, February 16, 1968, p. 24.

and among the laity generally, vary greatly. Paul Samuelson, one of the nation's leading mathematical economists, has said of him, "He is, *par excellence,* a non-economist's economist. . . . If J. K. Galbraith is the Pied Piper of the new generation, he is the *bête noire* of the corporate world. Sage of the Mixed Economy, he is part of our affluence."[2] Seymour Harris, another distinguished economist and friend of Galbraith, writes, "His tremendous vogue is very annoying to many university economists. . . . They reason that anyone with that kind of *rapprochement* with the general public just has to be a lousy economist. It's not true. He's the most read economist of all time. Not even Adam Smith has been read as much." While economist James Warburg asserts that Galbraith "is the most outstanding explorer of economics since Keynes," Dean Neil Jacoby of UCLA's Graduate School of Business Administration states, "Mr. Galbraith is a very talented journalist and a bad economist. I wouldn't have him on my faculty."[3]

The very success of some of Galbraith's books may have contributed to a degree of academic envy. Certainly the obsolescent public image of the college professor, one of shabby gentility, absentmindedness, and impecuniosity, is defied by this very alert, articulate "jet-prof" whose best-selling books have put him in the higher income brackets and in the sophisticated ranks of cosmopolitan society. All this has, of course, its adverse side. For example, someone told Galbraith after the publication of *The Affluent Society* that all he needed to finish him at Harvard was for Hollywood to make a movie of it. Sniping and carping criticism too comes from uninformed quarters. Thus Al Capp, the cartoonist, writing in a conservative business journal, calls Galbraith "the first hippie economist." Quoting him as writing, "Beauty is worth the sacrifice of some increase in the GNP," Capp adds, "We haven't had an economist like that since Edna St. Vincent Millay."[4]

Galbraith's incisive writing has been graced by a polished literary style and a mordant wit which have contributed to his popularity with readers. In his hands, economics is not the dismal science, as Carlyle dubbed it; his exposition of the subject can be read and understood "without tears." He develops his themes with a donnish, sardonic humor, as he portrays the ironies and paradoxes of the human com-

---

[2] P. A. Samuelson on Galbraith, *Newsweek,* July 3, 1967, p. 68.

[3] The two previous quotations are from *Time, loc. cit.,* p. 26.

[4] "The Hippie Economics," *Nation's Business,* September 1967, p. 64.

edy. He couples a skill as an aphorist with a talent for phrasemaking: the "conventional wisdom," the "affluent society," "countervailing power" are a few samples of his mintage. In argument, Galbraith employs a rhetoric of originality and iconoclasm which adds to the popular appeal of his work. He tends to present a somewhat charismatic image of himself as a breaker of idols and a prophet. But most fundamental of all is his propensity to be a moralist. Believing that the United States at least has reached a stage of economic development where it is confronted with the inevitable question of social priorities, he insists with Alfred Marshall that the economist "must concern himself with the ultimate aims of man." In this respect he is in a great tradition, extending from Adam Smith to John Maynard Keynes, that asserts the moral and humanistic relevance of economics. In the recently published work *Ambassador's Journal,* Galbraith delightfully reveals this tendency as well as his characteristic healthy self-esteem in summing up his background for the Indian office: "The job itself is amusing and interesting and one for which I have four considerable qualifications—a grasp of the economic situation, considerable ease in written and spoken communication, some knowledge of politics and an unquestioned willingness to instruct other people in their duty."[5]

In his writing for the general public on economics, Galbraith eschews pure theory. He generally seeks to relate economic principles to the social concerns of the day. As one fellow economist has said, "Galbraith seeks to infuse economics with a social relevance that is, on the whole, egregiously missing from most of its current output, particularly from that of the Chicago school."[6]

EARLY YEARS

Though no formal biography of Galbraith has yet been written, one can discern some of the elements that went into the making of this formidable critic in the available material on his family background and early life. Galbraith was born in 1908 in a Scotch farming community, near Iona Station, Ontario, close to the north shore of Lake Erie. His father had started out in life as a teacher and

[5] *Ambassador's Journal* (Boston: Houghton Mifflin, 1969), p. 72.
[6] R. L. Heilbroner, "Capitalism without Tears," *New York Review of Books,* June 29, 1967, p. 16.

---

later turned to farming. He was a tall man like the son and an active participant in local politics. (Galbraith facetiously explains his own propensity for politics: "My father thought we were obliged because of our enormous size to alter the world to our specifications.") He became the county auditor and a considerable figure in this rather isolated society. For close to half a century, according to the son's account, he was the leading liberal in that locality. In his son's words, he was a "Man of Standing" in the community.[7]

Galbraith, Senior, was an indefatigable orator, and at six or eight years of age the son began to accompany him to his political meetings. The boy learned some valuable lessons from these gatherings—among other things, the use of humor in politics. On one such occasion, a cattle sale, his father seized the opportunity to make a speech, to criticize his Tory opponents. He mounted a huge manure pile to speak to the assembled crowd. "He apologized with ill-concealed sincerity for speaking from the Tory platform. The effect on this agrarian audience was electric. Afterward, I congratulated him on the brilliance of the sally by which I too was deeply impressed. He said, 'It was good but it didn't change any votes.' "[8]

There are other revealing incidents from Galbraith's boyhood which suggest the emerging traits of the man, in this case his frolicsomeness and frankness. To be specific, it was summer and young Galbraith, under the influence of one of Anatole France's more explicitly sexual novels, was deeply in love with a compact, golden-haired girl who had come over to visit his sisters. They strolled through the orchard and climbed on a rail fence overlooking a field in which some of the family cows were grazing. Among the cows was a white bull which proceeded before their eyes to serve a heifer which was in season. Galbraith says he noticed the interest with which his girl friend watched these proceedings, and then, with some sense of his own courage, he said, "I think it would be fun to do that."

She replied, "Well, its your cow."[9]

Life had other compensations for young Galbraith in this uninteresting Canadian community, but religion was not one of them. His family belonged to a sect known as the

[7] *The Scotch* (Boston: Houghton Mifflin, 1964), p. 53. This is a charming memoir of Galbraith's boyhood.
[8] *Ibid.*, p. 75.
[9] *Ibid.*, p. 26.

Old School or Hard Shell Baptists. The faith of these hardworking, penurious people, says Galbraith, was completely accommodated to their culture. Their church was austerely plain and the service devoid of music, art, or inspired or inspiring sermons. The latter were so painful to him, he asserts, that even now he still partly associates churches with torture. ". . . To this day, I never sit down to listen to a speech or a lecture without making a mental calculation as to when it will be over."[10] Even the collection of money was banned in church. ". . . This was not to protect the worshippers from some momentary impulse to generosity. . . . Money was the weekday faith. To keep it out of church was to show that Sunday was sacred to a different deity."[11]

This Scotch congregation had a creed of uncompromising predestinarianism. A man was born either saved or damned, he tells us. Consequently they did not look to God for anything that they could do for themselves.

Young Galbraith attended a one-room, rural school that provided only the bare essentials of an elementary education. The teachers, for the most part, were "unlearned ladies" filling in the years between puberty and marriage. At the age of ten, he went to Dutton High School, a gaunt, two-story building with three teachers, presided over by a Mr. Thomas Elliot, principal. "Old Tommy," as he was "unaffectionately" called, was a tyrant and a taskmaster. He was particularly hard on the boys who came from the more elevated Scotch clans, of which Galbraith was one. His most distinguished pupil tells us that Mr. Elliot was grossly uninformed on most of the subjects he taught. In addition, his opinions on the many public questions which agitated post-World War I Canada were "worthless."

During the years that Galbraith attended high school a corps of cadets was organized for the purposes of military preparedness. A subsidy was paid for each student so trained. It was in that line of duty that Galbraith suffered some of his most painful experiences as an adolescent. "Old Tommy," the principal, who usually gave the military instruction, was very much of a terror to him because he couldn't keep step in the close-order drill which was practiced twice a week in the school yard. Accustomed as he was to keeping step with cows rather than with cadets,

[10] *Ibid.,* p. 98.
[11] *Ibid.,* p. 94.

Galbraith had a hard time. He was put in the Awkward Squad and frequently sent home to write five hundred times the sentence "My left foot is not my right." But Old Tommy's bite was not as bad as his bark. "As a result the brighter individuals [of whom Galbraith was presumably one] learned, as it was said, that you didn't need to be afraid of the Old Fart."[12]

Everyday life provided a considerable political education for young Galbraith. In the early post-World War I years, the village of Dutton was split by social conflict between the townspeople, who were mostly of English descent, and the rural Scotch. Apart from ethnic differences, politics too played a part as a source of community disharmony. Most of the merchants were Tories, while the Scotch were mainly members of the Liberal Party. On economic questions there were deep differences between the two groups. In the post-1918 years, while the village merchants prospered, the farmers were generally doing badly. Many of them concluded that the merchants' prosperity was due to their buying cheap and selling dear. This galled the Scotch because they believed—and Galbraith adds, "I have always thought right"—that they were superior to the townspeople who were exempt from manual labor. Thus the conflicts of this small town, like a social laboratory, provided this perceptive youth with valuable lessons in the difficult and dangerous art of social criticism.

FROM COLLEGE TO UNIVERSITY

However, at the time more mundane and practical matters confronted him. Upon graduation from high school, he gravitated to the Ontario College of Agriculture at Guelph, which was then part of the University of Toronto. He studied animal husbandry, among other subjects, but found most of his instructors either authoritarian or uninspiring, or both. Fortunately, he happened to notice on a college billboard in the fall of 1930 that the Giannini Foundation of Agricultural Economics was offering a number of research scholarships at the University of California. The annual stipend for unmarried scholars was a mere $720. Nevertheless, he grabbed at the opportunity because,

[12] *Ibid.,* p. 139.

as he later wrote, ". . . in that second year of the Great Depression, the monthly salary of $60, if not princely, was by far the best offer of any kind that I had. In fact, it was the only offer of any kind that I had."[13]

Borrowing five hundred dollars from an aunt, Galbraith and a college friend set out in a rickety gas-burner for California. Arriving far behind schedule and the limits of his meager budget, Galbraith immediately fell in love with the beauty of Berkeley. The International House at that campus struck him as "a place of unimaginable splendor." Even more important, he found the intellectual atmosphere far more stimulating and challenging than anything he had known at Ontario. He studied under such respected economists as Leo Rogin, Robert A. Brady, and Ewald Grether and discovered them to be professors who not only knew their subjects, but paradoxically invited debate on what they taught. Even then, it is evident, Galbraith was prone to challenge the authority of the accepted.

In his third year at Berkeley, he was sent to the campus at Davis. There, as he modestly recalls, he was head of the departments of economics, agricultural economics, accounting, and farm management. He says that he also taught all these subjects, but then, uncharacteristically, admits that with the exception of one elderly dean, he was the total teaching staff in these disciplines. His pay was now $1800 a year; out of this handsome income the frugal economist was able to repay his debts to his family by sending his younger sister to college. In 1934 he was awarded his doctorate for a thesis on agricultural economics. In the spring of that year Fortune smiled even more benignly; he was offered an instructorship at Harvard for the following year at $2400. Using an ancient professional ploy, he let it be widely known that they "wanted" him at Harvard. When he informed the dean of his attractive offer, he was dumbfounded to find himself being congratulated and given his release. As he recently wrote in retrospect, "The great love of my life was over."[14]

In the 1930s Harvard was a most exciting place for an economist. The great Schumpeter was expounding his conservative, penetrating analysis of the world's economic

[13] J. K. Galbraith, "Berkeley in the Age of Innocence," *Atlantic,* June 1969, p. 63. This essay has been reprinted in a revised form in Galbraith's *Economics, Peace and Laughter* (Boston: Houghton Mifflin, 1971), pp. 375–392.

[14] *Ibid.*

malaise. Alvin Hansen was displaying the elements of Keynes's "new economics," and Seymour Harris and others were exploring the implications of the new doctrine. Galbraith was also deciphering the complex theory of the great British economist. (In 1936 he spent a year at Cambridge, England, studying the new dispensation, but he did not personally meet the famous monetary heretic.) While tutoring at Winthrop House, he became a close friend of Joseph Kennedy, Jr., the eldest of the Kennedy brothers, and somewhat later met Jack Kennedy, the President-to-be. While he was at Harvard in this period Galbraith also met and married Catherine Atwater, a Smith College valedictorian who had come to study at Radcliffe, and who went on to become a respected professor of German at Cambridge.

At Harvard Galbraith's professional interests widened to include not only agricultural economics, but macroeconomics and industrial organization as well. In 1938, for example, we find him collaborating with H. S. Dennison in the study *Modern Competition and Business Policy.* In a work which adumbrates some of Galbraith's later views, the authors took a critical look at the competitive model of the economy and the underlying policy of antitrust. In place of the latter, they urged a more positive and comprehensive regulation of corporate enterprise.

In 1939 Galbraith taught briefly at Princeton, but his stay there was interrupted by several government assignments. Two years later President Roosevelt appointed him deputy administrator of the Office of Price Administration. In this almost thankless but vital role, he ran a staff that grew from a dozen to sixteen thousand employees. Finally, in 1943, under criticism from some but to the applause of others, Galbraith resigned from his post as price-fixer. He made a futile effort to join the Army, but was rejected because of his height. Instead he joined the staff of *Fortune* magazine, where, under the supervision of Henry Luce, he says he learned to write. Toward the war's end he returned to government service to head up the U.S. Strategic Bombing Survey of the effectiveness of Allied air raids on Germany and Japan. After this task and another brief stay at *Fortune,* he returned to Harvard to serve as Paul M. Warburg professor of economics. Since 1949, with generous leaves of absence (e.g., for his services as ambassador to India), this has been his principal academic post.

Upon returning to academia after World War II Galbraith published important articles summarizing his experiences as a government price-fixer.[15] Economists in these years, after having been away in military or government service, were catching up on wartime intellectual developments. Galbraith was chosen by members of the American Economic Association to survey progress in the preceding decade and a half in the field of "Monopoly and the Concentration of Economic Power."[16] His assessment of this subject was thorough, provocative, and in accordance with the highest standards of the profession.

In 1951 Galbraith rewrote and included two of his price-fixing articles with much new material in a book entitled *The Theory of Price Control.* The general lack of attention this book received seems to have disappointed him very much. His reaction has been reported subsequently as follows:

> I think most people who have read it would say that it is the best book I have ever written. The only difficulty is that five people read it. Maybe ten. I made up my mind that I would never again place myself at the mercy of the technical economists who had the enormous power to ignore what I had written. I set out to involve a larger community. I would involve a larger community. I would involve economists by having the larger public say to them, "Where do you stand on Galbraith's idea of price control?" They would *have* to confront what I said.[17]

THE ESSAYIST EMERGES

Whatever the motivations behind his decision to write for the general public, the fact is that his first "essay in social criticism," the book *American Capitalism,* appeared in 1952. Thereafter, Galbraith's productivity mounted steadily. In 1956 he began the practice of renting a chalet in the winter resort of Gstaad, Switzerland, and devoting several months to writing. Some of his writing was done also during the summer at his farm in Newfane, Vermont, and some while on trips or listening to routine politi-

[15] "Reflections on Price Control," *Quarterly Journal of Economics,* August 1946, pp. 475-489, and "The Disequilibrium System," *American Economic Review,* June 1947, pp. 287-302.

[16] See H. S. Ellis (Ed.), *A Survey of Contemporary Economics* (Philadelphia: Blakiston, 1948), pp. 99–128.

[17] V. S. Navasky, "Galbraith on Galbraith," *The New York Times Book Review,* June 25, 1967, p. 3.

cal speeches. The most important of his publications, other than those mentioned above, for the purposes of this book, are as follows: *The Great Crash, 1929* (1955), *Economics and the Art of Controversy* (1955), *The Affluent Society* (1958), *The Liberal Hour* (1960), *Economic Development* (1962), *The New Industrial State* (1967), and *Ambassador's Journal,* subtitled *A Personal Account of the Kennedy Years* (1969).[18]

In his general orientation to economics, Galbraith is usually classified as a member of the so-called institutionalist school of thought.[19] Such economists stress the influence of culture and social institutions on economic behavior; like Galbraith, they have frequently been critical of conventional wisdom and of analyses which excessively stress static formulations and ignore the dynamic ebb and flow of economic life.

In the early years of Keynesian economics, Galbraith became deeply involved in that subject and helped to draft a book entitled *Toward Full Employment.* In the years after 1945 Harvard was the center of a considerable amount of interest and writing about Keynes. Indeed, in the early fifties a conservative group of Harvard graduates who were opposed to the "new economics" investigated their school and concluded that "Harvard was the launching pad for the Keynesian rocket in America." Galbraith, they found, was being "groomed as the new crown prince of Keynesism [sic]."[20]

Actually, though Galbraith endorsed and advocated some measures of Keynesian fiscal policy in his early work, he soon saw its limitations in controlling inflation and was one of the first to detect that it was becoming the new orthodoxy. In this respect, he was acting in accordance with his own dictum: ". . . One of the most important and difficult of the responsibilities of the economist is to resist the authority of the accepted."[21]

In recent years Galbraith has not limited his writings to economics or public affairs. In addition to authoring *The Triumph,* a novel that lampooned the U.S. State Department

---

[18] All the above were published by Houghton Mifflin Co. of Boston, with the exception of *Economics and the Art of Controversy,* which was originally published by Rutgers University Press.

[19] See, for example, J. Oser, *The Evolution of Economic Thought* (2nd ed., New York: Harcourt, Brace and World, 1970), pp. 363–368.

[20] Z. Doobs, *Keynes at Harvard, Economic Deception as a Political Credo,* rev. ed. (New York: Veritas Foundation, 1962), p. 105.

[21] *American Capitalism* (Boston: Houghton Mifflin, 1960), p. xi.

and was a Book-of-the-Month Club selection, he has tried his hand at satire. In 1962–63, while recuperating from amoebic hepatitis, he wrote *The McLandress Dimension* under the pseudonym of Mark Epernay.[22] The chief figure of this clever little book is a Dr. Herschell McLandress, reputedly a former Professor of Psychiatric Measurement at the Harvard Medical School. He is the inventor of a coefficient which measures the longest span of time that an individual can concentrate on some subject other than himself. "Epernay" reported that the highest McLandress Coefficient in the federal government was that of Chief Justice Earl Warren—four hours, thirty minutes. "The lowest was that of Professor J. K. Galbraith, American Ambassador to India —one minute thirty seconds."

Another McLandress innovation was the Sonic Subliminal Support Apparatus, Mark II—nicknamed, for short, the Confidence Machine. This ingenious device was a small, transistorized unit which could be worn inconspicuously beneath the shirt of a businessman or of any other citizen who needed a "sustaining presence." It produced at a barely audible level speeches of Herbert Hoover, Calvin Coolidge, etc.

In summing up this sketch of the Harvard "worldly philosopher," we should note that Galbraith has many of the personal qualities that go to make an effective social critic. On his own accounting, his early life as a person of Scotch descent in a community that was dominated by the English made him critical of Establishment thinking. His subsequent status as a Canadian migrant to the United States afforded him the valuable perspective of something of a "marginal man" or outsider on the American scene. In the course of his professional career as an economist, writer, and adviser to Presidents, he acquired some of the other qualifications of the social critic. Hesketh Pearson, in his delightful portrait of George Bernard Shaw, describes what he regards as the four chief virtues of a great journalistic critic: readability, irreverence, individuality, and courage.[23] In various ways, as the following pages will disclose, Galbraith has strikingly exhibited some of these traits.

One personal feature that is almost as conspicuous as his stature is his highly developed sense of self-esteem. Gal-

[22] Both of these books were published originally by the Houghton Mifflin Co. of Boston; paperback editions have been published by The New American Library.

[23] H. Pearson, *G.B.S., A Full-Length Portrait and a Postcript* (New York: Harper and Row, 1942), p. 107.

braith himself has frankly said that his principal fault is "a towering ego." (On other occasions, he has contended that modesty is a much-overrated virtue.) In any case, even his friends have been impressed by his remarkably strong self-image. One of them, William F. Buckley, Jr., has amusingly said that when he meets Galbraith he always gives the impression of being on leave from Mount Olympus. Then there is that touching conversation that Galbraith had with General de Gaulle at a State Department reception in which he humorously remarked that the world belongs to tall men. ". . . They are more visible, therefore their behavior is better, and accordingly they are to be trusted. He [the General] said that he agreed and added, 'It is important that we be merciless with those who are too small. . . .' "[24]

At a social gathering a few years ago in honor of Galbraith, his friends not only showed the affection they had for him, but indirectly substantiated the existence of some of the personal qualities we have been describing. A one-night festival was held at the Plaza Hotel in New York by some four hundred of his "disestablishment intimates." "Galbraith was given the Calvin Coolidge Good Behavior Sash (for never speaking without being spoken to). Then he was awarded the Narcissus Medal (for self-evident reasons), next, the Croesus Peace Award (for devoting life to making money, not war), the Heart of Lion Award (for tireless service in losing causes), the Green Giant Gardening Award (for the most affluent and extravagant corn), the Odd Fellow from Canada Award (for helping his country by moving to Cambridge, Massachusetts), and finally the Pink Garter (for gallantry to all women without consideration of previous matrimony)."[25]

It is gratifying to be so honored by one's friends and associates. It is almost equally pleasant to be recognized for professional efforts by one's peers. Galbraith had this very agreeable experience in 1970 when he was nominated by a committee of the American Economic Association to serve in its highest office. At its meetings in Detroit in December he was chosen by the membership of this association, the principal and most prestigious organization of the nation's economists, to be president-elect, to take office in 1972.

In earlier years Galbraith had served on important com-

[24] J. K. Galbraith, *Ambassador's Journal, op. cit.*, p. 598.
[25] "Galbraith Is Honored for Newest Book," *The New York Times*, November 23, 1969, p. 76.

mittees of the AEA. Now he was selected for its highest post. Journalists at the convention marveled at the economists' election of one who was perhaps the most independent of them all. One reporter, noting that in the past Galbraith had "excoriated" the profession, speculated about what his election signified. ". . . It is difficult to say whether this is a sign of total security or insecurity on their part. It is more likely an expression of approval of Mr. Galbraith's efforts to restore richer social, moral and aesthetic qualities to a profession that shows signs of becoming desiccated by technical scholasticism and an ostentatious display of mathematical rigor."[26]

Whether one accepts this interpretation or not, it is a reasonable view that, in part, his election reflected the economic profession's recognition of the significance and impact of his famous trilogy. In the following chapters we shall be primarily concerned with these three books on economics, namely, *American Capitalism, The Affluent Society,* and *The New Industrial State.* In the next chapter we consider the first of these volumes, which was also the first in chronological order of publication.

[26] L. S. Silk, "The Economist Game," *The New York Times,* December 23, 1970, p. 37.

2 *American*

Capitalism Revisited

SOCIETY AS THE PATIENT

In his first best-seller, *American Capitalism,* published in 1952, Galbraith contended that Americans were suffering from a form of social neurosis, a sense of insecurity based on illusion.[1] Instead of individuals being sick, American society was the patient. Dr. Galbraith's diagnosis was that his fellow Americans were captives of ideas which caused them to view the world with misgivings and anxiety. "The ruling ideas of the period [1945–1950]," he wrote, "were better designed to maximize our alarm than our understanding of the economy."[2] Yet, on the basis of his and others' analysis, the economic performance of the nation in these years was satisfactory. Like the wing-heavy bumblebee which according to aeronautical principles shouldn't be able to fly, the economy was soaring for some inexplicable reason, at the very time that most Americans were worried. The design of Galbraith's compact essay was clever: like a mystery story it outlined a puzzling situation that defied the best efforts of the experts at solution, and then Galbraith came forth with the answer. He presented his theory of countervailing power to explain the operation of the economic system and strenuously advocated the revision of the antitrust laws to make them consistent with his new concept.

The historical context in which *American Capitalism* was written must be kept in mind. During the Great Depression some economists had accepted the stagnation thesis of Alvin Hansen, and others on the basis of Keynesian analysis

[1] Subtitle, *The Concept of Countervailing Power* (Boston: Houghton Mifflin, 1952). A new revision was published in 1956. Unless otherwise stated, we shall refer mainly to the text of the original edition and will note some of the major revisions.

[2] *Ibid.,* p. 196.

30

expected that we would face a massive depression with the curtailment of wartime production. On the other hand, conservative economists were agitated over the growth of planning fostered by the war and the development of the "welfare state." One Austrian professor, Friedrich A. von Hayek, in a widely read book argued that these policies were leading the nation down the road to serfdom.[3] In addition, economic liberals were being informed by the Federal Trade Commission that we were in the midst of a huge merger movement which was adding dangerously to the concentration of business power.[4]

Psychologists tell us that we respond to the environment that we perceive. According to Galbraith, in these post-World War II years the perceptions of both liberals and conservatives were biased by the conviction that the economy was unstable and that it had a strong tendency toward depression. Like a good psychiatrist, he sought to show Americans how they got their distorted ideas and to change their image of capitalism so that they could respond to reality rather than to a set of myths.

Galbraith next described the "foundations of the faith"—the theory of competitive capitalism—which had contributed to this insecurity Americans were displaying. These were the ideas of the classical economists, principally Englishmen and Scots, who had formulated their "alien doctrine" in the eighteenth and nineteenth centuries. The main requirements of this system were competition and the observance of Say's Law of Markets; the latter reassuringly held that the very act of producing goods provides the purchasing power necessary for buying them. With the passage of time the theoretical model of competition grew increasingly rigorous and, more significantly, it assured its believers of a high degree of social efficiency. If there were many sellers and buyers, no collusion among them, and rational pursuit of profit, the nation's resources would be fully employed in producing most efficiently what the people most wanted. Furthermore, if these conditions were satisfied in reality, there could be no misuse of private power because no one would have private power to abuse.

It was an ideal belief system that reassured those who held it. But there was one shortcoming in it. Except for a few manufacturing industries and agriculture, the number

[3] Friedrich A. von Hayek, *The Road to Serfdom* (Chicago: University of Chicago Press, 1944).

[4] Federal Trade Commission, *The Merger Movement: A Summary Report* (Washington, D.C.: U.S. Government Printing Office, 1948).

of sellers in many markets declined with the passage of time until there were just a few big survivors and a fringe of smaller hangers-on. Galbraith insisted that the cause of this growing industrial concentration was not greedy bankers or exploiters seeking monopoly, as many Congressional investigations had alleged. It rested instead, he asserted, on the technical economies of large-scale production and the advantages that growth provides in raising new capital. Furthermore, the established firms in the concentrated industries achieve "economies of experience" that are not available to the latecomers. This process of industrial concentration in the American economy has not resulted in a great many single-firm monopolies; the dominant pattern has been rather the concentration of output among a relatively few sellers.

Galbraith explained that in the 1930's economists eventually revised their theoretical models to take account of this new pattern of market control. Professors Edward Chamberlin and Joan Robinson almost simultaneously developed theories of monopolistic or imperfect competition which added an intermediate category to the old bipolar classification of markets—pure competition and pure monopoly.[5] A new category, competition among a few sellers or oligopoly, as it was called, was of outstanding importance.

The theorizing about oligopoly suggested that if the oligopolists recognized their interdependence—the effect of one's price on another—they were likely to avoid price competition because of its possible destructive nature. Competition would be channeled instead into such nonprice forms as new product development, salesmanship, advertising, and service. These new theories of competition, Galbraith argued, "although it wasn't wholly foreseen at the time, meant the end of the faith in competition in the old sense."[6] With elements of monopoly or market power becoming pervasive in the economy because of oligopoly or product differentiation, the old pressure for efficiency in production was lessened and a new premium was placed on expenditures for distribution. Thus, said Galbraith, "by evolution, from a system where nearly everything worked out for the best, economists found themselves with a system where nearly everything seemed to work out for the worst."[7]

    [5] E. H. Chamberlin, *The Theory of Monopolistic Competition* (Cambridge: Harvard University Press, 1932); J. Robinson, *The Economics of Imperfect Competition* (London: Macmillan, 1933).
    [6] *American Capitalism*, p. 44.
    [7] *Ibid.*, p. 51.

This academic recognition of the widespread existence of partial monopoly in the American economy dealt the liberal faith in antitrust a serious blow. As Galbraith archly said, ". . . It is possible to prosecute a few evil-doers; it is evidently not so practical to indict a whole economy."[8]

The new situation posed a difficult dilemma for the liberals, so far as public policy was concerned. Whereas formerly they could generally agree on the sovereign remedy of antitrust prosecutions against monopoly, there now developed something like a three-way split in opinion. One group advocated that the antimonopoly weapons should be used against oligopoly. A second argued that government regulation in some form would have to be substituted for antitrust. A third looked for elements in oligopolistic competition which could be considered "workable," despite its variance from the conditions of pure competition. Galbraith's conclusion about these approaches to the new state of affairs was pessimistic: "The common feature of all three enterprises has been a very large component of frustration."[9]

He felt that the liberal faith in antitrust was especially quixotic where oligopoly was concerned. ". . . To suppose that there are grounds for antitrust prosecution wherever three, four or a half dozen firms dominate a market is to suppose that the very fabric of American capitalism is illegal. This is a notion which can seem plausible only to the briefless lawyer."[10]

Public regulation or economic planning seemed to him also to be an impractical alternative. At the very least, it would require systematic price regulation by the state. This would be unpalatable to most contemporary liberals. Yet given their dissatisfaction with the old formulas, liberals tend, said Galbraith, to favor more state intervention in the economy. But their support of the latter is likely to be largely a verbal advocacy, witness the innocuous recommendations of the Temporary National Economic Committee—a veritable "miasma of words."[11]

Workable competition as an approach appealed to Gal-

[8] *Ibid.,* p. 55.
[9] *Ibid.*
[10] *Ibid.,* p. 58.
[11] *Ibid.,* pp. 59–60. The Temporary National Economic Committee was a joint executive and Congressional committee which investigated the economic concentration of power in the United States during the years 1938–1941. For a full account of its work, see D. Lynch, *The Concentration of Economic Power* (New York: Columbia University Press, 1946).

braith because of its pragmatism. But "the difficulty with the notion is that its authors have failed to make clear why what is unworkable in principle becomes workable in practice." Galbraith suggested here that there were other possible regulatory restraints on private market power that the advocates of workable competition were overlooking; in this suggestion he anticipated his own regulatory proposal.

At the time these theoretical difficulties concerning competition and the related questions of public policy were not agitating a large number of Americans. Galbraith observed that, to be a widespread source of alarm, such ideas would have to be reinforced by experience. The latter was provided in a most devastating degree by the Great Depression, which had led many to question the efficiency and stability of the national economy. Indeed, its consequences were so profound that it left millions with a sort of "depression psychosis."

In the thirties and after, liberals in the United States increasingly interpreted capitalistic instability in terms of the ideas of John Maynard Keynes. In his pathbreaking work, *The General Theory of Employment, Interest and Money,* this brilliant British economist had provided a most cogent analysis of business depressions and how they might be overcome. But many businessmen in the United States disliked the Keynesian remedies because they tended to make government an indispensable partner of business; and this would detract from the power and prestige of the business class. Instead most businessmen in these years continued to adhere to the old ideology of the competitive model (pure competition) and its corollary, antitrust. This body of ideas conveniently served to exonerate the big corporations from the charge of having objectionable market power.

Galbraith next turned to examine the substance of the contemporary doubts about the functioning of the American economy. What explained the paradox that the economy pleased no one in principle, while in practice it satisfied most? The efficiency of the American economy, he held, was disguised by the preconceptions fostered by the static competitive model. From the latter perspective, oligopoly encourages an avoidance of price competition and a corresponding restriction of production. But offsetting this, Galbraith insisted, is the fact that "the modern industry of a few large firms is an almost perfect instrument for inducing technical change. It is admirably equipped for financing technical development [innovation and new product development]. Its organization provides strong incentives for undertaking development and for putting it into use. The competition of the competitive model, by contrast, almost completely precludes technical development."[12] Furthermore, technical development is a safe rather than a "reciprocally destructive method" of competition for the oligopolists. And, in addition, the market power they possess protects their incentive to engage in technical innovation.

There is, however, another side to this phenomenon that is not so favorable. Both oligopoly and brand-name competition have promoted a tremendous amount of salesmanship and advertising which many economists have regarded as wasteful. Galbraith concedes that by the standard of efficiency of the competitive model the American economy is undoubtedly wasteful. But in truth this waste of excessive salesmanship and advertising is simply a symptom of our comparative opulence. We shouldn't worry too much about it. Indeed, the economist who frets unduly about such waste is deploying his own resources inefficiently. Moreover, our great wealth provides us with a margin for error in governmental decision-making. ". . . None of the real sources of well-being—the endowment of physical resources and the education and energy of the people—are ever seriously compromised by a government decision."[13] Our growing wealth has not only been a solvent for mistakes; it has served also to alleviate grave social strains.

THE CONCEPT OF
COUNTERVAILING POWER

Economists have sometimes distinguished in their professional discussions between the "tool-makers" and the "tool-users" of their craft. In introducing the "tool" or analytical concept of countervailing power, Galbraith entered perhaps the restricted ranks of the former. Actually, the idea and the phenomenon to which it refers have a long history. The concept has been alluded to in one form or another by writers as far back as Polybius, the Greek historian. In modern times, President Theodore Roosevelt seems to have envisioned the growth of countervailing

[12] *American Capitalism*, p. 91.
[13] *Ibid.*, p. 112.

organizations in our society. In economics, one of the first Americans to stress the importance of bargaining transactions in our economy was the late John R. Commons. Professors John M. Clark, Edwin G. Nourse, and others have dealt with collective economic action.[14] In addition, in American political science there is a vast literature devoted to pluralism, pressure groups, and the "group basis of politics."[15] So much for the antecedents of the idea.

Despite these anticipations of the basic idea by others, it must be said that Galbraith has given more currency to this politico-economic concept than any of his predecessors. In fact, the term "countervailing" seems to have acquired a new usefulness and relevance in social science literature since Galbraith used it. But we are running ahead of ourselves; let us next consider how he developed the concept and what role he saw it playing in the post-1945 American economy.

In his view our economy was maintaining its dynamism and performing tolerably well in the immediate postwar years because of two basic factors: (*a*) the innovative capacities of corporate oligopoly; (*b*) the neglected factor in accepted economic theory—countervailing power. We have touched on the first factor above; we need now to elaborate upon the latter.

In expounding the traditional theory of competition, economists have customarily explained the restraint on private economic power as being provided by other firms on the same side of the market. In recent decades, while price competition had declined on the seller's side of the market (the number of sellers had become fewer and collusion had become common), economists, according to Galbraith, had failed to see that buyers or customers had organized in self-defense against such concentrated economic power. Private economic power on one side of the market had begot a tendency toward similar concentration on the other. The long trend toward concentrated economic power had brought into existence strong buyers as well as strong sellers.

Those who are at a disadvantage in bargaining power,

---

[14] J. R. Commons, *Institutional Economics* (New York: The Macmillan Co., 1934); also, by the same author, *The Economics of Collective Action* (New York: Random House, 1948). J. M. Clark, *Alternative to Serfdom* (New York: Random House, 1948); E. G. Nourse, "Collective Bargaining and the Common Interest," *American Economic Review,* March 1963, pp. 1 ff.

[15] On this subject, see D. B. Truman, *The Governmental Process* (New York: Random House, 1951) and the literature cited therein.

Galbraith argued, had two incentives for resorting to counterorganization: first, to defend themselves against the unchecked power of others; second, to share in the monopolistic gains which the latter probably were making. Thus, even if competition was no longer a self-generating force because new firms could not break into tightly concentrated fields, there was the likelihood, for the above reasons, that countervailing power would arise on the other side of the market.

Galbraith stated that he had rejected the term "bilateral monopoly" to characterize the phenomenon he was describing. As treated in economic literature, bilateral monopoly, he said, was "an adventitious occurrence." He regarded countervailing power as being much more pervasive in the organizational economy of mid-twentieth-century America than most economists assumed.

THE FUNCTIONING OF
COUNTERVAILING POWER

Being well versed in the subject of industrial organization, Galbraith knew that he was advancing a very formidable contention that was likely to arouse controversy and opposition from more conventional theorists. In essence, he was arguing that competition, which since Adam Smith's time had been viewed as the autonomous and only available regulator of economic activity (apart from the state), had been superseded in oligopolistic markets. In such markets, he maintained, the active restraint is provided not by competition, but by strong buyers on the other side of the market. Under conditions of oligopoly, given the tacit agreement against price competition that is common in that type of market structure, the role of the sellers becomes passive. Nonetheless he held that "oligopoly facilitates the exercise of countervailing power by enabling the strong buyer to play one seller against another."[16]

In citing practical illustrations of countervailing power, Galbraith wrote that it could be seen most clearly in the labor market "where it is also most fully developed." The inequality of bargaining power between the large corporate employer and the individual, unorganized employee with all the abuses that such a relationship engendered called

---

[16] *American Capitalism*, p. 120.

for correction by counterorganization. In a much-quoted example, Galbraith asserted, ". . . In the ultimate sense it was the power of the steel industry, not the organizing abilities of John L. Lewis and Philip Murray, that brought the United Steel Workers into being." Furthermore, he argued, "as a general though not invariable rule there are strong unions in the United States only where markets are served by strong corporations." It is to be noted that Galbraith qualified the foregoing generalization by saying that he did "not advance the theory of countervailing power as a monolithic explanation of trade union organization."[17]

Galbraith also illustrated the functioning of countervailing power in retail markets (chain stores, mail order houses, and department stores bargaining with their suppliers) and in producers' goods industries (e.g., automobile manufacturers versus steel companies).

In certain markets, Galbraith explained, countervailing power is a self-generating force, but in others it is not easy for individuals to organize such power. He pointed out that those who organize to countervail the power of others usually have to gain the support of government to establish their organizations. And this policy of supporting the weaker economic groups has become in the last two decades perhaps "the major peacetime function of the federal government."

In holding that countervailing power had partially superseded competition as a social control in our economy, Galbraith sought to show that its exercise would often benefit the consumer. He admitted that it didn't perform this function when there was inflation or inflationary pressure on markets. On the other hand, when supply tends to exceed demand and there is slack in the economy and unemployment exists, countervailing power will benefit the consumer. Under these conditions of a so-called buyers' market, mass buyers, such as mail order houses, department stores, or chains, will tend because of self-interest to drive a hard bargain with their suppliers, and some of their gains, Galbraith held, will be passed on to the ultimate consumer. Under conditions of inflation and unemployment, however, countervailing power ceases to operate. "Under inflationary pressure of demand, the whole structure of countervailing power in the economy dissolves." And somewhat later, he adds, "It takes on, instead, a malignant form

---

[17] *Ibid.,* pp. 121, 122, and 123, successively.

which becomes part of the dynamic of inflation itself."[18]

Apart from its role in regulating product markets, Galbraith described the function of countervailing power in alleviating social tensions in American society. As a partial result of the government's subsidizing the countervailing power of workers and farmers, both groups, he insisted, had developed a greater sense of confidence and equality.

In this ambitious book, Galbraith not only presented a theory of the government's role in supporting groups which were weaker or disadvantaged compared to the possessors of original market power (usually big business); he also offered a new criterion for the government's antitrust policy. In practice, he would have the government attack positions of original market power only where these were not effectively offset by the countervailing power of other groups. And conversely, he argued that it was unwise for the government to assail positions of countervailing power and leave positions of original market power untouched. If this were done, the holders of original market power would be able to exploit their monopoly position without any check whatsoever. In his view, the development of organized economic blocs, some of which are sustained only by reason of their exemption from the antitrust laws, was not something to be deplored. In general, he contended, the growth of such countervailing power "strengthens the capacity of the economy for autonomous self-regulation and thereby lessens the amount of over-all government control that is required or sought."[19]

In broad perspective, Galbraith's economic philosophy in this book conceived the government's role as that of a make-weight or balance to maintain an equilibrium of power among the various economic groups of our society. During the New Deal, President Franklin D. Roosevelt had some such conception in mind in speaking of government's task as that of managing "a concert of interests." To Galbraith, the acceptance of this function by government and the beneficial technical dynamic of corporate oligopoly probably formed the basis for his differentiating American capitalism in these years from some of its less salutary manifestations in other countries and at other times.

One final point and we are finished with our summary of this provocative book. In the latter part of his treatment

[18] *Ibid.*, p. 196.
[19] *Ibid.*, p. 155.

of countervailing power, Galbraith displayed a curious inconsistency. At one place he asserted that countervailing
power had been dissolved as a result of the continuing
rounds of wage and price increases following World War
II.[20] Yet somewhat later in his analysis he argued that
during the years 1945 to 1950 "the economy possessed what
may loosely be called a deflationary potential. Its tendency
was to behave in such a manner that the internal regula-
tors including countervailing power would function and
with efficiency."[21] Then, toward the very end of the volume, he wrote, ". . . An unemployment of four million in
mid-1949, which except in a few industries appears to have
been enough to *rehabilitate* countervailing power in the
economy, seems to have produced no serious social
strains."[22] To be specific, our point of criticism is that if
countervailing power had to be rehabilitated after mid-
1949, it could hardly have been operating "with efficiency"
before then.

These conflicting statements must have made some readers wonder whether countervailing power was working or
not in the post-World War II period. But rather than pursue
that line of criticism at this point, we prefer to turn to a
consideration of the critical response to the book as a whole.

[20] *Ibid.,* p. 139.
[21] *Ibid.,* p. 191.
[22] *Ibid.,* p. 204 (our italics). In the revised, 1956 edition of
American Capitalism, the last two sentences in the paragraph that
contained this reference to the rehabilitation of countervailing power
were deleted by Galbraith.

3 Countervailing
Galbraith

Galbraith is so persuasive a writer and polemicist that it may be argued that there is a need to countervail his arguments with those of equally powerful critics. As this chapter will reveal, there has been no dearth of those who have sought to challenge his ideas, including the concept of countervailing power.

The initial response to *American Capitalism* on the part of critics reviewing the book was overwhelmingly favorable. Of some eight reviews listed in the *Book Review Digest* where an overall verdict was indicated, seven were favorable and only one was mixed. Thus Stuart Chase, in a highly laudatory review, said:

> The thesis of countervailing power makes sense to me, and is likely to make sense to most objective observers. It explains why the economy has not disintegrated. . . . It explains the place of the New Deal in history, not as a rush toward socialism . . . but as a strengthening of private decision-making, so that the system can still function after great sections of the free market have disappeared. . . . It explains the terms on which our free enterprise system can continue to function.[1]

Similarly, Professor C. L. Christenson of Indiana University praised Galbraith's volume as "a brilliant work of synthesis."[2] On the other hand, the late Paul T. Homan in a judicious, balanced review was impressed by the author's incisive analytical powers, but wondered about his decision to write for a nonprofessional audience.[3] He had misgivings about Galbraith's great emphasis on countervailing power

[1] "Capitalism without Tears," *The Reporter*, March 4, 1952, pp. 33–35.
[2] *Journal of Political Economy,* June 1952, p. 275.
[3] *American Economic Review,* December 1952, pp. 925–928.

as a *substitute* for competition. "Here he [Galbraith] appears to fall into a trap of his own making, that of contrasting countervailing power with the 'powerless' competition of theoretical models. In consequence, he nowhere pays attention to the extent and force of the 'real' competitive elements and the necessity of retaining them unless we are to embark upon a radically revised version of American capitalism." It was a respectful review, closing on the note that Galbraith's "outline of his ideas deserves the careful attention of his professional colleagues."

Professor Joan Robinson, a British economist and one of the co-founders of the economics of imperfect competition, considered the book to be "shrewd, witty and forceful."[4] She said Galbraith's analysis cut through many confusions of thought, and suggested new lines of analysis and policy. The analysis of imperfect competition, she remarked, was essentially a debunking of *laissez faire* ("though perhaps Professor Chamberlin did not see it like that"). She went on to say that "it is doubtful how far it [Galbraith's book] will succeed in rebunking *laissez faire*. . . . It will be interesting to watch the fate of the ideology which he proposes with the audience to which it is addressed." Galbraith was probably amused at the suggestion that he was engaged in his book in "rebunking *laissez faire*."

Daniel Bell, the American sociologist, in a longer, insightful treatment of the book, stated that countervailing power was "a phrase which in its imaginative simplicity crystallizes a feeling a number of observers have had about our society."[5] Galbraith, he added, had skillfully developed a realistic theory of political economy. He wasn't convinced, however, by the reasons Galbraith gave as to why the business community and the left were captives of a description of reality that no longer exists; "why, in effect, is the myth more compelling than the reality?" He perceptively noted too that Galbraith had avoided almost completely the problems posed by a permanent war economy. With remarkable prescience, he commented on the high rate of obsolescence to which social ideologies are subject in a period of sweeping change: "The intellectual rehabilitation of American capitalism is being completed while the reality itself is rapidly changing; the newest ideologies may become outmoded and require new revisions long before they have

---

[4] *The Economic Journal*, December 1952, pp. 925–928.
[5] "The Prospects of American Capitalism," *Commentary*, December 1952, pp. 603 ff.

had time to get themselves widely read, understood and accepted."

Adolph A. Berle, Jr., late professor of corporate law at Columbia University and a long-time student of social power as well as an influential adviser to governments, saw Galbraith's work as "a square challenge to some of the classic premises on which the current theory of capitalism is based."[6] Galbraith, he asserted, "has produced a theory of capitalism which cannot be disregarded by anyone, though it will disturb many." He was bothered, however, by the fact that "the author makes blanket statements which are justified, though the book would be stronger if the evidence was set out. . . ." Though sympathetic, Berle felt that Galbraith made some of his points with an "irritating lack of definiteness." He criticized the latter's conception that disadvantaged groups seek the assistance of the state to build countervailing power so that they may use it against market authority to which they previously had been subordinated. "Having studied many situations in which the state was called in, I question the generalization. More often, the community as a whole suffered from disruption of an economic service on which they had come to depend: there was an undersupply of steel, or an oversupply of oil. Not infrequently groups wielding the greatest market power were those who most wanted the government —of course, on their own terms—to get them out of situations imposing responsibilities they were unable to face. . . ." To much of this Galbraith would probably agree, but say that he was concerned with another type of state intervention.

Despite such reservations, Berle was very impressed with Galbraith's analysis, but saw it only as a beginning. "Galbraith has certainly opened a door which will certainly not be closed for a long time." His book was "an important" one. "The new territory he has sighted needs to be explored, mapped, and occupied. The service he has performed is a solid one. Properly exploited, the bridgehead gained may serve as a starting point for a true twentieth century theory of political economy—which is already a generation overdue."

Galbraith's book received its share of brickbats as well as bouquets in the first year after publication. The late Professor David McCord Wright of the University of Vir-

---

[6] "American Capitalism," *The Review of Economics and Statistics,* February 1953, pp. 81–84.

ginia was one of the hottest of the Harvard economist's
critics. In a long, blistering review, he let Galbraith have it
"between the eyes."[7] He admitted that the book was "re-
plete with interesting and challenging ideas. Two chapters
(IX and X) show qualities of real insight." But then,
". . . In all humility, I am obliged to say that both the first
and the last parts, and even occasionally the middle, show
an extraordinary proportion of error, coupled with extremely one-sided acquaintance with the literature, plus a
disturbing tendency toward sweepingly inaccurate generalization." Galbraith's generalizations about economics were
so extreme, said Wright, that his book is "very nearly a
wholesale libel of the economic profession."

By overlooking the shortage of equity capital and the
effect of the progressive income tax on the ability of small
business to finance itself, Galbraith's version of American
capitalism, according to Wright, came close to being Hamlet
without the Danish prince. In endorsing countervailing
power, Galbraith showed a preference for a stalemate
among contending groups rather than the limited, decen-
tralized power which makes for continuing growth and
adjustment.

BIG BUSINESS AND THE
ORGANIZATIONAL REVOLUTION

The critical reaction to Galbraith's work was
heightened by the publication in 1953 of another book
which attacked the orthodox position on competition and
big business.[8] David E. Lilienthal, a distinguished attorney
and former head of the TVA and the Atomic Energy Commission, urged a change in government policy to an affirma-

---

[7] "What Is Capitalism?" *Explorations in Entrepreneurial History,*
IX, Part 4, 223–228 (1951–1952). Professor Wright was the author
of *Democracy and Progress* (New York: Macmillan, 1948) and of a
book of his own entitled *Capitalism* (New York: McGraw-Hill,
1951).

[8] *Big Business: A New Era* (New York: Harper and Row, 1953).
Lilienthal, in writing his book, had read Galbraith's *American
Capitalism;* he spoke of it as "refreshing" (p. 74 of *Big Business*).
Incidentally, one critic of Lilienthal wrote of his book as "a less
sophisticated version of the Galbraith thesis" (W. Adams, "Competition, Monopoly and Countervailing Power," *Quarterly Journal
of Economics,* November 1953, p. 471, footnote 6.

tive attitude toward big business. He criticized the antitrust laws as antiquated, unrealistic, and ineffective. He contended that the growth of government's role in the economy, particularly since 1933, had made the danger of abuses by big business more manageable. He argued that we should encourage and promote big enterprise rather than view its growth with apprehension. With this defense of big business coming so soon after Galbraith's volume, it must have seemed to some defenders of traditional liberalism that the very citadel of the competitive market was under attack. One business journal reported, ". . . Signs like these made it look to many economists almost as though their shock troops were deserting to the enemy in a body."[9]

Still another volume appeared in 1953 that had an important relation to Galbraith's thesis. Professor Kenneth E. Boulding published a study for the National Council of Churches with the significant title *The Organizational Revolution*.[10] The author used this phrase to denote the great rise in the years since 1880 of organizations in the fields of business, labor, agriculture, and government itself. He analyzed the nature and causes of this extraordinary development and emphasized that it was not new needs for such organizations, but improvement in the skills of organizers and the opportunities for such bodies to grow, which accounted for the movement. Basically, he saw the labor and farm movements as "a revolt against the market." Stressing psychological and sociological factors as much as economic, Boulding said the great achievements of these two movements, "in America at least, has been the virtual abolition of the proletariat and the setting up of organizations which made the mass of the people feel that they 'belong' to the whole society."[11]

In his analysis, Boulding pointed to the dangers of organization in "politicizing" economic life. The greatest disadvantage, as he saw it, was that such massive organizations tended to make the economic structure more inflexible because "prices and money wages become more 'sticky.' " He contended too that a highly organized society will find itself with strong pressures toward inflation.

The commentaries on Boulding's ideas in his book are so relevant to the countervailing power thesis that we should

[9] "Clobbering Theory," *Business Week*, January 9, 1954, p. 94.
[10] Subtitled *A Study in the Ethics of Economic Organization* (New York: Harper and Row, 1953).
[11] *Ibid.*, p. 245.

take note of them. For example, the late Reinhold Niebuhr, the theologian, in his contribution criticized Boulding's neglect of the factor of power in his tacit model of the free market economy. He believed that Boulding had not adequately analyzed the pressures which had given rise to these diverse organizations. "The need is to balance the unbalanced disproportions of power introduced into modern life by large-scale production and distribution. This balance is necessary because disbalances of power prevent competitive bargaining from being as free and equitable as classical theory assumes."[12] "Justice in a technical society," wrote Niebuhr, "requires that the centralization of power inherent in the industrial process be matched by collective social power."[13]

Likewise, Jerry Voorhis, executive secretary of the Co-operative League of the U.S.A., challenged Boulding's analysis of power. He argued that the voluntary organizations that had developed in such large numbers since 1870 represented "a counterreaction to the concentration of control over capital and economic resources which came about in the later stages of the Industrial Revolution."[14] In his reply Boulding admitted that Voorhis' point about the improvement of weak groups in a society was a very important one, and one to which he had not perhaps given adequate attention. "The problem," he said, "is essentially not in economics, but in cultural anthropology, a field in which I cannot pretend to any special competence." Such modesty about interdisciplinary matters is strange in Boulding's case. But no matter; the exchanges cited above are interesting as showing recognition by other observers of what Galbraith had termed countervailing power.

THE DEFECTS OF

COUNTERVAILING POWER

The debate over Galbraith's new concept of countervailing power grew increasingly hot in the year following its presentation. The more orthodox economists, some of them specialists in industrial organization, began to attack the book more severely. One of the most capable reviews

[12] *Ibid.*, pp. 230–231.
[13] *Ibid.*, pp. 231–232.
[14] *Ibid.*, p. 266.

of this genre came from the typewriter of Professor Simon N. Whitney of New York University.[15]

At the outset of his criticism, Whitney noted the wide interest Galbraith's book had generated. "... The present writer has found an interest in the book on the part of graduate students and teachers which matches, or exceeds, that in any other book in our field since J. M. Keynes's *General Theory*."

Whitney systematically set out six defects in Galbraith's arguments for countervailing power. He classified them as follows: (1) cannot explain consumer benefits; (2) overlooks real reasons for the economy's success; (3) illogical examples; (4) defective cycle analysis; (5) fails to explain obvious successes; (6) not supported by history.

The central defect in Galbraith's theory of countervailing power, said Whitney, is that "it cannot explain why the consumer benefits. . . ." *"All it can do is explain how the possessors of countervailing power might force the possessors of original power to give them a share in the rewards."*[16] The only force which could compel mass buyers, for example, to share their gains with consumers is competition, which Galbraith minimizes. Furthermore, the low prices which mass buyers achieve may reflect more their attainment of economies of scale than their exercise of countervailing power. If they can economize through mass buying, the Robinson-Patman Act is not violated.

Whitney believed that Galbraith's effort to explain the "remarkable" performance of American capitalism puts too much emphasis on one factor and neglects others of equal or greater importance. Among the latter are "the profit and non-profit motives of business . . . as well as various fundamentals like the free and pioneering origins of the American people and the social mobility and ideals of self-help, enterprise, and material achievement (in contrast to culture or status) that thus grew up; our resources and the size of our relatively unstratified home market for mass-produced goods; comparative freedom since 1865 from losses due to war preparation and war itself; and perhaps the absence of cartels."[17]

Instead of mentioning these and similar factors, Whitney complained, Galbraith advocates something that resembles a cartelized economy, "for he hails each new instance of

[15] "Errors in the Concept of Countervailing Power," *Journal of Business*, October 1953, pp. 238–253.
[16] *Ibid.*, p. 239.
[17] *Ibid.*, p. 245.

power replacing competition on the ground that it balances the previous instances. . . ." Sarcastically, Whitney says, ". . . A theory of countervailing power is reminiscent of the plan to achieve riches by taking in each other's washing —only here it is by forcing down each other's prices."

Whitney regarded Galbraith's illustrations of groups that have sought monopolistic power in the sale of labor, coal, and farm products as illogical examples of countervailing power. He could not believe that the success of American capitalism could be attributed to a series of harmonies that have brought high prices down and low ones up. The experiments of the Bituminous Coal Commission in the years 1937–1939 and of the AAA in raising prices are strange illustrations, said Whitney, to explain why our system works well. Galbraith's defense of his analysis regarding organized labor has been noted above.

Under the heading of defective cycle analysis Whitney found Galbraith glaringly inconsistent in stating that the structure of countervailing power was dissolved during the "rounds" of wage increases following 1945, and yet he attributes the good performance in this period to the neglected factor of countervailing power. Galbraith reconciles this paradoxical performance with his theory by subtly arguing that the economy after 1945 possessed what may loosely be termed "a deflationary potential." We have called attention to this point of criticism above and will note later how Galbraith sought to meet it in the revised edition of his book.

Another defect in Galbraith's concept, according to Whitney, is its failure to explain the successful performance of industries in which countervailing power is not evident. Two such cases are automobiles and petroleum. Galbraith's stock reply to this criticism would probably be that he was offering only a partial model that couldn't be expected to explain everything.

Finally, Galbraith is criticized on the score that his countervailing theory of the rise of unions, mass distributors, and government price-fixing in coal and agriculture does "only a mediocre job of explaining the historical facts."

By way of conclusion, Whitney conceded that though much of Galbraith's theory comes to pieces under analysis, there are still fragments that are usable. "Countervailing power" as a phrase sums up well the power-group interactions between our large corporations, our industries, or between the former and other organized groups in the economy. Whitney, however, would stress that the interaction is in both directions—these groups tend to hold each other in check. " 'Countervailing power' is a good phrase and even a fruitful idea, but the author claims a great deal too much for both its scope and its effectiveness."[18]

Another slashing critique of *American Capitalism* was published the following month by Professor Walter Adams of Michigan State University.[19] Adams wrote as a staunch economic liberal with a long experience in industrial organization and as a government adviser. In his analysis he placed Galbraith in the school of economic thought associated with Edward S. Mason and the late J. M. Clark. Both of the latter had urged that we should judge the effectiveness of competition in terms of results rather than on the basis of market structure (i.e., industrial concentration).

In the first place, Adams argued that countervailing power is often undermined or vitiated by vertical integration or top-level financial control of the firms that are supposed, in Galbraithian terms, to countervail each other's power. Secondly, he pointed out that countervailing power is supposed to operate by establishing bilateral monopoly and/or oligopoly situations. In the labor market, however, where, according to Galbraith, this process is seen with greatest clarity, Adams stressed that unions and management have often jointly exploited the consumer, especially in times of inflation. He cited as illustration the 1952 wage dispute in the steel industry. Here, "bilateral monopoly, instead of providing countervailing checks and balances, was instrumental in wrecking price controls and supporting the inflationary forces which drove the economy into dizzy spirals of ever higher prices, wages, costs and prices."[20] Adams acknowledged Galbraith's concession that countervailing power becomes inoperative in inflationary periods.

Galbraith's reliance on research and product development by large corporate oligopolies was flatly rejected by Adams. "Inter-industry competition and technological innovation become a farce when public policy permits them to be subverted by merger and combination."[21]

Next, Adams attacked the role of the state in the Galbraithian system as resting on the doubtful assumption that there is a sharp separation between the economy and gov-

---

[18] *Ibid.*, p. 253.
[19] W. Adams, "Competition, Monopoly and Countervailing Power," *Quarterly Journal of Economics,* November 1953, pp. 469–492.
[20] *Ibid.*, p. 476.
[21] *Ibid.*, p. 480.

ernment. He effectively quoted the late V. O. Key, the political scientist, to show the dangerous contradiction upon which the theory of countervailing power relies. "The dilemma of the politics of economic control comes from the fact that governments must keep in check the pressures of particularism, yet at the same time governments derive their power in no small degree from the support of particularistic interests. . . ."[22] He cited some striking instances from our legislative, administrative, and regulatory history where special interests had manipulated the state to the detriment of the general public interest.

Finally, Adams criticized what he regarded as the basic assumption of the countervailing power thesis, namely, that the giant size of American corporations is attributable to modern technology and economics. This, said Adams, is the "cornerstone" of the whole countervailing power theory (we might note that not all economists, including Galbraith, would accept Adams' view in this regard). He cited economic theory and antitrust cases to disprove the notion that the present size of American corporations rests on the organic advantages of large-scale production or distribution. He contended that the giant firms, rather than being victors in a process of natural selection, owe their success very often to the benevolent support of government.

In concluding, Adams made a rather surprising concession concerning Galbraith's brainchild, considering the seeming finality with which he had condemned it earlier: ". . . The countervailing power thesis is not without merit; . . . it rightly calls attention to the existence of potential checks and balances which, in our economy, supplement competition as a device for counteracting concentrated economic power. This does not mean, however, that countervailing power is a suitable substitute for competition; or that it can long survive in the absence of competition; or that it affords any clear and administratively feasible guidelines for public policy."[23]

HOW THEY CLOBBERED GALBRAITH

There was considerable professional and academic interest in Galbraith's book throughout 1953, as the pre-

---

[22] V. O. Key, *Politics, Parties and Pressure Groups* (New York: Thomas Y. Crowell, 1944), cited in Adams' article at p. 481.
[23] Adams, *op. cit.,* p. 491.

Countervailing Galbraith 51

ceding reviews indicate. Presumably, it was for this reason that the subject of countervailing power in relation to competition and monopoly was put on the program of the American Economic Association in December of that year.[24] This major, annual conclave of the nation's economists was held at the Hotel Statler in Washington, D.C. As usual on such occasions, the lobby of the hotel was crowded and noisy, as acquaintances were made or renewed and professional views exchanged. Over the hubbub, one young economist was heard calling to his friend, "Hey! Aren't you coming to see 'em clobber Galbraith?"

One reporter on the scene stated that "the general mood of the audience was that Galbraith had had his fun and should now take his lumps like a good fellow. Galbraith himself didn't see it that way."[25]

He spoke first in defense of his theory, saying urbanely that he "had long been wanting to address a loving word to some of his critics." He admitted that, as a result of criticism, he wanted to revise his contentions on two or three important points. First, he felt that he hadn't made explicit the welfare criteria he had employed in his analysis. In defending countervailing power, he hadn't made sufficiently clear whether his normative standard was that of consumer welfare or the minimization of social tensions. He confessed that if he had been less under the influence of the former norm, he would have defended the concept in terms of its promoting social harmony. An opulent society, he argued, can afford to sacrifice material welfare for social contentment.

Second, he yielded to his critics' contention that the reason mass buyers pass some of their countervailing gains along to the consumer is because retailing is still a competitive industry. Galbraith said that he "suspected" that on this point they were right; he had been reluctant in presenting his argument for countervailing power to admit reliance on competition. "After all, it is a bit embarrassing after one has just murdered his mother-in-law to disinter the lady and ask her to do the cooking."

Most of the other criticisms he brushed off lightly. For those who argued that countervailing power can be circumvented by vertical integration or defeated by inflation, he said that he readily conceded these imperfections in the

[24] *American Economic Review, Papers and Proceedings,* May 1954, pp. 1–34.
[25] "Clobbering Theory," *Business Week,* January 9, 1954, pp. 93 ff., for this quote and that of the preceding paragraph.

concept. Countervailing power, he had stated, was uneven in its effects, but there was a use for such "partial models." As for those who pointed to the inflationary tendency of countervailing power, Galbraith said that he had admitted this, but some apparently made him responsible for these untoward effects. "Such criticism, in effect, requires that the social phenomenon described be both universal in application and socially benign in effect. This is silly."

On another point, Galbraith reiterated that his espousal of countervailing power did not mean an end to the antitrust laws, but merely some discrimination in their use.

Professor George J. Stigler, a University of Chicago liberal and a highly respected expert on industrial organization, was the first to dissect Galbraith's thesis at this convention. With characteristic wit and sarcasm, he entitled his remarks "The Economist Plays with Blocs."[26] Stigler asserted that at the very outset of his book, Galbraith had eschewed presenting a rational explanation of the doctrine of countervailing power. Bilateral oligopoly was what countervailing power was all about. But the economic theory of the former can hardly be said to exist; in general, it should lead to relatively monopolistic results. But Galbraith's "proxy-minded oligopolists" pass their savings along to consumers in "a welter of irrational competitive moves." On the other hand, in labor markets and under agricultural programs the parties with countervailing power are pictured as using it to their own advantage—a result that Stigler thought was inconsistent with Galbraith's previous argument. In view of these contradictions, he concluded that Galbraith's concept was more of a dogma than a theory.

Stigler then considered the empirical evidence adduced in support of the "dogma." As to one concentration of economic power begetting another, while this view has a "limited plausibility," most of the unions that came into existence in concentrated industries did so with the aid of the New Deal. Here, Stigler pronounced a dogma of his own: ". . . We cannot use government-sponsored blocs as an illustration of the natural emergence of countervailing power, unless this is a political rather than an economic dogma." Certainly, Galbraith had made it clear in his book that he was describing a political economy in which the state had such a supporting role.

In analyzing the functioning of countervailing power in

[26] *American Economic Review, loc. cit.,* p. 7.

retail markets, Stigler cited cases to show that the emergence of large-scale retailing did not parallel that of concentration in production. Furthermore, he challenged the idea that the mass retailers were able to sell for lower prices than the independent retailers, citing Federal Trade Commission studies to support his view. One of Stigler's strongest points was that if bilateral oligopoly leads, as Galbraith contended, to socially tolerable results, then that microeconomic hypothesis should be tested on an industry-by-industry basis, not demonstrated in terms of the macroeconomic performance of the economy as a whole.

Another Stigler criticism was that Galbraith's practice of proving his case by citation of examples was dubious. Galbraith had pointed to the Great Atlantic and Pacific Tea Company's savings on corn flakes as demonstrating the benefits of countervailing power; Stigler replied that the number of industries having oligopolistic structures where the performance was generally considered to be unsatisfactory overcame any presumption resting on the one case of corn flakes.

Finally, Stigler expressed his skepticism about bilateral monopoly (countervailing power) as a method of redistributing the national income. Combination alone, he insisted, will not place groups on a basis of equality with one another. "The economic power of a group depends upon its ability to control its numbers and upon the elasticity of the demand for its services. In a cold January, coal miners will always be able to do better than college professors." Expressing his antistatist philosophy, he concluded that even at the Christmas season Galbraith could not persuade his listeners that "we should turn our economic problems over to Santa, i.e. the Welfare State."

Another industrial specialist, Professor John Perry Miller of Yale, presented a thoughtful critique of countervailing power in which he deplored the economics profession's inadequate understanding of the competitive *processes* (as contrasted with equilibrium states) in the American economy.[27] Miller saw Galbraith's concept of countervailing power as an effort to develop an understanding of these competitive processes that was more adequate than the conventional static models. He admitted that "there is much good sense in Professor Galbraith's tract." But he had the "uneasy feeling that Professor Galbraith is straining to

[27] "Competition and Countervailing Power: Their Roles in the American Economy," *American Economic Review, loc. cit.,* pp. 15 ff.

force under the single rubric of countervailing power, several [kinds] of phenomena the essential differences between which are as great, if not greater, than their similarities." He granted that a case could be made that the development of unions and of agricultural reforms had reduced social tensions, "although Professor Galbraith has certainly not marshalled the evidence [for this]." But did the rise of mass distribution allay social tensions? The agitation for the Robinson-Patman Act, the taxation of chain stores, and the drive for fair trade [resale price maintenance] indicate, said Miller, that the development of the mass distributor created rather than alleviated social tension, whatever its initial effects on the original power of manufacturers. For these reasons, Miller concluded that "a catchy phrase is being used to cover a variety of situations. It is doubtful whether so used it is a very useful tool of analysis. I doubt, also, that it is good history. And as an instrument of policy it is at best one in a crowded kit of tools along with the traditional tools of the policy of competition."

In the discussion that followed these papers, Professor David McCord Wright attacked Galbraith rather intemperately as a Platonist who was advocating the checks and balances of a stalemate.[28] "His few big business units countered by a few big unions, locked in a perpetual balance which neither side dares disturb, form a picture about as far removed from creative, democratic, competitive development as one can well conceive." For failing to espouse the fluid society, Wright judged Galbraith to be "one of the most effective enemies of both capitalism and democracy."[29]

COUNTERVAILING POWER:

SOME EMPIRICAL EVIDENCE

Another critique of Galbraith's work appeared in 1954, written by Professor Arthur Schweitzer of Indiana University.[30] He, like so many others, gave Galbraith his due —he deserved credit for formulating correctly the problem of economic power. Yet Schweitzer could not accept the

[28] *Ibid.,* pp. 26 ff.
[29] *Ibid.,* p. 30.
[30] A. Schweitzer, "A Critique of Countervailing Power," *Social Research,* Autumn 1954, pp. 253–285.

theory of countervailing power because of its two central
deficiencies. First, it made no attempt at a general theory
of power. Galbraith, said Schweitzer, advances the view that
all power originates in markets, or is the result of monopolistic positions in markets. Reasoning thus, Galbraith
neglects "all the differences between the power in the market, in the concentrated power structure, in economic organizations, and in the state."

The second deficiency, related to the first, consists in the
failure of countervailing power to show how it determines
prices, how it transfers the original power to itself, and
why it has to pass on the excess profits to consumers. This
last point, it will be noted, is identical with one made by
Whitney and others.

In 1955 a book was published that has a peculiar and
important relevance to Galbraith's thesis about countervailing power, particularly as it pertains to distribution or marketing.[31] The author, Joseph C. Palamountain, tells us that
he conducted his research independently of Galbraith. He
submitted it as a doctoral dissertation at Harvard and it
was filed in Widener Library in 1951, a year before the
publication of *American Capitalism.* In this little volume,
Palamountain explored the economic bases of conflict in
wholesale and retail distribution in the United States. In
the course of his analysis, he distinguished among three
basic forms of distributive conflict: horizontal, that is,
among sellers of the same type; intertype, or competition
among different methods of distribution; and vertical conflict, or the struggle between different levels of distribution,
such as that between manufacturer and wholesaler, wholesaler and retailer, or manufacturer and retailer. Palamountain observed that this general type of conflict had been
most neglected by economic theoreticians, but then added
in a footnote that "this neglect was in part recently cor-
rected with J. K. Galbraith's penetrating and well-written
American Capitalism. . . ."[32]

After analyzing the struggle for control of marketing
channels in the American economy (and Palamountain insisted that this involves a study of *process*), he asserted
that "a principal factor differentiating vertical conflict from
horizontal and intertype competition is that it is so directly
a power conflict." Power had multiplied in many of the
newer marketing channels. "Power," he went on to say,

---

[31] J. C. Palamountain, Jr., *The Politics of Distribution* (Cambridge: Harvard University Press, 1955).
[32] *Ibid.,* p. 48, footnote 60.

"is a two-sided relationship, and organization tends to breed counter-organization. Dominance by one end of the distributive chain often promotes groupings at the other end, for those subordinated to economic power will naturally tend to organize in attempts to create and use economic or political power. . . ."[33]

Palamountain carefully studied competition and vertical power in the distribution of groceries, drugs, and automobiles and described the political maneuvering of different groups in the passage of chain store taxes, the Robinson-Patman Act, and the Fair Trade laws. He acknowledged that power at one distributive level may, as Galbraith contends, balance and restrain power at another level. But he concluded that "Galbraith's apparent belief in the almost beneficent consequences of 'countervailing power' is not justified."[34] The druggists used their power to inflate retail margins and the auto dealers, in checking the power of the manufacturers, also restrained competition in ways that were detrimental to consumers.

Similar conclusions appear, on the whole, in a 1958 study which examined the concept of countervailing power in a British context.[35] This investigation found that mass distributors in Great Britain did not develop as a direct reaction to the market power of the oligopolistic producers. The former were organized more with a view to achieving economies of scale through organizational and merchandising techniques.

Contrary to Galbraith's thesis was the discovery that the British cooperatives had neglected their opportunities to exercise countervailing power. On the other hand, Hunter did discover some empirical evidence of countervailing power in interindustry and interfirm transactions in manufacturing. Furthermore, these cases of bilateral monopoly often tended to benefit the ultimate consumer by keeping prices down and stimulating efficiency. They did not, however, develop, as Galbraith would expect, in response to the market power of suppliers. Hunter too complained that Galbraith ignored countervailance by associations of manufacturers and distributors formed to restrict competition.

In general, this British economist doubted that countervailing power was "a universal panacea for inequality."

[33] *Ibid.*, p. 56.
[34] *Ibid.*, p. 261.
[35] A. Hunter, "Notes on Countervailing Power," *The Economic Journal*, March 1958, pp. 89–103.

And as to minimizing social tensions, he believed that the economist could not be the main authority on such a subject; this was a task for the other social science disciplines. On this point we can see the methodological differences between Galbraith and his British critic; the former as an institutional economist is inclined to include such matters as falling within the economist's jurisdiction.

American Capitalism—
THE REVISED 1956 MODEL

In 1956 Galbraith brought out a new edition of his book which he said in the foreword constituted "a substantial revision" of the original volume. Apart from small changes necessitated by the passage of time, he magnanimously admitted that the discussion of his ideas had convinced him "in some instances I was wrong and in others, either through brevity or ambiguity, I had conveyed the wrong impression."[36] Despite these amendments, the substance of the original argument of the book remained and was perhaps strengthened. He remarked that this would disappoint those who had sought "to extirpate the notion of countervailing power from the otherwise pure stream of economic thought."

In one of the most important revisions, Galbraith in a rather veiled way admitted that mass buyers are compelled by competition to pass on their gains to consumers in the form of lower prices.[37]

In his chapter "Countervailing Power and the State," he elaborated somewhat on the former's role in reducing social tension. He conceded that rather than reducing prices to consumers, the development of such power by workers and farmers might redistribute income and it might, by increasing marginal costs of enterprise, raise prices to the consumer.[38]

In another place, as already noted, he deleted some sentences regarding the "rehabilitation" of countervailing power during the recession of 1949, thus seeking to eliminate the inconsistency referred to earlier. Finally, he in-

[36] *American Capitalism,* 1956 edition, p. xi.
[37] *Ibid.,* p. 118.
[38] *Ibid.,* pp. 146–147.

serted a new chapter, "The Problem of Restraint," in which he dealt more fully with inflation and its threat to the "character and constitution" of American capitalism.

COUNTERVAILING POWER AS
AN IDEOLOGY

The preceding review of the criticisms of *American Capitalism* amply indicates the extent of the discussion that it stimulated. In addition, and perhaps as a reflection of its aptness, the phrase "countervailing power" came into wide use. Galbraith, says one economist, had the experience of seeing his concept become immensely popular in less than a decade after its introduction. "The use of the term 'countervailing power' has become so common in business and sociological writing about contemporary America that it is hard to find current popular discussions in print that do not make at least some use of the idea."[39] This author, writing in the early 1960s, went on to say, "While there is no organized group as such that espouses a Countervailing Power Ideology, yet its popular acceptance, despite its many critics among professional economists, has already given it nearly the form of a modern capitalistic ideology."[40]

Countervailing power's appeal as an ideology rests in part, says Monsen, on its *post hoc, ergo propter hoc* ("after this, therefore on account of this") approach to institutional development. Galbraith's presentation of the evolution of countervailing power makes certain institutions, such as trade unions, appear as inevitable historically. Furthermore, because they now exist, they had to exist. Such an argument serves to buttress existing institutions. "This is undoubtedly what helps give the ideology of countervailing power much of its 'persuasive' appeal."[41] Galbraith must be somewhat bewildered and amused by this interpretation which seems to convert him into a champion and supporter of "the establishment." Disclaiming such a role, he probably would say that countervailing power has the potential of serving new, disadvantaged groups that need to challenge the status quo; in that sense and from that

---

[39] R. J. Monsen, Jr., *Modern American Capitalism, Ideologies and Issues* (Boston: Houghton Mifflin, 1963), pp. 29–30.
[40] *Ibid.*, p. 30.
[41] *Ibid.*, p. 35.

perspective, it does not necessarily buttress the existing social structure.

Monsen, after evaluating some of the criticisms of countervailing power, asserts that Galbraith's approach is far more effective than the traditional ideology of capitalism in explaining the industrial structure of the United States. In his book he discusses the other ideologies (the managerial, people's capitalism, and enterprise democracy) and notes that frequently the concept of countervailing power is adopted by each of these within its own ideology as a way of coping with the problem of oligopoly. "Thus, in a sense, countervailing power as an ideology is in a state of transition in which it is apt either to be merely absorbed by other ideologies or else to absorb some of them."

In concluding, Monsen remarks that the concept of countervailing power "appears far more adaptable as an ideology for the defense of American capitalism than as an economic theory to explain it. . . ."[42]

Galbraith's book had stirred up considerable interest abroad as well as at home. It is not surprising, therefore, that in 1958 he was invited by the University of Warsaw and the Polish Economic Society to give a series of lectures on economics and the American economy. Subsequently, a Professor Stanovik of the Institute of International Politics and Economics asked him to extend his trip to Yugoslavia. So in the spring of that year he traveled through these countries, lecturing, meeting economists, and even having dinner, by way of diversion, with a high-class member of the oldest profession in the world![43] The Ford Foundation, through the Institute of International Education, arranged for the journey. Galbraith rather proudly informs his readers that "this was—at least so I was told—the first comprehensive series of lectures on capitalism to be given by a non-socialist in any Communist country since the Russian Revolution."[44]

In speaking about economics in these talks, Galbraith had an opportunity to publicize his concept of countervailing power. Characteristically, he didn't miss it and, in fact, presented his idea in its most acceptable, revised form. Thus, in his lecture entitled "Economic Power in the American Setting," he gave more emphasis to the role of interest

[42] *Ibid.,* pp. 35–36.
[43] J. K. Galbraith, *Journey to Poland and Jugoslavia* (Cambridge: Harvard University Press, 1958).
[44] *Ibid.,* p. v.

groups such as labor unions and the farm bloc in alleviating social tensions than he did to countervailance by the mass distributors. At one point he said: ". . . I have argued, subject to a good deal of dissent from my economic colleagues, that this also represents a version of countervailing power. . . . No one, I believe, claims that the position of the American consumer would be as favorable in the absence of these buyers." To this statement, one can only say, "True," but that was not exactly the proposition that was originally advanced in his book.

In his remarks to his Communist audiences, Galbraith observed that the prosperity of the post-World War II years was a notable solvent for social tensions in the United States. He claimed that this was so because, in contrast with the prosperity of the 1920s, labor's share of the national income had increased. He cited some statistics of Selma Goldsmith to show that in 1929 wages, salaries, and other income constituted 59.6 percent of the national income; in the years 1950–1955, they averaged 67.5 percent of the total.[45] On the whole, these European lectures demonstrated rather nicely the ideological use that could be made of the countervailing power theory in international politics.

Galbraith was courteously and respectfully received by his Polish and Yugoslav hosts, but he does not tell us how convinced his listeners were by his economic philosophy. For that matter, one may wonder how convinced he himself was at that time concerning some of the propositions and interpretations he had advanced in his 1952 opus. Actually, on the eve of this European journey he had another book "poised for publication" in which he came to much less optimistic conclusions about the functioning of the American economy.

In *American Capitalism* Galbraith had contended that an expanding gross national product, the operation of countervailing power, and the resultant income distribution were lessening social tensions in the nation. During the years of the Eisenhower Presidency, however, he came to see things differently, but he didn't mention this in his European lectures. In the latter, as we have noted above, he said that the post-1945 prosperity was dissolving social tensions. But in *The Affluent Society,* published later in 1958, he found that a grave social imbalance had developed in the economy

---

[45] S. F. Goldsmith, "Income Distribution: Changes in Size Distribution of Income," *American Economic Review,* May 1957, pp. 504–518.

against which countervailing power was of no avail.[46] In fact, some of the beneficiaries of countervailing power, such as the trade unions, had acquired a vested interest in production and the related employment that was aggravating the economic distortions. We can, of course, account for some of these discrepancies in Galbraithian thought and policy by attributing them to the passage of time and the emergence of new circumstances. Perhaps there is a reference to these depredations of time on his interpretations as well as an element of self-consolation in this remark in the second edition of the aforementioned book: "It is unwise to reflect excessively on one's past writing and especially on one's foresight, for to do so is to invite critical attention to those other forecasts which brings one's score back to normal."[47]

A SUMMING UP

In appraising *American Capitalism* it is appropriate to see it as an essay which significantly reflected the spirit of post-World War II America and, in particular, that of the five years after the Japanese surrender. In those years, as others have pointed out, American intellectuals often looked at their society and its institutions in a new way.[48] Galbraith's book suggests this tendency to find something good about American society after the disillusionment caused by the Great Depression and the horrors of totalitarian tyranny. However, to an important degree it was summing up intellectual currents that had been set in motion years before, in the Progressive era and during the New Deal. Ironically, the power of circumstances, so frequently cited by Galbraith, was conspiring against it. The accelerating pace of social change in the fifties and sixties speedily made several of its formulations rather obsolete. Still, some of its basic ideas appear to have a more enduring significance.

The book as a whole can be viewed as a seminal institutional analysis of what has been termed the "organ-

[46] In his introduction to the second edition of *The Affluent Society,* Galbraith stated flatly, ". . . We have had many years of expansive Gross National Product. Social tension has increased, not lessened" (Boston: Houghton Mifflin Co., 1969, p. xxiii).

[47] *Ibid.,* p. xxii.

[48] For evidence of this tendency in writings of others, see *The Partisan Review,* May-June, pp. 282–326; July-Aug., pp. 420–450; Sept.-Oct., pp. 562–597; all preceding are for 1952.

izational economy." This phrase, in the words of the economist who first gave it currency, refers to "the vastly increased role of industrial and financial corporations, labor unions and farm organizations and of the largest and most powerful of all organizations, the state, in an economy in which competition in old and new forms still plays a strategic role."[49] Galbraith might balk at the emphasis in this definition on the primary role of competition, but he would accept the overall characterization of the economy that it embodies.

In economics, Galbraith's emphasis on the emergence of countervailing power in product markets has been regarded by some as an important contribution to the study of competition as a dynamic process. In this view conventional static theory leaves offstage the responses of those with whom a competitor deals in the way of market canvassing and bargaining. But such maneuvers are an essential part of a dynamic analysis. The late John M. Clark acknowledged this in these words: ". . . Galbraith has taken advantage of theory's neglect of this process to annex it as one sector of his rather heterogeneous category of countervailing power, treating it as a substitute for competition which has lapsed into passivity."[50]

The classical economists had looked upon production as a process. Galbraith, like Palamountain, insists that distribution or the marketing of goods should likewise be analyzed in process terms. This approach brings out the elements of bargaining in the price determination process and thus makes for a more rounded analysis than is accepted in pure theory. Incidentally, Galbraith did not explore the effects of this countervailing type of bargaining on the improvement of products and production processes. There would appear to be important evidence of this tendency in American industry.[51] As indicated in some of the criticism above, Galbraith was apparently too optimistic about countervailing power benefiting the ultimate consumer. In some striking instances, the tactics of counter-

---

[49] C. B. Hoover, "Institutional and Theoretical Implications of Economic Change," *American Economic Review*, March 1954, p. 12.

[50] J. M. Clark, "Competition: Static Models and Dynamic Aspects," in American Economic Association, *Readings in Industrial Organization and Public Policy* (Homewood, Ill.: Richard D. Irwin, Inc., 1958), p. 253.

[51] For example, see C. H. Hession, "The Metal Container Industry," in W. Adams (Ed.), *The Structure of American Industry* (4th ed., New York: Macmillan, 1971), p. 328.

vailance have been employed to restrict competition and raise prices, even in periods of slack demand.

The opinion that countervailing power is too broad and heterogeneous a category would also seem to be sound. Countervailing power by mass buyers may be justified, as Galbraith argues, as a partial model. But will a partial model suffice when one advocates countervailing power for whole interest groups? A more holistic model seems to be required where such major processes of societal functioning are involved. Furthermore, if such countervailance is urged in terms of minimizing social tensions, we are dealing with questions that transcend price or distribution theory; economistic diagnosis and remedy are not adequate. The functioning and implications of a society of countervailing blocs must be analyzed in sociopsychological terms as well as economic ones, if the possible effects on democracy, individual freedom, and social stability are to be understood.[52]

Finally, some skepticism must be expressed about explaining the post-World War II performance of the American economy wholly in terms of the neglected factor of countervailing power. Other analyses that point to the backlog of consumer demand and the massive monetary liquidity in the economy in that period seem equal or superior to countervailing power as explanations. Better still, what is needed is a comprehensive evaluation of the conjoint effect of the several forces at work at that time. Galbraith is admittedly a provocative and persuasive writer, but our review of his book certainly suggests that some countervailance of his literary power has contributed to a more balanced evaluation of his contribution to the understanding of our complex economy.

[52] Some elements of such an analysis will be found in C. H. Hession et al., *The Dynamics of the American Economy* (New York: A. A. Knopf, 1956).

4 The Affluent

Society in Its Historical

Context

THE POWER OF CIRCUMSTANCES

Toward the close of his last great book, John Maynard Keynes philosophized about the influence of ideas on the course of history as follows: ". . . The ideas of economists and political philosophers, both when they are right and when they are wrong, are more powerful than is commonly understood. Practical men, who believe themselves to be quite exempt from intellectual influences, are usually the slaves of some defunct economist."[1] In his various books, on the contrary, Galbraith has often stressed the power of circumstances in influencing the impact and reception of ideas. Thus in one of them he writes: "The enemy of the conventional wisdom is not ideas but the march of events."[2] In this chapter we shall be concerned with the events, the circumstances, that led Galbraith to write *The Affluent Society* as well as with the historical developments that helped to make it a best-seller.

Our task in doing this is made lighter by the fact that Galbraith has provided an introduction to the second edition of that volume in which he reviews the ideological background against which his book was written. In the post-World War II years, he explains, there occurred something of a revival of free enterprise or market economics in the United States. The proponents of this movement were mainly Republicans or other conservatives who were

[1] J. M. Keynes, *The General Theory of Employment, Interest and Money* (New York: Harcourt, Brace, 1936), p. 383.
[2] *The Affluent Society* (Boston: Houghton Mifflin, 2nd ed. Revised 1969), p. 12.

weary and critical of what they regarded as intolerable government regimentation under the New Deal and wartime administration. They were aided in their agitation by the publication of a widely read tract by Professor Friedrich A. von Hayek, *The Road to Serfdom*.[3] In this book the author pictured the horrible despotism that inevitably awaited America if it continued its dalliance with economic planning. This market revival was strenuously promoted also by the publishers of such journals as *Reader's Digest, Fortune,* and *The Wall Street Journal*. It received some aid from free-enterprise economists at the University of Chicago and some other academic centers as well as from a number of intellectuals who were in ideological retreat from the Stalin-Hitler pact.

There were still other historical circumstances that favored the market revival. Among these were the general discontent with economic controls—rationing, price-fixing, and so on—and wartime deprivations. Furthermore, during World War II business claimed credit for the "miracle of production" and this led many to yearn for a return to normalcy, as had been the case after World War I. These reactions manifested themselves in the election of many conservatives in 1946. On the whole, however, during the Eisenhower years the market revival produced more rhetoric than action. Nevertheless, in Galbraith's view it had a restraining effect on new federal activities and on state and local expenditures for public projects. In addition to the ancient complaint about the burden of taxes, there was now the new argument that public spending threatened freedom itself and that it carried the nation nearer to Communism.

Liberal economic policy in these years tended more and more to concentrate on Keynesian fiscal action as the main answer to the nation's economic problems. Maintenance of a high level of aggregate demand and of output and employment was thought to be the way to solve national ills. And in the atmosphere of the Cold War and later of actual hostilities in Korea, large defense expenditures provided the fiscal support necessary to preserve prosperity or stimulate recovery from recession. In the current liberal view such "military Keynesianism" did not require a major revision in the role of the state. This fact made possible, in effect, a tacit coalition between the conservatives and the liberals. The conservatives approved because it assured a strong

[3] London: George Routledge and Sons, 1944.

military defense against Communism. These were the ideas, says Galbraith, "both the market revival and the Keynesian preoccupation with employment *qua* employment and production *qua* production, that seemed to me damaging."[4]

There was another inducement, says Galbraith, for his writing *The Affluent Society*. For a number of years as an agricultural economist he had wondered at the persistence of rural poverty in the United States, the richest nation in the world. Indeed, his first intention was to write a book with the title "Why People Are Poor." In the development of his thought he came to see that the neglect of government services, such as education, health, and welfare, had much to do with the persistence of poverty in an increasingly affluent society.

The social climate of America in the fifties was growing critical of the national obsession with private goods and consumerism. While there was a general euphoria in the early years of the Eisenhower administration, intellectuals were beginning to look askance at the new postwar style of life. David Riesman was one of the first to criticize the nation's consumer orientation and conformity in his *The Lonely Crowd* (1950). The late C. Wright Mills analyzed the emptiness of life and political apathy among the new middle class in his brilliant book *White Collar* (1951). Later, William H. Whyte, Jr., drew a dismal picture of the life of "orgman" at work and in his homogeneous suburbia in *The Organization Man* (1958).

In the Presidential election of 1956 this questioning of the nation's goals became quite explicit, especially in the campaign of Adlai Stevenson. (Galbraith served as a writer and agricultural adviser on the Stevenson staff in the 1952 and 1956 campaigns.) In one of his speeches, the Democratic candidate said:

> But free society cannot be content with a goal of mere life without want. It has always had within it a visionary spark, a dream that man, liberated from crushing work, aching hunger and constant insecurity, would discover wider interests and nobler aims. If quantity comes first so that men may eat, quality comes next so that they may not live by bread alone. Free society in the West has brought most of its citizens to that great divide. The next frontier is the quality, the moral, intellectual and esthetic standards of the free way of life.[5]

4 *The Affluent Society*, 2nd ed., p. xxi.
5 S. E. Harris *et al.* (Eds.), *The New America*, by Adlai E. Stevenson (New York: Harper and Row, 1957), p. 260. In 1956 Arthur

There was wide recognition of the increasing potential of our economy and the possibilities of abundance in the fifties. In 1956, in collaboration with two colleagues, I published a book, *The Dynamics of the American Economy,* that stressed the potentialities of our future growth, and urged expansion of collective consumption (expenditures for schools, health, improved communities).[6] With the satisfaction of many wants that had gone unfulfilled in the war years, by the middle fifties there was talk of satiation of demand for durable consumer goods. The auto industry, the major industry of that category, frantically pushed its efforts at salesmanship and planned obsolescence to new heights. The "insolent chariots" were made longer and were more lavishly ornamented. The horsepower race among the car manufacturers accelerated, increasing the hazards to life and the pollution of the atmosphere.

Demand creation in other industries also became extreme. In addition to tail-fins, excessive chrome, and the like, there were reports that the rich were receiving Christmas presents of electric swizzle sticks and other useless gadgets. Walter Lippmann wrote a column denouncing the triviality of such consumption, and other journalists did likewise. Professor Alvin Hansen, leading Harvard economist, wrote a book that questioned the sanity of the nation's priorities. "After ten years of almost incredible *output* performance," he wrote, "we need to assess not merely the speed of our growth and progress but also the direction in which we are going. What qualitative goals shall we set up? These are matters that we dare not overlook, lest we perish, as a great nation in the midst of material plenty."[7]

Galbraith, like others in this period of McCarthyism and often flagrant anti-intellectualism, was oppressed by the intellectual atmosphere and the general euphoric mood of the nation. "These are the days," he wrote, "when men of all social disciplines and all political faiths seek the comfortable and the accepted; when the man of controversy is looked upon as a disturbing influence; when originality is

---

Schlesinger, Jr., chief of Stevenson's brain trust, wrote an essay entitled "The Future of Liberalism—The Challenge of Abundance," in which he defined the difference between the "quantitative liberalism" of prewar America and the "qualitative liberalism" which was possible with America's increasing mastery of production.

[6] C. H. Hession, S. M. Miller, and C. Stoddart, *The Dynamics of the American Economy* (New York: A. A. Knopf, 1956), pp. 434–441, 481.

[7] A. H. Hansen, *The American Economy* (New York: McGraw-Hill, 1957), p. 146.

taken to be a mark of instability; and when, in minor modification of the scriptural parable, the bland lead the bland."[8]

In the early summer of 1955, Galbraith sailed for Switzerland to begin work on what became *The Affluent Society*. Before its publication he had some misgivings about its eventual reception. He feared that it would be dismissed as "another semi-socialist case for public spending and by my Keynesian friends as apostasy." But then, most opportunely, circumstances favored him: in the autumn of 1957, on the very eve of the book's publication, the Russians sent up the first Sputnik. Galbraith was overjoyed.

> No action was ever so admirably timed. Had I been younger and less formed in my political views, I would have been carried away by my gratitude and found a final resting place beneath the Kremlin Wall. I knew my book was home. A vastly less productive society had brought off a breathtaking and also, who could tell, very alarming achievement. It couldn't be because they had more wealth—more automobiles, more gasoline, more elegantly packaged food, or anything comparable in depilatories and deodorants. Surely they were using their more meager resources more purposefully.[9]

Galbraith sensed that the launching of Sputnik meant that we would be in for "one of those orgies of anguished soul-searching which are a recurrent and distinctive feature of our social history." And, of course, he was right. The nation became alarmed about the quality of its education and turned introspectively to inquire about the "national purpose." Indeed, President Eisenhower characteristically appointed another commission to investigate the subject.[10] None of this national concern about the nation's goals hurt the sales of Galbraith's book. Quite the contrary, after the first Sputnik, he was confident, at least, that it would be a "major success."

OUR LEGACY OF ECONOMIC DESPAIR

In the opening chapters of his book Galbraith seeks to demonstrate that the ideas by which we interpret "the great and quite unprecedented affluence" in the United States are derived from an older culture of economic

[8] *The Affluent Society*, 2nd ed., pp. 4–5.
[9] *Ibid.*, p. xxviii.
[10] U.S. President's Commission on National Goals, *Goals for Americans* (Englewood Cliffs, N.J.: Prentice-Hall, 1960).

scarcity and mass poverty. Our economic attitudes, he tells us, are rooted in the poverty, inequality, and economic uncertainties of the past. As a result of our being guided, in part, by ideas more relevant to another world, "we do many things that are unnecessary, some that are unwise, and a few that are insane." We are victims, in short, of a disastrous cultural lag in our thinking; in his words, we are captives of that "greatest of vested interests, those of the mind."

Anthropologists teach us that men in all cultures need a belief system to give meaning and direction to their lives. Similarly, Galbraith argues that in an economic life that is often complex and difficult to understand, men need a body of ideas, an ideology, to provide a rationale for their existence. Economic phenomena are not so unambiguous as the facts of physical life. Consequently there is more room for different interpretations and views of it than of the physical world. One can believe what one pleases within a relatively wide range. Still, for the generality of men the ideas that are familiar and convenient—that contribute to their self-esteem, comfort, and self-interest—these constitute what Galbraith calls, in a memorable phrase, "the conventional wisdom." The latter may have its drawbacks, but it does have an important social function: it provides stability and continuity in thought and action.

Following these preliminary conceptions, Galbraith sketches out in broad strokes the development of economic thought in the Western world. His purpose, he says, is not to describe the evolution of economic theories, but to see what economics "assumed in its origins about the ordinary individual and his fate." In another place, he suggests that he is tracing the ideas that were taught and read and by which the properly qualified were guided. His treatment, extending over several chapters, is necessarily brief, but it is readable and filled with human interest.

Starting with Adam Smith (1723–1790), the founder of what he calls the "central economic tradition," Galbraith notes that the Scotch philosopher is generally considered hopeful and optimistic about human progress. In his classic work, *An Inquiry into the Nature and Causes of the Wealth of Nations,* Smith placed his reliance, in the main, on the competitive market and on self-interest rather than on the mercantilist state. But Smith, says Galbraith, was more concerned with the production of aggregate wealth than with its distribution. And even he was not too hopeful about the improvement of the economic condition of the

working masses. The latter, he saw, in his day were at a
great disadvantage in bargaining power compared to the
merchants, manufacturers, and the landlords. Smith even
suggested that wages tended toward a minimum set by subsistence and thus anticipated that most despairing principle
of classical economics—the iron law of wages.

But it was in the hands of David Ricardo (1772–1823)
and Thomas Robert Malthus (1766–1834) that economics
truly became the "dismal science." In their writings, says
Galbraith, "the notion of massive privation and great inequality became a basic premise." He refers, of course, to
the functioning of the Malthusian principle of population
which, together with Ricardo's subsistence theory of wages,
tended, in theory, to keep the ordinary man on the edge
of starvation. Even the political economy of John Stuart
Mill (1806–1873), which emphasized the malleability of
the institutions controlling the distribution of income, was
not overly optimistic about the fate of the common man.

In the latter part of the nineteenth century Alfred Marshall (1842–1924) continued and elaborated on the central
economic tradition. Galbraith quotes a passage from his
work to prove that even Marshall held that under stationary conditions the tendency of wages was still to a minimum. Likewise, Galbraith argues that Professor Frank W.
Taussig, the leading American economist in the early decades
of the present century, was not optimistic about the prospects
for improvement in the wages of ordinary labor in the United
States during the years 1900–1910. In general, according to
Galbraith, the legacy of ideas of the central tradition taught
that poverty was normal, inequality inevitable, and individual insecurity inherent in the working of the competitive
order and in the periodic recurrence of business depressions.

In describing the "American mood" implicit in the developing body of economic thought in this country, Galbraith continues to press his thesis about the predominance
of the economics of scarcity. He rightly observes that in
the early years of the nation there were few figures comparable to those of the British tradition. He concentrates
in his summary on three economists who were the "most
heard." Henry Charles Carey (1793–1879) rejected the
pessimistic Ricardian tradition and expounded an optimism
more appropriate to the new republic. But Henry George
(1839–1897) and Thorstein Veblen (1857–1929), Galbraith contends, were "prophets of a gloom that was, in

some respects, more profound than that of Ricardo." George, basing his famous doctrines on Ricardo's law of rent, saw only a continuation of poverty and depressions, so long as there was private property in land. Galbraith does acknowledge that George and his followers show typically American optimism in their faith in his panacea, the single tax. Given the opposition to such a proposal, the mood of George's sympathizers was often one of "misanthropic or frustrated radicalism."

Veblen, a most indigenous and original American economist, substituted only a "grandiloquent iconoclasm" for the Ricardian gloom. He emphasized, says Galbraith, the businessman's sabotage of production and the tendency of the economy to chronic depression. In *The Theory of the Leisure Class* he dramatized, as no one had before him, the amazing spectacle of social inequality in the Gilded Age. Nor did he hold out any hope of change; exploitation and invidious display of wealth were inevitable in an acquisitive, pecuniary culture.

Having set out Veblen's mordant conclusions, Galbraith admits that his ideas were not widely read or taught. He goes on to say that the teachers influenced by Veblen taught the central tradition, but they had "a disbelief, even a contempt, for the notion that economic progress could much benefit the masses, or indeed, that there was such a thing." It is not clear to whom he refers in this passage.

After treating American economic thought proper, Galbraith turns to the doctrines of the Social Darwinists because they had a profound influence on the attitudes concerning the fate of the ordinary man. These writers, drawing on the thought of the British philosopher Herbert Spencer, held that competitive society was governed by the evolutionary principle of the "survival of the fittest." Galbraith shows how the Spencerian principles of the survival of the fittest were used to justify the competitive economic struggle. Poverty, insecurity, and inequality were thus made inherent even in the economy of this most favored of nations. Although one might think that the economic contest would be moderated in the rich, continental environment of the United States, Social Darwinism suggested the opposite.

Galbraith wisely qualifies the picture he has drawn of American economic ideology toward the end of his summary, saying, "One would not care to claim that this chapter exhausts the influences which have borne distinctively on American economic attitudes.[11] He observes that the frontier and West had their own expansive mood. And he admits that the political debate at the end of the nineteenth century and the beginning of the present one expressed the idea that any American—"at a minimum any properly energetic American of Anglo-Saxon and Protestant antecedents"—could attain a comfortable affluence by his own efforts. But he insists that "the ideas which were taught and read, and by which the properly qualified were guided, were far from sanguine."[12]

In his last chapter on economic thought, Galbraith discusses the "Marxian pall." He asserts that Marx subtly affected those who were least supposed to be subject to his influence. For example, American businessmen often reason like economic materialists. For those who came under his influence, Marx's prediction of increasing economic concentration, of more severe and devastating depressions, of mounting economic inequality, and of the ultimate collapse of capitalism cast a pall over the future. In summary, says Galbraith, up until the middle thirties the broad impact of the ideas, whether classical or Marxian, left the typical individual with "a sense of the depth, pervasiveness, and burden of the economic problem and, on the whole, with the improbability of a happy outcome."[13]

While this is not the place for a full analysis, we must express some dissent with Galbraith's sketch of our recent intellectual history. His treatment ignores altogether the more optimistic outlook on the American destiny which was reflected at the turn of the century in the work of William James and John Dewey. The pragmatic revolt against formalism affected the Progressive movement and helped to shape its general belief that American society could be reformed by the use of man's creative intelligence.[14]

In saying also that the broad impact of conventional economic ideas left the nation pessimistic and uncertain of

[11] Professor Allen M. Sievers has pointed out that the passage of Marshall's work Galbraith quoted was most unrepresentative of his thought; he was a believer in progress and dynamic evolutionary change and his optimistic philosophy reflected the spirit of the Victorian era. (A. M. Sievers, *Revolution, Evolution and the Economic Order,* Englewood Cliffs, N.J.: Prentice Hall, Inc., 1962, pp. 88–89.)

[12] *The Affluent Society,* p. 63.

[13] *Ibid.,* p. 75.

[14] On this important subject, see E. Goldman, *Rendezvous with Destiny* (New York: Vintage Books, 1956), and M. G. White, *Social Thought in America* (Boston: Beacon Press, 1957).

a happy outcome, Galbraith neglects the euphoria of the 1920s, the famous New Era. It was not all politics that led Herbert Hoover in the campaign of 1928 to speak repeatedly of the "abolition of poverty." On August 11 of that year, Hoover said, with his characteristic earnestness, "We in America today are nearer to the final triumph over poverty than ever before in the history of any land. The poorhouse is vanishing from among us. We have not yet reached the goal, but, given the chance to go forward with the policies of the last eight years, we shall soon with the help of God be in sight of the day when poverty will be banished from this nation."[15]

Galbraith does not sufficiently convey to his reader that the twenties were actually the period which witnessed the dawn of the affluent, mass-consumption society. He seems to date its emergence from the advent of Keynesian economics in the thirties, but many close observers of our history differ with him on this point. During the hectic twenties America was making the painful, but important adjustment to a consumer's culture.[16] The institutions of advertising and of installment finance were vigorously expanded by the new managers of "welfare capitalism" in order to accommodate the nation to an emerging economy of abundance. The doctrine of high wages and the faith in the capacity of the Federal Reserve System to maintain economic stability reflected the optimism of the business class of that period. Curiously, Galbraith's formulation of the evolution of the industrial system in *The New Industrial State* provides a better historical perspective on what was happening in the twenties than will be obtained from his chapter on the American mood in *The Affluent Society*. His concentration on the formal ideology, on "the ideas which were taught and read," imposed very severe restraints on his exposition, as he himself indicated in the last paragraph of that chapter.

In the Galbraithian perspective, then, the central tradition made productivity, inequality, and insecurity the main preoccupations of economics. This was never more the case than in the Great Depression of this century, just

[15] Quoted in A. M. Schlesinger, Jr., *The Age of Roosevelt, The Crisis of the Old Order, 1919–1933* (Boston: Houghton Mifflin, 1957), p. 89.

[16] See especially D. Potter, *People of Plenty, Economic Abundance and the American Character* (Chicago: The University of Chicago Press, 1954), and C. H. Hession and H. Sardy, *Ascent to Affluence: A History of American Economic Development* (Boston: Allyn and Bacon, 1969), pp. 666–674.

before the nation was to experience "a mountainous rise in well-being." Yet, despite the fact that we have passed that great divide and have seen the advent of affluence, the older preoccupations still remain. Not completely, however —because we can see the modifications that have been wrought in conventional economic attitudes toward inequality and insecurity as a result of the increase in the nation's productive capacity.

INEQUALITY AND INSECURITY

Inequality and insecurity of income have long been a source of controversy, writes Galbraith, between the rich and the poor, the radical and the conservative. These conditions have frequently led to proposals for redistribution to alleviate the tension between social classes. In the nineteenth century the classical economists defended inequality in terms of natural law, the equity of property rights, and the danger of disrupting a functioning social order. In modern times it has been more common to defend inequality in terms of its functional economic role. The prospect of riches and of retaining what one has earned serve, it is alleged, as an incentive to effort. Furthermore, the concentration of income in the hands of the rich augments saving, and therefore capital formation is greater than it would be with more equal distribution.

In the mid 1950s Galbraith concluded that though inequality was still great, there had been a noticeable decline of interest in equality as an economic issue. A variety of reasons could be found for this: For one, inequality, at least between the late 1920s and the mid-1950s, did not grow worse; second, the power and prestige of wealth have waned as the nation's economy moved from the Age of the Moguls to that of the Corporate Managers; the rich have become more common, while household service as maids and butlers has contracted; the conspicuous display of wealth, as in the late nineteenth century, has become passé. All these reasons have been related in one way or another to a more basic one—the vast increase in production. Increased production has come to be seen as an alternative to the more difficult policy of redistribution. Production is regarded as "the great solvent of the tensions associated with inequality." Liberals as well as radicals have accepted the goal of an expanding economy. Thus the old question of the distribution of income, though not resolved, has fallen largely into abeyance and attention has been concentrated on the objective of increased productivity.

Galbraith next turns to examine the mythology concerning economic security. Liberals and conservatives have long been divided on this issue. The conventional wisdom of the latter insists that the quest for security is a terrible threat to economic progress. The liberals, on the other hand, frantically search for new forms of security legislation as tokens of social progress and as a basis for preferment at the polls. All this has an unreal character, because as economic insecurity has been eliminated or reduced in economic life, it survives as ideological underpinning in the conventional wisdom.

In the economy dominated by the central economic tradition insecurity was an inevitable outcome of the competitive market system. While preaching free enterprise, the businessmen were among the first to seek escape from market insecurity. Through such means as monopoly, collusive action, advertising, diversification, and joint decision-making, business has sought to stabilize its income. Anticipating his theme in *The New Industrial State,* Galbraith minimizes the monopoly motive of the businessman, and flatly states that "the development of the modern business enterprise can be understood only as a comprehensive effort to reduce risk."

Likewise, other economic groups have sought security, especially in the thirties, through a variety of microeconomic measures designed to stabilize their prices, wages, or income. For the small man there was social security; for the farmer, parity prices; and for the worker, unions. At about the same time, there was a great development of interest in what one can call macromeasures to stabilize the economy, thanks to the influence of Keynesian thinking and the pragmatic mood inspired by the New Deal.

Rather than reflecting dire poverty, this search for security was more often the result of improving fortune; people had more to protect, and the more affluent were generally the most energetic in their own behalf, though they frequently recommended competition for the other fellow.

As these measures for individuals and groups are instituted, there is a declining urgency for such policies. Galbraith announces confidently that "the elimination of insecurity in economic life can be a finished business." The preoccupation with economic security, he says, is largely in the past; but the success of all the separate micro-measures is dependent on the avoidance of business depression.

Contrary to the conventional wisdom, there is no fundamental conflict between security and progress. But the notion that economic insecurity is essential for efficiency and economic advance is erroneous—"a major miscalculation." The facts show that along with the drive for security there has been an unparalleled advance in productivity. And conversely, the nation has recognized the close relation between a high level of production and economic security. Indeed, it pursues production compulsively because a high level of output is essential for the security of businessmen, farmers, and workers. In all this there is a paradox: "Why is it that as production has increased in modern times concern for production has also increased?" The answer, says Galbraith, is that "production has become the center of a concern that had hitherto been shared with equality and security." Bolstered and reinforced by modern advertising, production has managed to maintain a priority more suitable to the poor world of Ricardo.

THE MYSTIQUE OF PRODUCTION—
CAUSES AND CONSEQUENCES

The central preoccupation of Americans, says Galbraith, is production—the gross national output. On this object, Americans of all political persuasions, all religions, ethnic groups, and occupations have common ground. Production is identified with the sensible and the practical. Indeed, its prestige and importance transcend our national boundaries. The American standard of living—based on production—is the "marvel of the world." Yet this attitude toward production is based on tradition and social myth rather than reason. Our preoccupation with a growing GNP is "the culminating consequence of powerful historical and psychological forces—forces which only by an act of will we can hope to escape. . . ."[17]

Our conventional attitude toward production is revealed by the stylized manner in which we go about increasing it. In peacetime we concern ourselves mainly with the efficiency of resource allocation and the promotion of thrift

[17] *The Affluent Society,* 2nd ed., p. 124.

and diligence, but we irrationally neglect other means of raising output. In many of our backward industries we ignore the low rate of capital formation and the small investment in innovation. We don't expand the labor force to increase production, nor do we worry unduly over the output lost during depressions. Our concern tends to be focused on those dimensions which were relevant a century ago. In wartime, however, the conventional wisdom on production is rejected; we seek to expand production along all the relevant dimensions.

The conventional wisdom molds our attitudes in still another way. Private goods produced by the market are highly esteemed and even viewed with pride, no matter how frivolous they may be; public goods and services, provided by government, tend to be viewed as a burden. Tradition, the old suspicion of tyrannous governments and bad kings, and the rich man's opposition to taxation have contributed to these negative attitudes about public services. Private goods, on the other hand, suffer from no such preconception. On the contrary, they are extolled by "the massed drums of modern advertising."

Our national preoccupation with production has been provided with a rationale by economic theory. While this theory has an impeccable position in the conventional wisdom, "it is illogical and meretricious and in degree even dangerous." Economists have a vested interest in the view that production is eternally urgent and human wants unlimited. The orthodox theory of consumer demand which upholds this view is based on two broad propositions. The first, the principle of the insatiability of human wants, holds that the urgency of wants does not diminish appreciably as more of them are satisfied. When physical wants are satisfied, then psychologically grounded wants take over and these can never be completely satisfied. Second, the economist assumes that wants originate with the consumer; they are given data for his analysis. He does not need to inquire how they are formed.

SCARCITY, NATURAL AND CONTRIVED

Galbraith then undertakes a review of the theory of consumer demand. He shows how in the evolution of value theory the paradox of high utility and low exchangeability was resolved by the economics of marginal utility.

Yet this doctrine of diminishing marginal utility would seem to have supported the view that production will be of diminishing importance under conditions of increasing affluence. As per capita real income increases, men can satisfy additional wants beyond those for food, clothing, and necessary shelter. The production that satisfies these less urgent wants would appear to be of smaller and ever-declining importance. Increasing affluence should lead to a minimization of economic goals. But orthodox theory did not admit any such diminishing urgency of wants as production mounted. This feat was accomplished in the name of a refined scientific method that has proved to be a bulwark of the conventional wisdom.

The orthodox economists achieved this remarkable outcome by divorcing economics from ethics. To be more specific, they contended that it is impossible to make comparisons of utility for different persons. The burglar's jimmy is of as much value to him as the food which keeps the poor man from starving. In Bentham's famous expression, "Pin push is as good as poetry." (Perhaps, in terms of our culture, we could paraphrase this to mean that "bingo is as good as Bach.") Furthermore, according to the orthodox theory, intertemporal comparisons of utility cannot be scientifically made. This means that the economist cannot say anything useful about the satisfactions individual consumers obtain from goods consumed at different periods of time. What this amounts to is that economists have a theory of individual demand, but not of consumption. Contrary to the prevailing view, Keynes in one of his essays argued that man's absolute needs were capable of being satisfied and therefore the economic problem need not be the permanent concern of the human race. But Keynes had no success in this endeavor at persuasion because his advocacy of the idea was not supported by historical circumstances.

Galbraith then turns to refute the orthodox theory of demand, noting that there is a basic flaw in its reasoning. The accepted theory assumes that the consumer's wants are autonomous. If the individual's wants are to be considered urgent, they must be original with him, says Galbraith; they cannot be contrived. And certainly they cannot be legitimately contrived by the various processes of production that seek to satisfy them. The urgency of the wants stimulated by the producers cannot be used to defend the urgency of production. Galbraith notes that Keynes recognized the insatiability of wants that arises out of one man's desire to emulate or outdo his neighbor in consumption. Furthermore, those who acknowledge that many goods in our affluent society are prestige symbols, in effect admit that the production of goods creates the wants the goods are supposed to satisfy.

The major link between production and wants is established by the powerful institutions of modern advertising and salesmanship. These institutions actively seek to synthesize or create wants for the goods which are being produced. This relationship between wants and the process by which they are satisfied Galbraith terms the "dependence effect." The teaching of economics, he contends, continues "almost undefiled" to pretend that wants are independently or spontaneously generated and to minimize the role of advertising in want creation. In so doing, it maintains the myth of the prime urgency of production as a social goal. But this approach is perilous and cannot long withstand close examination. "Among the many models of the good society no one has urged the squirrel wheel."

In the original edition of *The Affluent Society* Galbraith dealt in one chapter with what he called "The Illusion of National Security." In the revised edition, though he said that he liked the chapter and would miss it "as a favorite child," he deleted it. He did so because he believed that the idea, so strongly held during the Cold War, that our national security depended on our excelling the Russians in the rate of increase in production was now more widely rejected. The myth that he attacked was the belief that military power is a function of economic output; in short, that victory would tend to crown the efforts of the nation with the greatest GNP. However true that may have been in the days of old-fashioned war with its more leisurely mobilization, it has little to do with the waging of atomic or thermonuclear war. Furthermore, Galbraith argues, even in a time of limited war, as in Korea, the stimulus to production of consumer goods increases the demand for consumer goods *pari passu* because of the dependence effect, so that much of the nation's economic potential is not available for military purposes, barring drastic curtailment of civilian consumption.

THE PROBLEMS OF THE
AFFLUENT SOCIETY

Having examined the sources of the conventional wisdom that makes production paramount in the affluent society, Galbraith next considers the three unsolved problems or tensions that these economic attitudes generate. The first is the artificial creation of demand through advertising and high-pressure salesmanship. Closely related to this is the process of debt creation via the institution of installment finance. Galbraith points to the psychological tensions associated with the massive debt that consumer borrowing entails. "The legacy of wants, which are themselves inspired, are the bills which descend like the winter snow on those who are buying on the installment plan. . . . Can the bill collector be the central figure in the good society?"[18] Installment finance not only contributes to inflation in boom times, but increases the instability of aggregate demand and makes the economy more liable to depression, unless prompt and effective countercyclical action is taken to offset the decline in the rate of consumer debt creation. A greater allocation of resources to the public sector, where installment financing is not practiced, would therefore contribute to economic stability. "Mass persuasion leading on to mass encouragement to indebtedness" seems to Galbraith a perilous course for the nation. His views on this subject rest on close analysis of the difficult choices public policy faced in seeking to check the 1955 boom which culminated in the recession of 1957–1958.

In Chapters XV to XVII Galbraith deals with inflation, the second major problem of an affluent society infatuated with production. While there are a variety of reasons why inflation has been extraordinarily difficult to control in the post-World War II years, the main one has been that our commitment to all-out production leads us to operate the economy so close to capacity that price advances are very likely. The responses of our industries to increases in demand are not uniform. In those which are concentrated or oligopolistic, the big firms may not increase prices as demand goes up; they have a degree of market control and therefore can postpone price revisions in line with their long-run goals. When unions demand increased wages, however, the big firms can grant these demands and raise prices to cover their increases in costs at the opportune time. Their discretionary market power permits them to do this, but it also contributes to the familiar wage-price spiral. The price increases in the oligopolistic sector spread through the whole economy. Those who operate in the less concentrated industries or whose compensation is not

---

[18] *Ibid.,* p. 201.

readily adjusted suffer from the market power of the big firms and the big unions. It is of no use to increase production or investment to counteract inflation, because both of these actions will increase demand correspondingly. Control of inflation is difficult because to create sufficient slack in the economy to moderate inflation conflicts with the desire for economic security and maximum production. And to adopt wage-price controls clashes with the criterion of efficiency and the nation's commitment to free enterprise as a means of attaining the latter.

Faith in monetary policy as a control of inflation has deep historical roots. In Great Britain in the nineteenth century the mystique of the banker was highly developed, and given the conditions of the world economy, it gained a reputation of magical effectiveness. But in the United States in the twenties monetary policy failed to check the speculative boom; nor did it stimulate recovery from the Great Depression of the thirties. The faith in monetary policy declined, only to regain some of its luster after 1950 as the favorite instrument of the conservatives.

Despite its high position in the conventional wisdom, Galbraith contends that monetary policy makes "only secondary contact with the problem of inflation." Its only effect on inflation comes through reducing the aggregate demand for goods. It cannot effectively control consumer demand because it clashes with the imperatives of demand creation and can be evaded by those selling goods on installment. Still worse, monetary policy is grossly discriminatory. The big, oligopolistic concerns are able to contract out from the effects of monetary policy, because of their possession of market power and ability to borrow outside the influence of central bank controls, while those selling in competitive markets—farmers and small businessmen—will be severely curbed by high interest rates. Finally, there is a great danger in monetary policy because it operates on the most volatile element of aggregate demand—private investment—and its effects are often unpredictable. Putting on the monetary brakes can land us in a depression.

Galbraith next considers fiscal policy, the weapon of the liberals, as a means of controlling inflation. In *American Capitalism* he was optimistic in his appraisal of its effectiveness. But in this work his faith in this article of the Keynesian doctrine has collapsed. "In the years since World War II in the United States, fiscal policy has also revealed itself as a very poor defense against inflation. The reason was not that it failed to work but that not even its principal proponents argued for its vigorous use. It was favored in principle but not in practice. . . ."[19] The reasons for this peculiar fact are to be found in the social and political context of policy-making. There is a certain asymmetry about fiscal policy; it is easier to spend public money to stimulate recovery than to advocate an increase in taxes to counter inflation. Increases in taxes in peacetime mean the end of the truce concerning economic inequality. Liberals are loath to see this occur, and conservatives oppose it. In seeking to hold production below capacity to achieve price stability, fiscal policy inevitably sacrifices economic growth. Such a policy obviously clashes with the nation's commitment to production and full employment. "The politics of an anti-inflationary fiscal policy could scarcely be less promising." Even the possibility of combining fiscal policy with price and wage controls is slim. The latter are generally regarded as impractical and un-American in peacetime. There seems to be no alternative to "recurrent inflation."

The third problem, and probably in Galbraith's mind the most serious of the affluent society, is what he terms social imbalance. He defines this condition somewhat loosely as "a satisfactory relationship between the supply of privately produced goods and services and those of the state." The crux of his analysis is that "our wealth in privately produced goods is, to a marked degree, the cause of the crisis in the supply of public services."[20] He argues that just as there must be balance among the products which go into the productive process, there must also be a balance in what the community consumes. Increased use of one product requires additional consumption or availability of others. But the irrational fetish of our society for consumer goods has produced a condition of "private opulence and public squalor."

Three causes are given for this extraordinary state of affairs. While the conventional wisdom holds that the consumer by voting makes an independent choice between private and public goods, the facts are quite otherwise. Because of the powerful dependence effect, he makes no such choice. The social context in which decisions are made to purchase private goods is so subject to high-pressure salesmanship and advertising, while there is no similar promotion of public goods and services, that there is no chance

---

[19] *Ibid.*, p. 211.
[20] *Ibid.*, p. 251.

for an equal choice between the two types of goods. This is the first of the causes of social imbalance.

The second is that expenditure for public goods conflicts with the emphasis on production and with the truce on inequality that liberals and conservatives have worked out. Increased income taxes would endanger this truce. At the state and local level the usual sources of revenue, especially the general property tax, are quite inadequate to finance the need for growing public services. In the case of the federal government, a large proportion of its revenue is preempted by defense or it has been impossible to raise taxes because of the common belief that they were already at wartime highs.

Finally, social imbalance is caused by persistent inflation. The pay scales of government employees tend to lag behind a rising price level, with the result that there is a deterioration in the public services.

The social imbalance between private and public goods tends also to distort the relationship between investment in material things and investment in people. Investment in human beings increases in importance as industry becomes more complex and scientific in its operation. While the capital market allocates material investment with tolerable efficiency, there is no comparable institution which allocates resources as between material and human resources. Investment in individuals is in the public domain, and this fact subjects it to some peculiar handicaps. In the past, education was considered a consumer expenditure, not a productive investment, and this conception still shapes our policy with respect to it. In the terminology of the economist, education is an external economy, beneficial even to those who do not finance its cost. Similarly, scientific research, especially of a basic nature, is neglected in favor of applied research on specific products that are profitable to particular firms. In general, the conventional wisdom in its obsession with the production of goods and its neglect of human investment stunts man's capacity for enjoyment of the less readily synthesized wants and in so doing narrows the range of human fulfillment.

"WE MUST DISENTHRALL OURSELVES"

Having analyzed the causes and historical context of what he calls "the thralldom of a myth"—the idea that

production should be the central concern of our lives—
Galbraith next considers how we might emancipate ourselves, reminding us of Lincoln's words concerning another
kind of servitude, "We must disenthrall ourselves." He
recognizes that the nation's preoccupation with production
and the declining urgency of the latter pose major problems
of values. Philosophically, men must see a purpose in their
efforts. In the past and even today many economic policy
questions—the tariff, the place of the large corporation, the
progressive income tax, and so on—have been considered
in relation to the efficiency of production. But now with
the reduced urgency of goods other considerations—com-
passion, individual happiness, the minimization of social
tensions—become relevant. In short, we are not faced with
mere questions of economic policy, but with fundamental
value choices.

In a nation of growing affluence, the old Puritan gospel
of work that was rooted in an economy of scarcity loses its
relevance. Yet the stigma of unemployment and the inflationary pressures generated when the economy is worked
close to full employment demand a new solution. Economic
security must be freed from its dependence on production.
Galbraith offers a scheme called CGC, or Cyclically Grad-
uated Compensation, to supplement unemployment compensation, particularly in time of recession. Under his plan
the loss of a job would not mean loss of well-being, nor
would unemployment constitute a threat to security. In
order to prevent malingering, he provided for a gap between
earned income and unemployment compensation.

In seeking to redress the social imbalance, Galbraith contends that the economy would be more secure if it were
based on the whole range of human needs rather than on
the less urgent need for private goods. The solution of this
problem is make available to government for public services
a pro rata share of rising national income. Unfortunately,
the federal government cannot do this at present because
national defense preempts an overwhelming share of tax
revenue. Liberals must see the necessity of separating the
issue of income equality from that of social balance, and
must favor the latter. Galbraith does this forthrightly himself by favoring at the state and local level (where the imbalance is most conspicuous) an expanded use of the sales
tax. The general property tax is inadequate for this purpose;
it is too rigid and inflexible and, consequently, is "a poor
servant of social balance." Though the sales tax is a regres-
sive tax, it does have the virtue that its yield varies directly

with the sales of private goods. The coverage of this sales tax, says Galbraith, should be on all consumer products and services. Rather than tailoring tax policy to the needs of the poor, an affluent society should use its sales tax and other revenue to eliminate poverty.

In the first edition of *The Affluent Society,* in a short chapter entitled "The New Position of Poverty," Galbraith contends that, in contrast to the situation in Alfred Marshall's day, poverty in the United States was no longer "a universal or massive affliction." Poverty, in consequence, had ceased to be a problem of a majority, but remained one for a minority. It was a special case rather than the general one. He did not offer a precise definition of poverty. Poverty in his mind was relative because, as he says, "People are poverty-stricken when their income, even if adequate for survival, falls markedly behind that of the community. Then they cannot have what the larger community regards as the minimum necessary for decency. . . . They are degraded for, in the literal sense, they live outside the grades or categories which the community regards as acceptable."[21] He cited the statistic that in the mid-fifties, one family in thirteen in the United States had a cash income, from all sources, of less than a thousand dollars; in addition, there were a large number of unattached individuals in this income class. The hard core of the very poor, he informed his readers, was declining but not with great rapidity.

Poverty, he explained can be classified into two broad categories: (1) the case poverty of those who are unemployable because of bad health, mental deficiency, inability to adapt to industrial life, and so on, or a combination of these handicaps; (2) insular poverty—that which manifests itself as an "island" of poverty. Nearly everyone in such a community, regardless of individual circumstances, is poor. Galbraith traces the origin of this type of poverty to a sort of "homing instinct" that causes a comparatively large number of people to prefer to spend their lives at or near the place of their birth. This reluctance to migrate dooms them to a pattern of employment or unemployment that keeps them in relative poverty. The very poverty of such a community results in poor schools and health facilities and these conditions perpetuate low income and inability to migrate. Though he did not deal with it at any length, Galbraith treated the poverty of the poor black or other ethnically disadvantaged groups as falling within this class of insular poverty.

[21] *Ibid.,* pp. 286–287.

The most certain fact about modern poverty, both case and insular, says Galbraith, is that it is not effectively eliminated by a general advance in income. Some may escape from such poverty in a time of improving business, but this is of no help to those who, because of self or environment, cannot participate in the economic process.

The political position of the poor is not what it was when they constituted a majority of the population. As a small and relatively inarticulate minority, they have few politicians to speak for them. The remedy for both case and insular poverty, Galbraith asserts, is to invest more than proportionately in the children of the poor. To a great degree, the remedy for such poverty is the same as that for correcting social imbalance—increased investment in persons.

The penultimate chapter in Galbraith's book deals with labor and leisure in the affluent society. After noting that the decline in the length of the work week reflects a tacit and unmistakable acceptance of the declining marginal urgency of goods, Galbraith observes that there are other alternatives to reducing the work week as our efficiency grows. One of these is to make work easier and more pleasant. Another is to have fewer people work. Since the 1890s large numbers of the young have been retired from the labor force but, in general, such is our obsession with productivity and efficiency that we still do not make the investment in education that we should.

As affluence has increased in advanced industrial societies, we have had a growth in leisure, both voluntary and involuntary, and we have also seen the appearance of a New Class, a group to whom work is pleasurable rather than disagreeable. Those who do such creative, fulfilling work expect to do their best regardless of compensation. The members of this New Class seek to perpetuate themselves; they raise and educate their children for work which is enjoyable and creative rather than the most lucrative. The prime qualification for entry into this New Class is education. Galbraith concludes very confidently that "the further and rapid expansion of this class should be a major, and perhaps next to peaceful survival itself, *the* major social goal of the society. . . ."[22]

In his last chapter, "On Security and Survival," Galbraith states that he has avoided considering the relation of the pursuit of private affluence to happiness and settled for the more manageable task of showing how our preoccupation

[22] *Ibid.,* pp. 307–308.

with the production of goods is compelled by tradition and myth. If we can be released from these compulsions, we become free for other opportunities which have a more plausible relationship to happiness. On national security, he asserts that the launching of Sputnik, the first earth satellite, by the Russians, demonstrated the importance of a rational allocation of our resources rather than the present irrational emphasis on the production of private goods. And even apart from the Russians, there remain vast millions of hungry and discontented people in the underdeveloped world who are ripe for revolution unless they are aided in improving their condition.

Furthermore, when the arms race ends, there remain huge tasks on the scientific and technological frontiers to be accomplished. But a society that is preoccupied with the production of private consumer goods is woefully ill equipped for many of these frontier challenges.

5 Critics,

Conventional and Otherwise

Despite his inclination to take his critics lightly, Galbraith was extremely anxious about the early reviews of *The Affluent Society*. At the time of its publication, he was in Europe on a lecture tour and he has told of how he returned to London and feverishly scanned the American magazines at his hotel newsstand for their reactions. Finally he discovered one in *Time*, though its comments, he was disappointed to find, were relegated to the business section.[1] The reviewer conceded that his book was well written, but it seemed to be "a vague essay with the air of worried dinner-table conversation." Galbraith, said the critic, having pointed his bat at the bleachers, had stepped away from the plate. His "sonorous generalizations" about the need to expand the public sector were left in the air; he had sketched the problem of social imbalance, but had failed to provide the answers.

Galbraith was dismayed at the possibility that his book could be thus dismissed. By coincidence, the late John Steinbeck happened to be standing next to him, reading the review at his shoulder. His comment lifted Galbraith's spirits: "Unless a reviewer has the courage to give you unqualified praise, I say ignore the bastard."[2]

One reviewer who had such courage is the British writer John Strachey. Shortly after the appearance of Galbraith's book he gave it the following striking encomium: ". . . Let me take my courage in both hands and predict that twenty years after its publication, *The Affluent Society* will be exercising an influence comparable, though of a very different

---

[1] *Time*, June 2, 1958, p. 78–80.
[2] *The Affluent Society*, 2nd rev. ed., p. xxix.

kind, to that exercised by *The General Theory* [of Keynes] today."[3]

Since its publication *The Affluent Society* has not been received by all reviewers with such acclaim, but it has been very widely read. It first made the best-seller list in the summer of 1958 and remained on it for much of that year. In January 1962, *Time* reported that the book had achieved a sale of 154,000 copies in 12 languages. In 1969 Galbraith himself stated that he had earned $138,000 on the American edition and perhaps an additional $20,000 on the British edition and the 20 or 30 translations.[4] Apparently, however, the wide popularity of his book did not exactly delight all of Galbraith's professional peers. One of them, Professor George Stigler of the University of Chicago, some years ago in the course of criticizing the tastes of the American people, illustrated their lack of literary judgment by remarking, "I consider it shocking that more Americans have read *The Affluent Society* than *The Wealth of Nations*."[5]

Never disposed to dismiss a barb such as that, Galbraith subsequently shot back: "I am reluctant to reply to Professor Stigler for I could seem to be urging the claims of my book against those of a very great classic. And I could conceivably be missing the deeper cause of Professor Stigler's sorrow which may be not that so many read Galbraith and so few read Smith but that hardly anyone reads Stigler at all."[6]

One interesting semantic consequence of Galbraith's volume was to give the word "affluent" new and greater currency. Less than ten years after it was published, one perceptive reporter noted that

affluent came into use as a vaguely conscious way of saying "rich" after the publication of JKG's book. . . . Even when a writer or speaker appears to mean nothing more complicated than "rich" in the sense of having a lot of money, often as not he will eschew the word (or "prosperous" or any other variant) for the newly portentous "affluent." It brings intimations of economic doctrine . . . and it also manages to imply, without the addition of a single word or thought, that the group of persons or the community that is affluent wouldn't be

[3] "Unconventional Wisdom," *Encounter*, October 1958, p. 80.

[4] J. K. Galbraith, "Professor Gordon on 'The Close of the Galbraithian System,'" *Journal of Political Economy*, July/August 1969, p. 497, footnote 6.

[5] G. J. Stigler, "The Intellectual and the Marketplace," in A. Klaasen, *The Invisible Hand* (Chicago: Henry Regnery, 1965), p. 34.

[6] J. K. Galbraith, "Economics versus the Quality of Life," *Encounter*, January 1965, p. 34.

nearly as affluent if it were putting its money to better use or it had a more highly developed sense of public duty and private values.[7]

Another index of the book's extraordinary influence on the "American mind" was its choice by one author for inclusion in a work entitled *Books That Changed America.*[8] The purpose of the latter was not to list outstanding literary gems, but "to identify those writings which have exerted the greatest impact on our national history, direct or indirect." In a list of twenty-five authors (or twenty-seven, including joint authors) that ranges from Tom Paine to Rachel Carson, Galbraith is included for his vivid presentation of the problem of private opulence and public poverty. In his introduction, the author of this collection states his belief that perhaps a majority of the writers included in this book belong in the category of "great disseminators" of ideas. Probably without exception, he says, the authors who wrote these influential works "brought new interpretations to ideas they found floating in the air, dramatized situations, and caught the public imagination with their manner of expression."

"The secret of success of the chosen books," he further remarks, "is that the world was ready to receive them and *in toto* they carried messages appealing to millions of people. . . ."[9] Along with Gunnar Myrdal's *An American Dilemma* and Miss Carson's *Silent Spring,* Galbraith's book was one of those published since World War II that was regarded as having stirred the consciousness and conscience of Americans.

THE VERDICT OF THE
POPULAR JOURNALS

The Affluent Society was received very favorably, on the whole, by the reviewers in the popular periodicals. Of nineteen reviews cited in the *Book Review Digest* for 1958, eleven were positively favorable and eight were mixed in their appraisals.

Both Edwin L. Dale, Jr., and Robert Heilbroner in the

---

[7] M. Greenfield in *The Reporter,* June 1, 1967, p. 35.
[8] By R. B. Downs, published by Macmillan, New York, 1970.
[9] *Ibid.,* pp. xiii, xv.

New York Times and *Herald Tribune* book reviews, respectively, praised it. The former wrote, "It is frequently annoying, some of the reasoning is not impeccable, and some of the iconoclasm that pervades it is deceptive." Still, ". . . This reviewer has the unequivocal belief that it is a very good thing indeed that this book was written." Heilbroner thought it to be "a book with which it is easy to cavil or disagree, but which it is impossible to dismiss." He hoped that "technical criticism would not obscure the basic issues which it raises."[10]

In *The New Republic*, Robert Lekachman, a capable academic economist, extolled "this impressive book" and said in a rather general piece that he was "convinced that Galbraith has done an enormous service to the cause of intelligent economic and social debate. In the end, he may have done as substantial a service to the prestige of economics itself."[11]

Michael R. Reagan, a political scientist, wrote in *The Nation:* ". . . A more refreshing examination of the stereotypes of both liberal and conservative economic thought has not appeared in many a year." Nevertheless, he had three objections to make to the book's arguments: (1) Productivity, he argued, outruns needs today only in terms of the domestic market; (2) Galbraith disposed too easily of the problem of poverty in America; (3) his reliance on state and local governments to correct social imbalance was dubious. "The liberal influence which would approve Galbraith's social program is much stronger in national politics."[12]

The late David N. Potter was a distinguished American historian and author of the penetrating volume *People of Plenty*. (This study of economic abundance and its influence on the American character was unaccountably ignored by Galbraith in his analysis of our national affluence.) Potter in his review praised *The Affluent Society* for its force, originality, and constructive imagination.[13] Yet he had some thoughtful criticism to offer. The title of Galbraith's book, he asserted, especially in view of its content, was something of a misnomer, "for the study takes more ac-

[10] "Are We Living Too High on the Hog?" *The New York Times Book Review*, June 1, 1958, pp. 1 ff., and *New York Herald Tribune Books*, June 1, 1958, p. 3.

[11] "Galbraith's New Economics," *New Republic*, June 9, 1958, p. 18.

[12] "Private Wealth and Public Poverty," *The Nation*, June 14, 1958, pp. 546–547.

[13] *Saturday Review*, June 7, 1958, pp. 31–32.

count of economics than it does of society." Potter continued:

> ... With fuller attention to society Mr. Galbraith might have reckoned with the fact that our Puritan aversion to idleness and our pioneer urge to subdue a new continent have contributed more than economic theory to our obsession with productivity and that the one-horse individualism of our agrarian past has done more than classical economics to breed distrust of extensive community services. He might have taken more account also of the fact that democracy adopts given measures because organized groups believe it will be to their advantage to do so, and not because of any criterion of optimum social good.

Despite his criticism, Potter in his conclusion ventured an interesting prediction: "But at a more basic level it [*The Affluent Society*] ranks as a work which, Utopian or not, ought to contribute in the long run to the reshaping of some of our basic ideas."[14]

The conservative reaction to *The Affluent Society* was illustrated in these years by Colin Clark's "The Horrible Proposals of Mr. Galbraith."[15] The world-famous statistician deplored Galbraith's "fatal fluency" and thought that his "New Class" was ominously reminiscent of Orwell's 1984! He magnanimously conceded that *American Capitalism* was "a real contribution to economic theory" and agreed that "the facts about social imbalance so graphically here described, are, in many regions, correct." But Galbraith's solution for this extraordinary problem was not.

THE PROFESSIONALS BEAR DOWN

In 1959 several professional journals evaluated Galbraith's essay. As one would expect, the points raised became more technical, the critical flak thicker. Chronologically, Kenneth E. Boulding's review was one of the earliest in such publications. This erudite scholar was generous in his praise of "this penetrating tract." He considered it "a moving and important work, addressed to the conscience and good sense of our times. One hopes that its effect will be as great as its popularity and that it will

---

14 *Ibid.*
15 *National Review,* October 11, 1958, p. 237.

help to rescue us from the paradox of public stinginess in the midst of private affluence."[16]

The University of Virginia's Rutledge Vining analyzed *The Affluent Society* in a more technical review article in the *American Economic Review*.[17] After noting the favorable popular reviews, he remarked that "much of that part [of the book] which purports to be factual and much that is interpretative seem grossly casual; and much of that part that takes the form of deduction seems somewhat loose and questionable." Vining was critical about "a sustained note of something resembling presumption" and "the author's lively sense of being naughty." The book, he said, was written in the tradition of Veblen, but lacked "the deft touch of the master or so it may seem to some."

Vining appraised Galbraith's work from the standpoint of modern statistical decision theory. Disregarding the fact that the book was not written for a technical readership, he stated that its analysis from that standpoint was "most awkwardly, haphazardly, and unreliably [done] as compared with the way modern statisticians do these tasks for their restricted field of choice phenomena." But Galbraith's work, unreliable and unsystematic in itself, had a major redeeming feature in Vining's opinion; it had the virtue at least of "trying to do the relevant things."

A much more fundamental attack on the book appeared the following month in *The Journal of Political Economy*.[18] Proctor Thomson, professor at Claremont Men's College, enjoyed Galbraith's "urbane and engaging essay" with its "spritely and entertaining rhetoric." But "the ironic and unfortunate feature of the entire performance," claimed Thomson, "is that the central position, the saturation of physical output, is neither necessary nor sufficient to support the conclusions the author eventually advances." Citing the adage which Leibniz used and of which Alfred Marshall, the British neoclassical economist, was so fond— *Natura non facit saltum* (literally, "Nature doesn't make jumps," that is, there is a continuity in natural phenomena) —Thomson raised what he thought were three crucial questions for Galbraith's thesis:

(1) . . . At what point in the onward march of economic progress did relative scarcity become suddenly transformed

[16] *Review of Economics and Statistics,* February 1959, p. 81.
[17] March 1959, pp. 112–119.
[18] April 1959, pp. 201–202.

into burdensome abundance? (2) is the insistence that economy no longer matters and the conviction that no one wants
the goods we waste a useful contribution to the solution of
economic problems? (3) is an attitude of miscellaneous hos-
tility toward the private economy an appropriate foundation
for responsible decision by the literate electorate to whom this
book is addressed?

Some of these questions are answered by Galbraith in his
remarks below;[19] in the meantime the reader will have to
judge their value as best he can.

SOME FOREIGN VIEWS

Somewhat later in the year Galbraith came in for
a similar criticism from across the Canadian border; the
economists of his native land showed him no leniency.
Professor H. Ian MacDonald was of the opinion that Galbraith had directed such sweeping challenges to the American economy that his book should be considered more in
the class of "social criticism" than of "moral science." He
too was skeptical of Galbraith's deemphasis of production.
"If the United States is to provide for the social consumption and public services which Galbraith proposes, as well
as for those he ignores and does not stress, production must
be paramount, as it was during the war." Nevertheless, he
ended on a complimentary note: "Galbraith has turned a
mirror directly on the American economy of abundance,
and the image which we see is the clearer for his work."[20]
The reviewer in the influential journal *The Economist*
expressed doubts about the influence of Galbraith's book
on public opinion in Great Britain.[21] He added, *"The
Affluent Society* is penetrating, fresh, knowledgeable, humane, and . . . entertainingly written. It is also perverse,
muddleheaded, provincial and dangerous." He complained
that the central notion of affluence remained vague. "At
what level of income per head does it replace poverty and
make the 'conventional wisdom' obsolete?" Answering his
own question, he asserted that Galbraith gave no hint of an
answer, nor did he recognize that the conventional wisdom

[19] See pp. 123–124 and 131.
[20] "The American Economy of Abundance," *Canadian Journal of
Economic and Political Science,* August 1959, pp. 352–357.
[21] "The Price of Affluence," *The Economist,* September 20, 1958,
pp. 928–929.

may not be totally obsolete but rather that dependence on it may be a matter of more or less, depending on the gradually changing urgencies and problems of an evolving society. In the reviewer's opinion, there were a good many questions to ask about Galbraith's diagnosis of the affluent society. For example, "is 'social imbalance' . . . necessarily the fruit of conventionally guided affluence, or simply an American weakness?" In short, this British critic was questioning the relevance of Galbraith's analysis to his country. *"The Affluent Society* may, on balance, make very salutary reading in its native land. In Britain, it may only encourage delusion."

In striking contrast to this view, the reviewer of another famous British publication, *The Times Literary Supplement,* believed the very opposite to be the case.[22] He felt that Galbraith's book, grounded in the common culture of the two continents, might "serve as a link between them" and was of "foremost importance for them both." He concluded that Galbraith had not solved the problem he posed, but his attempt was "intensely provocative of thought."

THE PROS AND CONS OF
The Affluent Society

In the years following its publication *The Affluent Society* stirred up a considerable amount of controversy and debate, in the course of which some basic issues in its analysis and interpretation became evident. One such intellectual exchange occurred in the columns of *Commentary* magazine.[23] The participants were Ernest Van den Haag, economist and practicing psychotherapist, and Professors Lewis A. Coser and the late Ben B. Seligman, a sociologist and an economist, respectively. Van den Haag aggressively challenged the Galbraith essay, saying: "Galbraith has written a lucid muddle; the whole is far from coherent, though all the arguments are brilliantly put, most of them make sense—and none lead to Galbraith's conclusions."

22 "Problems of Prosperity," *The Times Literary Supplement,* November 21, 1958, p. 675.
23 E. Van den Haag, "Affluence, Galbraith, the Democrats," *Commentary,* September 1960, pp. 206 ff.; also L. A. Coser and B. B. Seligman, *Commentary,* January 1961, p. 70.

Among the faults Van den Haag found in Galbraith's work were the following:

1. A failure to define social imbalance specifically as well as offering no evidence that it exists. Furthermore, he wrote, "Unless some standard of balance between public and private expenditures is supplied, Galbraith's view that there is an 'imbalance' owing to low taxes is as good as but no better than Westbrook Pegler's (or Colin Clark's) that there is an 'imbalance' owing to high taxes." (Parenthetically, we might note that Galbraith does not attribute social imbalance primarily to the level of taxation.)

2. Galbraith's ideas about excessive private production. "[His view that] production and productivity become less and less important seems not only fanciful, but also frivolously parochial."[24]

3. Galbraith's use of the concept of "contrived" demand. "Are all contrived desires bad?" Van den Haag asked.

4. Galbraith's advocacy of more public spending on roads [?] and schools was questionable. Van den Haag's conservatism leads him to fear an expansion of the public sector. He says in this connection, ". . . to abandon the individualism which is the *raison d'être* of liberalism in favor of increased government domination is always dangerous, and perhaps in principle immoral even if we knew the government to be wise—and we don't." He reveals a liberalism more rigid and doctrinaire than any espoused by Adam Smith himself when he asserts, "No collective decision can do as much justice to individuals as they can by deciding each for himself."

As a student of dynamic psychology, Van den Haag questioned whether Galbraith had provided a sufficiently deep explanation of the American's pursuit of private affluence. "Just as a people do not overeat because of food, so they do not overbuy because of goods—let alone advertisements for them. Both actions spring from a feeling of dissatisfaction and emptiness. They are symptoms, not causes. . . ."

[24] The notion that Galbraith ignores the needs of the underdeveloped world in his preoccupation with affluent America disregards his remarks in the closing chapter of *The Affluent Society:* ". . . Were the Russians to disappear from the world, or become as tractable as church mice, there would remain vast millions of hungry and discontented people in the world. Without the promise of relief from hunger and privation, disorder would still be inevitable. The promise of that relief requires that we have available or usable resources . . ." (*The Affluent Society*, 2nd ed. revised, p. 315).

On this point, it should be noticed that while Galbraith emphasizes the deliberate synthesis and management of consumer demand by sellers and seems to make Madison Avenue the main villain, there are passages in *The Affluent Society* that suggest a broader, more psychodynamic explanation of American consumer behavior. For example, consider this statement: "Our preoccupation with production is, in fact, the culminating consequence of powerful historical and psychological forces—forces which only by an act of will we can hope to escape. . . ." At another place in his book, Galbraith speaks of our being released from "compulsions."[25] While these passages suggest a recognition by Galbraith of the irrational forces at work in our culture, it must be admitted that his emphasis in explaining social imbalance is on advertising, emulation, and the vested interest in output.

Coser and Seligman sought to refute Van den Haag by arguing that he had relied on incompatible ideologies, that he had "one foot in the liberal camp and one in the conservative."[26] "We must reject," they say, "the model of hedonistic and acquisitive man on which he bases his whole approach. He cannot maintain at one and the same time that men are hedonistic calculators, maximizing pleasure, and that they are anxious, frustrated, and bored creatures yearning for human fulfillment." Van den Haag replied to this point by stating simply, "They are the latter because they are the former."

Coser and Seligman contended that "the shallow, individualistic hedonism of the nineteenth century economists and their fantasies of a free market" provide no answers to the problems of the affluent society. They accused Van den Haag of a nihilistic position in that in his social system one desire is as good as any other. They generalized to this effect: "When the fetishism of commodities tears apart the fabric of human solidarity, then only a policy asserting the primacy of the community is likely to bring human benefit."

Van den Haag answered this line of argument by stating that he did not hold that one desire is as good as another, but merely that "the right to decide which is better ought to be vested ordinarily in the individual citizen and not in the government." He explained that he saw "no way of giving up the mass-producing style of life which mass

[25] *The Affluent Society*, 1958 ed., pp. 124, 351, respectively, for above quotes.
[26] *Commentary*, January 1961, p. 70.

production produces without giving up the latter—and people do not want to." With finality, he concluded, "This is the problem. Galbraith evaded it elegantly, Coser and Seligman furiously."[27]

THE DEPENDENCE EFFECT
RECONSIDERED

In all the criticism of *The Affluent Society,* certain basic issues have been raised again and again. One of these recurrent points of controversy has to do with Galbraith's so-called "dependence effect." This is his contention, it will be recalled, that in the affluent society wants, rather than being original with the consumer, are "contrived" for him by modern advertising and salesmanship. As a consequence, instead of production being the servant of the consumer, it "only fills a void that it has itself created." So long, says Galbraith, as wants are thought to be independently determined by the consumer, the production that serves such wants can be regarded—and is so considered by the conventional-minded—as urgent.

In his critique of the orthodox theory of consumer demand, Galbraith attacks a basic premise in the classic rationale of the functioning of the free-enterprise system, namely, the concept of consumer sovereignty. (In this reasoning, the consumer is "king" because it is alleged that the expenditure of his income on various consumer products indirectly dictates the allocation of society's resources.) In support of his position Galbraith cites one of Keynes's most provocative essays, in which the latter observed that the needs of human beings "fall into two classes—those needs which are absolute in the sense that we feel them whatever the situation of our fellow human beings may be, and those which are relative only in that their satisfaction lifts us above, makes us feel superior to, our fellows." Keynes went on to state that while the second class of wants might be insatiable, the first was capable of being satisfied. From this he concluded that "assuming no important wars and no important increase in population the *economic problem* may be solved, or at least within sight of solution, within a hundred years. This means the economic problem

[27] *Ibid.,* p. 75.

is not—if we look into the future—*the permanent problem of the human race."*[28]

Galbraith, having quoted Keynes to demonstrate the role of emulation in want creation, argues that a more direct link between production and wants has been created by the modern institutions of advertising and salesmanship. The latter cannot be reconciled with the conception of independently determined wants because their very function is to synthesize wants that previously did not exist. Production, in short, creates the wants it seeks to satisfy. And "as a society becomes increasingly affluent, wants are increasingly created by the process by which they are satisfied. . . ."[29]

This whole line of reasoning was later challenged by Professor Friedrich von Hayek of the University of Freiburg.[30] At the outset of his critique he attempted to discredit Galbraith's argument by associating him with a nineteenth-century socialist sect, the Saint Simonians, who he said likewise contended that the problem of production had been solved and all that remained was the problem of distribution. After this ideological overture, Hayek criticized Galbraith's assertion that wants that are not spontaneous with the individual cannot be urgent or important. This conclusion, he maintained, is a *non sequitur* and "it would seem that with it the whole argument of the book collapses."

Hayek insisted that the two Keynesian types of wants which Galbraith cites are only extreme classes of wants and that such a classification disregards the overwhelming majority of goods on which civilized life rests. Most of our wants, he continued, are the result of our cultural inheritance. He thought that Galbraith's illogic was most clearly shown if one applied his reasoning to the arts. An individual's want for literature or great music is not original with him, but is cultivated by the producers of important literary or musical works. And yet, in Galbraith's words, here "the process of satisfying the wants creates the wants." The tastes of men and much of their personality are largely molded by their cultural environ-

[28] J. M. Keynes, "Economic Possibilities for Our Grandchildren," in *Essays in Persuasion* (London: Macmillan, 1931), pp. 365–366, cited in *The Affluent Society,* 2nd ed., p. 145. (Italics in Keynes's original essay.)

[29] *The Affluent Society,* 2nd ed., p. 152.

[30] F. A. von Hayek, "The Non Sequitur of the Dependence Effect," *Southern Economic Journal,* April 1961, pp. 346–348.

ment. The producers of goods through their joint but un-
coordinated efforts to sell their products merely create one
element of the environment by which the wants of consumers are shaped. Galbraith's obscurity, said Hayek, does
not make it clear whether he is contending that producers
"determine" the wants of consumers; though that is skillfully suggested, it is nowhere made credible. Granted that
producers seek to make their products more attractive than
their rivals', but each consumer still has a choice among
all the different offers. In Hayek's view, "keeping up with
the Joneses" is usually greatly exaggerated; in addition, it
is not really relevant to Galbraith's main thesis. Hayek
closed on the note that, despite all its shortcomings, "there
is some originality in this latest version of the old socialist
argument."

It is not possible to examine here all the subtle aspects
of the complex controversy over consumer sovereignty;
some matters pertaining to it are considered later.[31] Galbraith is not alone in his skepticism about the orthodox
doctrine. Apart from Marxists who are critical of this
phase of capitalist functioning, there are other more conservative thinkers who believe that the consumer is no
longer king. For example, Professor E. J. Mishan, a respected British economist, in a recent work flatly asserted:
". . . To continue to regard the market, in an affluent and
growing economy, as primarily a 'want-satisfying' mechanism is to close one's eyes to the more important fact that
it has become a 'want-creating' mechanism."[32]

Rather than pursue the subject further in theoretical
terms, it may be useful at this point to consider briefly the
role of advertising in the American economy from a historical perspective. Mass advertising assumed a new importance in the 1920s for the first time. In the United States
the per capita volume of newspaper and periodical advertising almost doubled between 1919 and 1929. Expenditure
per capita in the latter year almost quadrupled compared
to its level in 1914.[33] As the nation developed a surplus
capacity to produce in the post-World War I years, new
styles of consumer behavior were necessary, if that capacity was to be utilized to the full. A society which had

---

[31] See below, pp. 124–126.
[32] E. J. Mishan, *The Costs of Economic Growth* (New York:
Frederick A. Praeger, 1967), p. 111.
[33] C. H. Hession and H. Sardy, *Ascent to Affluence: A History
of American Economic Development* (Boston: Allyn and Bacon,
1969), p. 670.

been previously oriented toward production now had to be converted into "a consumer's culture." Professor David Potter has contended that advertising fulfilled this function. In his view it was the only institution that we had to instill new needs, to train people to act as consumers, to alter their values, and, in general, to hasten their adjustment to potential abundance.[34]

There is another historical development which Hayek disregarded in his critique of Galbraith on this subject. He ignored the fact that the development of oligopoly (fewness of sellers) which became more common in American industry in the twentieth century tended to shift the emphasis in business rivalry from price to nonprice competition. Advertising was a major form of the latter. It is important to note too that in the 1920s advertising began to appeal more to the nonrational side of human nature. It played on the emotions, the fears and anxieties of Americans to a greater degree; this strategy apparently helped to sell more goods. For these and other reasons we are led to conclude that Hayek's criticism of the Galbraithian dependence effect is defective itself.

A more penetrating criticism of Galbraith's dependence effect has been written by Professor Cyril Zebot of Georgetown University.[35] He suggested that Galbraith may be inaugurating a revolution in the field of demand theory. In his view both the classical and Keynesian economics have been based on a "rather unilluminating" theory of demand. In these systems individual wants are taken as given; they are considered as originating and behaving independently of the economic system. In other words, "the determination of wants is left outside the analytical scope of both micro- and macro-economic theory."[36] The novelty and analytical significance of *The Affluent Society,* said Zebot, lies in its presentation of a new theory of demand which deals with the generation and nature of wants. Most of the rest of Galbraith's analysis derives from this theory.

[34] D. N. Potter, *People of Plenty, Economic Abundance and the American Character* (Chicago: University of Chicago Press, 1954), p. 173.

[35] C. A. Zebot, "Economics of Affluence," *Review of Social Economy,* September 1959, pp. 112–125. Similar ideas are presented in Zebot's *The Economics of Competitive Coexistence, Convergence Through Growth* (New York: Frederick A. Praeger, 1964), Chapter 5 and Appendix C-2.

[36] Zebot, "Economics of Affluence," *op. cit.,* p. 115, footnote. For a lucid discussion of demand theory, see D. Hamilton, *The Consumer in Our Economy* (Boston: Houghton Mifflin, 1962), Chapters 1–3.

In Galbraith's conception many of the wants catered to by modern production have little real urgency, in so far as they are contrived by the sellers of goods. As he points out, received theory has little to say about these matters because it avoids the psychological complexities of want generation. Furthermore, it denies the possibility of interpersonal and intertemporal comparisons of utility. Behind its "façade of sterile theoretical neutrality," as Zebot expresses it, there is an assumption that human wants over time are without significant limits. (The older texts spoke of a law of satiety in accordance with which individual wants were subject to diminishing utility, but human wants in general were considered to be insatiable.) In traditional marginal utility terms, this means that the marginal utility of income or of money does not diminish, as its quantity increases. As Zebot sees it, Galbraith's attack fundamentally is on this tacit assumption of demand theory.

Instead of treating wants as given or independent of the productive process, Galbraith regards many of them as dependent variables in economic analysis; this, says Zebot, is "the most important single element in Galbraith's thinking."

According to the Georgetown economist, Galbraith has a "new vision of wants," but he provides no systematic history or psychological analysis of social emulation or of advertising in his book. He arrives at the dependence effect by a direct inference from the everyday facts of emulation and advertising. "Galbraith makes wants and demand depend on production by inferentially assuming that emulation and advertising in pushing an ever growing and changing variety of *products* (means) in the process actually also creates the underlying *wants* (and implied ends) themselves. . . ."[37] "This reasoning," argues Zebot, "implies that specific economic goods are related exclusively to specific wants and *vice versa*. Only on the assumption of such a narrow goods-want relationship is it possible at all to argue that seeing a product used by others or hearing about it from advertisers can *create* in the consumer a new want that he did not have before."

Zebot objects that such a view implies that the individual consumer is "a psychological vacuum to be filled in a purely accidental manner." But "individual consumers are not mere *tabula rasas*. While people are subject to environmental influences, advertising and emulation make no sense

[37] *Ibid.,* p. 115.

unless they are related to some pattern of pre-existing human aspirations."

Zebot sees advertising and emulation, not as generators of new wants, but as producers of specific ways and means for the attainment of human ends. He admits that, even within his conception of the matter, advertising and economic emulation may still be charged with the contrivance of wants to varying degrees. "But such a change of consumer behavior now refers to the specific goods rather than to the underlying wants and ends themselves." The difference in phrasing, he thinks, is not simply verbal or trifling.

> If it were true, as Professor Galbraith claims, that emulation and advertising create wants from scratch, as it were, then it might be possible to treat such extraneous wants as *ipso facto* unimportant with all the policy conclusions that such a conclusion entails. If, however, in accordance with any realistic humanistic interpretation, economic emulation and advertising are viewed as operating on the level of specific ways and means for the attainment of inherent human ends rather than being a sort of substitute for the ends themselves, then no such conclusion is warranted. . . . But one cannot automatically dismiss as psychologically unimportant an end in itself for the sole reason that the specific means by which the end happens to be served passes through the conventional channels of emulation and advertising.[38]

Zebot then argues that emulation and advertising as media of social learning must be constructively criticized to improve them and thus lead to more discriminating individual and social choosing. "This is very different from a summary condemnation of emulation and advertising on Galbraith's assumption that they create wants which are therefore *ipso facto* unimportant."[39] Zebot's line of criticism is interesting and possesses some merit, but it will be noticed that he ignores the manipulative use of advertising with its nonrational appeals; the latter would seem to have the power to distort "inherent" human ends to a considerable degree.

In closing his critique of Galbraith's book, Zebot praises it as "a highly original work. . . . With all its analytical exaggerations, *The Affluent Society* deals with the two weakest links in economic theory. It breaks new ground and provides invaluable leads for further work. Again, Galbraith has proved himself a daring pioneer. As such he

[38] *Ibid.*, p. 117.
[39] *Ibid.*, p. 119.

cannot be blamed for having used heavy equipment rather than precision instruments."[40]

An equally cogent and incisive analysis of the Galbraithian economics of affluence has been written by Professor Harry G. Johnson of the University of Chicago.[41] He asserts that Galbraith's reasoning concerning the dependence of wants on production strikes at the heart of liberal economics. He considers Galbraith's thesis as containing two parts: The first is the proposition that as income rises, less urgent wants are satisfied by marginal production; the latter's value, therefore, is decreasing. From the strictly economic point of view, says Johnson, this proposition is a tautology ("less urgent wants are those you do not satisfy unless you are rich enough to afford to satisfy them"), but in Galbraith's argument, it assumes the nature of a value judgment. It amounts to holding that as society grows more affluent, it becomes less important and worthwhile to stress the maximum efficiency of production. Of course, one can reject that kind of value judgment and argue that the activities of the rich are of superior social value to those of the poor. But, adds Johnson, while this is a tenable position, it is not the popular view. ". . . On the contrary, common sense would seem to be on Galbraith's side on this issue," and therefore the community seems willing to tolerate more wasteful uses of resources as national income rises.

Johnson then turns to the second part of Galbraith's thesis, namely, that since wants are created either socially or commercially, the satisfaction of these wants cannot be regarded as a "genuine" increase in satisfaction. In Johnson's view, Galbraith's inclination to value such created wants adversely is "essentially a trivial matter of opinion." Jokingly, he says that it illustrates his own Law of Social Intransitivity, to wit, "everyone has good reasons for considering himself superior to other people."[42] But the very fact that people think this way offers a clue to the proper treatment of created wants.

The notion that new wants emerge with the advance of production and economic progress, says Johnson, is not original with Galbraith. The British neoclassicist Alfred

[40] *Ibid.,* p. 125.

[41] H. G. Johnson, "The Consumer and Madison Avenue," *Current Economic Comment,* August 1960, pp. 3–10; also reproduced in P. Bliss (ed.), *Marketing and the Behavioral Sciences* (Boston: Allyn and Bacon, 1963), pp. 115–125.

[42] Johnson in Bliss, *op. cit.,* p. 120.

Marshall and the American economist Frank H. Knight, in fact, had ideas on this subject which seem to offer the correct answer to the Galbraithian challenge to liberal economics. For example, Marshall introduced his analysis of demand as follows: "Speaking broadly, therefore, although it is man's wants in the earliest stages of his development that gave rise to his activities, yet afterwards each new step upwards is to be regarded as the development of new activities giving rise to new wants, rather than of new wants giving rise to new activities."[43] Marshall recognized the influence of social emulation on wants, but he also stressed the desire for excellence as a stronger motive. Knight also emphasized the desire for "the cultivation of better and better wants."

Essentially, Marshall and Knight's answer to Galbraith is "to admit that the aim of economic activity is not the fuller satisfaction of *given* wants [our italics]—wants conceived of as wants for specific commodities do not stay given, but instead evolve as the commodities themselves change in the course of economic growth—but to assert that the evolution of wants itself is motivated, fundamentally, by the desire to increase satisfaction. . . ."

This type of argument, says Johnson, asserts that the changes in taste are influenced ultimately by accepted standards of good and better taste, all of which are learned from fellow consumers and from advertising. Johnson also insists that it is not possible, as Galbraith assumes, "to dismiss wants as valueless simply because they have been acquired under the pressures of social emulation and advertising. All economically relevant wants are learned. Moreover, all standards of taste are learned. It is therefore both arrogant and inconsistent to assume that those who have acquired their standards from general culture and advanced education can choose and pass judgments according to standards possessing independent validity, while those who have acquired their standards from social pressures and advertising can neither understand nor learn to understand the difference between good and bad taste."[44]

Johnson's analysis leads him to the "comforting conclusion" that "the mere fact of want-creation does not destroy the assumption that an increase in the national income carries with it an increase in welfare. . . ." Galbraith's contrary contention that "the marginal utility of present

[43] A. Marshall, *Principles of Economics* (8th ed., New York: Macmillan, 1948), p. 89.
[44] Johnson in Bliss, *op. cit.*, p. 122.

aggregate output, ex advertising and salesmanship, is zero," says Johnson, is "sheer semantic chicanery: one might with equal logic argue that the marginal utility of income is negative to a man who supports an administration which spends some of his tax payments on purposes of which he disapproves or to one who reduces his life expectation by heavy smoking. . . ."[45]

Anticipating Galbraith's exposition of the function of advertising in *The New Industrial State,* Johnson expresses the opinion that the future of Madison Avenue will be as prosperous as its recent past. He expects more emphasis on discriminating taste, on what used to be termed the "art of gracious living." Even the psychiatric treatment embodied in much "hidden persuasion" is likely to spread since it is probable and not entirely deplorable, he says, that the less affluent will enjoy this luxury of the rich by buying it with their groceries.

Johnson's values and perception of social reality, it is evident, differ considerably from those of Galbraith; for example, he believes that in purchasing an automobile today "the consumer is offered his last chance to buy a piece of the frontier spirit." Galbraith's answer to Johnson's neoclassical defense would take the form, I suspect, of challenging the relevance of Marshall's reasoning about the relationship between wants and activities to consumption under the auspices of the industrial state. Marshall, he might argue, was writing of activities in a society that celebrated individual achievement and sensibility; the context of the affluent, industrial state with its fetish-like worship of production is not conducive to personal autonomy and the "art of gracious living." Furthermore, the "sick" joke about the masses buying psychiatry with their groceries suggests a contempt or disregard for the freedom of the individual that does an injustice to the heritage of liberalism.

SOCIAL IMBALANCE AND ITS CAUSES

Another salient point of controversy between Galbraith and his critics has to do with the concept of social imbalance, the question of its existence and its alleged causes. It will be recalled that Galbraith defines social balance loosely as "a satisfactory relationship between the

[45] *Ibid.,* p. 117.

supply of privately produced goods and services and those of the state. . . ." He describes the tendency toward social imbalance as being "implacable" and says that it is a problem that is "ubiquitous" and "frequently obtrusive" in the affluent society. He insists that "this disparity between our flow of private and public goods and services is no matter of subjective judgment. . . ."[46] As evidence he cites the newspapers of any major American city since World War II and states that they were filled with reports of shortages and deficiencies of vital municipal services and discussions of the pervasive public poverty. New York City's newspapers were "an excellent example" of such complaints, and Los Angeles was "a near-classic study in the problem of social balance."

Next, he argues in abstract terms that just as there must be a balance among the components of the productive process, there must also be a balance in what the community consumes. Having made the case for social balance, as he says, negatively, he turns to the causes for "the inherent tendency . . . for public services to fall behind private production." He advances the dependence effect as the primary cause of this phenomenon, stating, "Advertising operates exclusively, and emulation mainly, on behalf of privately produced goods and services." He analyzes the truce on inequality and the tendency to inflation as two additional causes. We have reviewed Galbraith's treatment of social imbalance at this point so that the reader may better understand the counterarguments of his critics.

Some of the latter have questioned the very existence of social imbalance, stressing that it is very difficult to measure. "A conception of an efficient allocation of resources ultimately rests upon a value judgment as to what the optimum composition of output ought to be. As a result, there is obviously no scientific way of proving (or, by the same token, of disproving) that social imbalance actually exists."[47] It is argued, for example, that the casual empiricism, if we may call it that, of citing random illustrations and statistics of social imbalance may exaggerate the problem.

Other critics, cited by McConnell, call attention to the fact

[46] *The Affluent Society*, 2nd ed., pp. 221, 222.
[47] C. R. McConnell, "Social Imbalance: Where Do We Stand?" *Quarterly Review of Business and Economics*, May 1961, pp. 6–23, as quoted in A. L. Grey, Jr., and J. E. Elliot, *Economic Issues and Policies: Readings in Introductory Economics* (2nd ed., Boston: Houghton Mifflin, 1965), p. 180.

that "expenditures for all kinds of durable consumer goods, including automobiles, run about 14% of personal consumption" and most of this is for essential equipment rather than gadgetry and frills.[48]

Professor Henry Wallich of Yale University challenges Galbraith on several grounds, arguing that public goods production has frequently been encouraged rather than inhibited because the unrelatedness of taxation and public spending creates the impression that the latter is costless. Moreover, some groups, especially in the lower income levels, who pay little direct taxes are inclined to favor and vote for increased public spending. In addition, the realities of "pressure politics" and "logrolling" are such that special interest groups can press for and achieve larger public expenditures. For these reasons, Wallich concludes, "As between the forces that inhibit and those that advance public expenditures, no one can say for sure where the balance lies. . . ."[49]

Zebot, in the article cited above, is also critical of Galbraith's analysis of social imbalance. Pointing out that Galbraith blames social imbalance largely on the dependence effect, he denies this, stating that whether a community will be better served by more public goods and less private is "a question that cannot be answered by any categorical Dependence Effect. Such answers must be based on the technical and economic merits of each case, whatever they may be."[50] The burden of proof, he contends, for good psychological and democratic reasons is unavoidably on the proponents of more public goods. "In summary, Galbraith's Dependence Effect reveals nothing about the desirable proportion between private and public goods. In democratic societies the case for public goods can only be based on the facts and analysis of specific instances. Even socialists in Europe, at least, begin to grasp this point."[51]

Professor Allen M. Sievers of the University of Utah is very critical of Galbraith's ideas about social imbalance,

[48] *Ibid.*

[49] H. C. Wallich, *The Cost of Freedom* (New York: Harper and Row, 1960), p. 169.

[50] Zebot, "Economics of Affluence," *loc. cit.,* p. 118. Zebot questions Galbraith's implied equation: Public Goods = Governmentally Provided Goods. "Actually this equation is not necessary, or desirable, for a variety of public goods (such as schools, hospitals, recreational facilities, cultural institutions of all kinds, etc.) either is, or can be, provided on non-governmental levels" (*Ibid.,* p. 119, footnote 8).

[51] *Ibid.,* p. 120.

among other things.[52] After lecturing him to the effect that it is "a curiously provincial assumption" to think that social balance is only attainable in an affluent society, Sievers finds several faults with his reasoning on this subject:

1. If the American people prefer private goods to more public goods, Galbraith may believe that they are mistaken in this choice, but he is not free to assume axiomatically that they are. He can merely try to *persuade* them to change their values; his arguments seem to imply the substitution of his judgments for the collective judgment of the American people.

2. Galbraith overstates the diminishing marginal urgency of goods. He is within his rights to join the chorus of those who regard America to be overly materialistic, commercialized, and conformist, "but the inferences he makes are greatly exaggerated." Sievers asks us to consider, by way of illustration, household appliances, which are to some the essence of our "Sybaritic effeteness." If women have become emancipated from drudgery because of these appliances and have thus achieved more leisure—a Galbraithian goal—what is there to criticize in this? "The class structure in America and the pattern of middle-class living are not only functions of income but of modern appliances." Without servants, middle-class women can only maintain a standard of living equal to that of their predecessors because of labor-saving appliances. Essentially, Galbraith is contending that people do not get satisfactions from their middle-class way of life and that they have been hoodwinked into believing that they do. To Sievers this is clearly not the case. The moral problem posed by America's prosperity is an ancient one—"how to use goods as a means and not as an end. To foreswear prosperity is an extreme solution to this problem. . . ." And this raises the question again of just how affluent we are. In Sievers' opinion, Galbraith is a bit premature in announcing our deliverance from poverty and scarcity. "The American economy will have to grow at customary rates for another generation or two before poverty can possibly be eliminated and the middle class be able to enjoy the kind of affluence which means genuine emancipation from concern about scarcity."[53]

3. On the central question of Galbraith's advocacy of

[52] A. M. Sievers, *Revolution, Evolution and the Economic Order* (Englewood Cliffs, N. J.: Prentice-Hall, 1962), Chapter III.
[53] *Ibid.*, p. 77.

more education to correct social imbalance and promote human fulfillment, Sievers thinks that his rhetoric and his polemical style of writing have led him to neglect the qualitative side of the matter, which is far more important than the quantity of money spent on educational plant and staff. Since Galbraith is concerned with ends and basic values rather than mechanics, he needed to devote more attention to "what he expects education to accomplish and how he thinks his objectives can be implemented."[54]

At this point we cannot forebear interpolating some comments on the above criticisms of Galbraith's work. One shortcoming that they tend to share is that they do not consider Galbraith's separate points in the context of his whole essay. In saying this, on the other hand, we do not wish to imply that none of these lines of argument have any merit. But one must remember that Galbraith wrote a popular essay addressed to the general reading public rather than to a professional audience. His stress on the so-called dependence effect is not substantiated by elaborate statistical analysis, but is offered instead as an interpretation in a broad, holistic, institutional treatment of the contrasting influences at work in private and public choices. Similarly, on the matter of the quality of education, Galbraith undoubtedly has as many questions about this as Sievers, but after all he was writing only one book. Educational philosophy was not exactly the principal focus of his study in *The Affluent Society*. Nevertheless, Sievers' contribution on this subject is valuable as an addendum and postscript to Galbraith's broader generalizations.

THE DISPUTED FACTS OF
SOCIAL IMBALANCE

The debate over the question of social imbalance spread from academic circles and periodical reviews after the publication of *The Affluent Society* to the nation's capital itself. *The New York Times* reported early in 1960: "More and more people in the capital are convinced that the most important continuing issue of American policy and politics over the next decade will be the issue of public spending—what share of America's total resources should

[54] *Ibid.*, p. 84.

be devoted to public as distinct from private purposes."[55]

Mr. Dale, the *Times*'s economic reporter who wrote this dispatch, went on to sum up his view on "private affluence and public poverty" as follows:

> Our society has reached a level of private wealth never before seen on this earth.
> Yet at the same time there is poverty in the public sector of the economy. Education is underfinanced. Streams are polluted. There remains a shortage of hospital beds. Slums proliferate, and there is a gap in middle-income housing. We could use more and better parks, streets, detention facilities, water supply. The very quality of American life is suffering from these lacks—much more than from any lack of purely private goods and services. The share of government in the total economy has been stable or even declining, while private affluence grows."[56]

The dissenters from this social imbalance view were not slow to counterattack in the public journals. Thus there appeared in a widely circulated bank letter an answer to the situation described by Mr. Dale.[57] In it the authors stated: "It is hard to see evidence of the alleged shriveling of the share of government in the total economy. Such evidence does not appear in statistics of government employment, tax revenues collected, or funds disbursed." In fact, this account asserted that there had been spectacular increases in outlays for social welfare, highways, sanitation facilities, jails, and the rest. It showed that where government expenditures in the mid-1920s were 10.8 percent of the gross national product, in 1940 they were 20.8 percent and in the late 1950s, 31.0 percent.

A chart was presented in this article to show how generous the American citizen had been with government, comparing what he kept for himself with what was paid in taxes to the federal, state, and local governments over the years 1927 to 1959. Compared to the former year the federal government's cash intake was shown to have grown twenty times. State and local revenue rose to an index of 567 in the latter year, contrasted with a base of 100 in 1927—more than a fivefold growth. Personal disposable

---

[55] *The New York Times*, Mar. 13, 1960, IV, p. 5. See also the same publication for Feb. 7, 1960, p. 1.

[56] *Ibid.*

[57] "Private Affluence and Public Poverty," *First National City Bank Monthly Letter*, June 1960, pp. 62–66.

income, on the other hand, was "not much more than four times the level of 1927."[58]

As for expenditures on schools, perhaps the most widely used illustration of "public poverty," the article pointed out that total public and private expenditures for education in the United States amounted to $22 billion in 1959, almost treble their level ten years before.

Those critical of the nation's private affluence say that the nation's schools are "old and overcrowded." Yet, says this article, this collides with the fact that state and local communities built 680,000 classrooms between 1945 and 1959, more than half the 1,330,000 in use in the latter year. The U.S. Office of Education reported in 1958 that there was a shortage of only 141,000 classrooms, whereas three years earlier it had predicted that we would be short by 600,000. The article contended that the peak demands in the future would be for high school and college facilities, since we had already passed over the hump of elementary school enrollments.

The authors of this influential economic publication explained the whole phenomenon of social imbalance in terms of a "vicious circle" in which we were caught: "The truth seems to be that we are caught in a vicious circle in which people's abilities to take care of their own needs are hampered by the burden of taxes. Paying so much in taxes, the citizen is tempted to think it only right to get something back. Hence the 'needs' government sees for more and bigger subsidy programs which in turn require to be financed by still higher taxes. And inflation, hitting the weak and helpless hardest, creates still more 'needs.' "

Arguing that more public spending clashes with the traditional beliefs of our people, it nostalgically recalls our rural individualism, saying, "The right to be different, the right to live according to our own lights is rooted too deeply in the American soil to be passively given up." Mr. Maurice H. Stans, U.S. Budget Director, speaking before the U.S. Chamber of Commerce, is quoted in a fashion that Galbraithians would marvel at: "We must not be charmed by the notion that Government is a wiser manager of our economic fortunes than is private enterprise." Shades of consumer sovereignty!

Another view of the postwar trend in government expenditures as it affected social imbalance appeared that same year (1960) in a study by Professor Francis Bator of

[58] *Ibid.,* p. 64.

M.I.T.[59] He itemized government spending for defense in these years and came to rather different conclusions from those of the First National City Bank. His technique was to compare government's nondefense purchases of goods and services with the size of the nondefense GNP over a number of years; in other words, he sought to measure the share of the public sector, so defined, in the civilian GNP. Nondefense expenditures of government as a percentage of the nondefense GNP, according to his analysis, stood at 7.5 percent in 1929 and rose to 13.4 percent ten years later; but by 1957 they had declined to 10.3 percent. On a per capita basis, evidence of a deficit in the public sector was even more pronounced. Per capita real nondefense spending by government was approximately the same in 1957 as it had been in 1939, despite the fact that total real civilian output per head increased from $1514 to $2281 over the same period. Bator's analysis, even though it was couched in aggregative terms, was superior to the National City Bank statistics, because the latter, on the whole, did not take account of the changing value of the dollar over the period studied, nor did they consider properly the sizable effects of military spending on the federal budget.

Incidentally, a similar conclusion was indicated in the Rockefeller *Report on the U.S. Economy,* issued in 1960, particularly in a chart on per capita expenditure on public works in the United States from 1915 to 1957.[60] This report clearly showed that in the period 1915–1940 per capita spending in constant dollars on schools, roads, waterworks, and other public works rose at an average annual rate of 4.5 percent. Such expenditures dropped sharply in the Great Depression and did not regain their previous rate until 1936. During the post-World War II decade these expenditures on public works increased rapidly from their 1945 low, but in 1957 they were no higher than they had been in 1936. Moreover, in the years 1952–1957 they seemed to have leveled out. "Total public expenditures have lagged behind the growth of total national output— the ratio to GNP declined from 4½ per cent in the late 1930's to 3 per cent now."[61]

Still another researcher to find a growing deficit in the

[59] F. M. Bator, *The Question of Public Spending* (New York: Harper and Row, 1960).

[60] Rockefeller Brothers Fund, *The Challenge to America: Its Economic and Social Aspects* (Garden City, N.Y.: Doubleday, 1958), p. 26.

[61] *Ibid.*

public sector was Professor Walt W. Rostow, an eminent economic historian, then also at M.I.T. Examining the dynamics of American society in the years 1940–1956, he reached two significant conclusions about social imbalance:

> First, the quiet, unexpected choice of postwar Americans for enlarged families over enlarged stocks of durable consumer goods and services—a decision which reflected at the margin a rejection or dilution of material objectives—is having and will have profound material consequences. Second, an unbalanced extension of private consumption since 1940 has left the society with an enormous backlog of social overhead requirements at precisely the period when the population and family formation increases are about to enlarge current requirements for social overhead capital. . . .[62]

Rostow expressed the belief that the problems of allocating resources between the private and public sectors, traditionally made at state and local levels, would likely be carried to a national plane. Reflecting on our national style of decision-making, predominantly that of the *ad hoc* solutions of the operator, the pragmatic manipulator rather than that of the man of reflection, he eloquently summed up the predicament of affluent America in 1958: "As of the summer of 1958, Americans live in a world where moralism serves the nation ill in its relation to the world and in its vision of itself; where the rate of increase in material output is an insufficient measure of the society's performance; where the operator's simple empiricism, combined with heavy immobile staff procedures for innovation, fails to keep pace with the challenge of the environment: and where even the image of American success is clouded."[63]

So much for the professional criticism of Galbraith's analysis of social imbalance. In the following section we offer an interpretation of that phenomenon which supplements Galbraith's treatment and puts it in a more defensible context.

[62] W. W. Rostow, *The United States in the World Arena: An Essay in Recent History* (New York: Harper and Row, 1960), p. 462.

[63] *Ibid.*, p. 536. Rostow differed strongly with Arthur F. Burns, President Eisenhower's chief economic adviser, with regard to the criteria for judging the performance of the economy in these years. It was not sufficient to think that public outlays must be accommodated in some quasi-Keynesian, compensatory fashion to an exuberant private economy. ". . . The composition of output directly matters as well as its level and rate of growth" (p. 524). On the other hand, he differed with Galbraith in stressing that "a rapid and steady rise in our GNP will, in fact, be necessary if the nation is to meet the multiple claims of security and the good society at home . . ." (p. 471).

THE CULTURAL AND POLITICAL
CONTEXT OF SOCIAL IMBALANCE

As an institutionalist, Galbraith has always stressed the importance of context in explaining social behavior. Thus in *The Affluent Society* we find him stating at one point: ". . . The calm decision between public and private consumption pictured by the conventional wisdom is, in fact, a remarkable example of the error which arises from viewing social behavior out of context."[64] The context he refers to, of course, is the market environment in which the "sovereign" consumer makes his choices of private goods, subject to all the subtle and powerful appeals of the advertisers, whereas public goods are acquired by the community, if at all, without the services of Madison Avenue and under a cloud of fiscal orthodoxy and of almost Puritan morality about the sinfulness of public spending.

There is some ideological and cultural heritage implicit in the disparate nature of American private and public decision-making as Galbraith describes them, but he does not make it very clear. Perhaps we can say that the shortcomings of Galbraithian economics, to paraphrase him without malice, lie not in logical error, but in a failure to specify context fully. In the case of social imbalance, he failed to describe the full cultural and social context of the 1950s in which advertising and emulation operated. By leaving American culture and social structure in the murky background, he gives his reader a distorted sense of the importance of the single institution of advertising.

To make this criticism specific, let us examine his treatment of social imbalance in the services performed by local governments. The problem here, he asserts, is much more severe than it is at the national level. The revenues of the localities lag behind increased private production because they are based on the inflexible general property tax, and the borrowing powers of local governments are more circumscribed than those of Washington. Increased services for states and localities require more money, but generally "the question of social balance is lost in the debate over equality and social equity."[65] In other words, the urban crisis is the result of ideological and philosophical differences among the citizenry; this explanation of social imbal-

---

[64] *The Affluent Society,* 2nd ed., p. 231.
[65] *Ibid.,* p. 233.

ance at the local level is distressingly general and undetailed.

Clarity and accuracy in the diagnosis of social imbalance are very important because they are essential for correct remedial action. In what sense do we say that Galbraith treats advertising and emulation outside their social context? By this we mean that he does not take adequate account of the whole American cultural heritage with its stress on the individualistic pursuit of success and social status. These elements in our social behavior go back to the foundations of the nation, to Lockean conceptions of the individual and the contract theory of the state. They bear the imprint of Jeffersonian and Jacksonian democracy and of the post-Civil War scramble for wealth and power. They were accentuated and revitalized again in the long struggle of the new immigrants along the "tenement trail" from the East Side to Brooklyn, to Long Island, and so on, as the urban frontier moved on in New York and other American cities.

The mobility drive of the American people manifested itself in the post-1945 years in the great migration to suburbia. "To map the growth of almost any of our larger cities since the turn of the century," says S. Lubell, "is to map this upward, outward push of the masses toward the greener suburbs, propelling the older residents before them. . . . The exodus was not accomplished in a single, mass evacuation, but through successive moves, from one neighborhood to the next. Each new neighborhood represented a higher rung on the social and economic ladder. . . ."[66]

The dependence effect and emulation must be analyzed against this cultural heritage of individualism and in relation to the social structure of the nation's metropolises, the changing pattern of residential segregation, and the massive automobile boom that accompanied the quest for subtopia. Such questions as these suggest themselves: Did social imbalance exist in suburbia in the late 1950s, or did the suburbanites enjoy public affluence as well as private affluence? What was the relationship between the mass movement to suburbia in the post-World War II years—David Riesman called it the "suburban dislocation"—and the development of social imbalance? Was it cause or effect?

[66] S. Lubell, *The Future of American Politics* (New York: Harper and Row, 1951), p. 61. The social and economic ascent of Americans is described in *Ascent to Affluence: A History of American Economic Development,* by C. H. Hession and H. Sardy (Boston: Allyn and Bacon, 1969), *passim.*

These queries need to be raised in any constructive criticism or appraisal of *The Affluent Society*.

The metropolitan explosion after 1945 which vastly enlarged suburbia was a continuation of a trend begun earlier. But in the postwar years that expansion was greatly accelerated. During the period 1950–1960 the central cities of the nation's 212 metropolitan areas increased 5.6 million in population, but 85 percent of that increase resulted from annexation of surrounding regions. The suburban population swelled in numbers from 36.9 million to 54.8 million in that decade.[67] The massiveness of the hegira to suburbia has been aptly compared in terms of size to the trans-Atlantic migration of the earlier decades of this century. In 1907 when the latter was at its height, 1.2 million Europeans landed in the United States. As of 1953, an average of 1.2 million Americans was moving to suburbia every year, and the exodus from the central cities by no means ended at that time. As is well known, white people constituted the predominant part of those migrating to suburbia in those years.

Accompanying this shift in population there were a substantial change in employment opportunities and a vast increase in the sale of houses, automobiles, and other durable consumer goods. Consumer expenditures for automobiles grew from about $6 billion in 1946 to close to $30 billion in 1956. Car registrations in the nation soared from 25.8 million in 1945 to 54.3 million in 1956.[68] This surge in automobile sales reflected the fact that many had not been financially able to buy new cars in the depressed thirties and that new automobiles were not available during World War II. Considering the long love affair of Americans with the internal combustion engine, their behavior in these years was not altogether inexplicable nor was it to be wholly explained by the dependence effect.

Suburbanites purchased a large share of new automobile output in those years. According to the Automobile Manufacturers Association, 61 percent of new car buyers lived outside the central cities in 1955.[69] The automobile was becoming an integral part of the middle-class style of

[67] B. McKelvey, *The Emergence of Metropolitan America, 1915–1966* (New Brunswick, N.J.: Rutgers University Press, 1968), p. 154; Y. Willbern, *The Withering Away of the City* (University, Ala.: University of Alabama Press, 1964), p. 20.

[68] The Editors of Fortune, *The Exploding Metropolis* (Garden City, N.Y.: Doubleday, 1957), pp. 53–54.

[69] Automobile Manufacturers Association, *Automobile Facts and Figures* (37th ed., Detroit, Mich.: 1957), p. 33.

life in suburbia; children had to be transported to school, the supermarkets were at a distance, and so on. While tailfins and other model changes were being extensively used to sell cars and to differentiate product in these years, the increase in demand needs to be seen in relation to the concurrent rise in national income and to this emergent pattern of suburban living.

An ingenious study has estimated that in the latter 1950s the cost of the automobile industry's model changes amounted to as much as $5 billion a year to the consumer.[70] This was a substantial cost, and one can rightly question whether the pace and character of many of these model changes were worth it, but the sum involved has to be seen in relation to the $30 to $34 billion spent on automobiles in those years. The automobile industry undoubtedly synthesized the demand for a sizable share of its product, but can we credit it with contriving suburbia? A similar argument can be made with regard to the household appliances which suburbanites and others purchased in such large quantities in these years. If such appliances provided women with more leisure in servantless households, it is difficult to believe that the want for such products was entirely synthesized by Madison Avenue.[71]

The demographic and industrial changes cited above were transforming American urban life at the very time that Galbraithian social imbalance was becoming evident. The change in the composition of the nation's central cities had a profound effect on the social and economic characteristics of these areas. The shift in racial, age, and income distribution in our central cities significantly affected the demand for public services placed on local governments and at the same time weakened their revenue resources.[72] Furthermore, the political fragmentation of American metropolitan government was creating the most serious tax and expenditure disparities among the constituent local bodies. The resulting discrepancies between needs and resources in our central cities lie at the heart of the so-called urban crisis in the United States. This aspect of the etiology of

[70] F. M. Fisher, Z. Griliches, and C. Kaysen, "The Cost of Automobile Model Changes Since 1949," *Journal of Political Economy*, October 1962, p. 433.

[71] Sievers, *op. cit.,* p. 76.

[72] Advisory Commission on Intergovernmental Relations, *Fiscal Balance in the American Federal System,* Vol. 2, *Metropolitan Fiscal Disparities* (Washington, D.C.: U.S. Government Printing Office, 1967), pp. 27, 58.

social imbalance was not adequately dealt with in Galbraith's first edition of *The Affluent Society*.

In dealing with the cultural elements underlying social imbalance, Galbraith did not show how these factors affected the development of our cities. The lopsided growth of our urban areas can be traced to the tradition and legacy of "privatism" (individualism) that they inherited. For example, in a study of Philadelphia, Professor S. B. Warner has shown that social imbalance existed in the "city of brotherly love" long before the post-World War II years.[73] Social imbalance was evident in that community during the nineteenth century and was most obvious during the bitter years of the 1930s. In the Depression, he writes, the industrial metropolis was "a private city and the public dimensions of urban life suffered accordingly."[74]

In his view, and it is one with which we agree, privatism is the most important element of our culture for understanding the development of our cities. Its essence is concentration on the individual and his search for wealth. Psychologically, it has meant an emphasis on the individual's independence in this quest for affluence. Socially, it has required that the individual should see his primary loyalty as his immediate family. The community is regarded as a mere aggregation of such money-making families. Politically, this tradition has resulted in the public agenda being heavily dependent on the changing focus of men's private economic activities.[75] Culturally, as Warner's study demonstrates, with the exception of the earlier creative years of the Republic, a city such as Philadelphia did not develop a social structure or a powerful group who understood the city as a whole and wanted to deal with it "as a public environment of a democratic society."[76] And Philadelphia was not unique in this respect; in Warner's opinion, it was quite representative of the ethos of American urban life. The institutions of advertising and of social emulation must be interpreted, so far as their functioning is concerned, in this context; they cannot be understood in a cultural vacuum.

In his chapter on inequality in *The Affluent Society*, Galbraith argued that Americans concentrated on production during the 1950s and thus sought to avoid the contro-

[73] S. B. Warner, Jr., *The Private City: Philadelphia in Three Periods of Its Growth* (Philadelphia: University of Pennsylvania Press, 1968), p. 202.
[74] *Ibid.*, p. 202.
[75] *Ibid.*, pp. 3, 4.
[76] *Ibid.*, p. 223.

versial question of income distribution. He presented some
evidence that between 1941 and 1950 income inequality
in the nation had been reduced. But he did not examine the
effects of the flight to suburbia or the results of the increased white residential segregation and its relation to
economic and social equality.

Over the years of our national history the evolving industrial and social structure of our cities has produced a distinct pattern of residential segregation of social classes and
of ethnic groups. The ghettos of our central cities and the
"gilded ghettos" of suburbia are merely the latest manifestation of this long-persisting social tendency.

The President's Advisory Commission on Intergovernmental Relations recently described this condition, which
was steadily growing worse at the time *The Affluent Society*
was published. "The *paradox of the poverty in the midst of
plenty* emerges most strikingly in the central cities of the
large metropolitan areas—and especially in the older central cities of the industrial Northeast and Midwest. The
decline in absolute poverty and increase in absolute affluence is overshadowed by the economic disparities between
the large central cities and their suburbs."[77]

Contrary to the impression that Galbraith's treatment of
social imbalance may suggest, the suburbanites were not
neglecting the public sector in their own communities in
the postwar years. Rather, we have been told that the flight
to suburbia "accounted for enormous outlays for public
services; social overhead capital, such as power facilities,
highways, streets, sewerage plants, water systems, schools,
etc. . . ."[78] Granted that the public sector in suburbia did
not have the services of Madison Avenue to contrive demand for schools in the postwar years; but it did have the
potent and indefatigable efforts of innumerable parent-
teacher associations to press the case for education and
"school betterment." In most instances, too, such groups
had the political clout to win a majority of the electorate
on this issue.[79]

[77] *Metropolitan Fiscal Disparities, op. cit.,* p. 5 (italics in original).
[78] H. C. Vatter, *The American Economy in the 1950's* (New York:
W. W. Norton, 1963), p. 23.
[79] R. C. Wood, *Suburbia: Its People and Their Politics* (Boston:
Houghton Mifflin, 1959), pp. 186–191, 205. "After raising the ade-
quacy and quality of their school plants in the late 1950's and early
1960's, these suburbs were able to concentrate more of their energies
on enriching instructional programs and improving teacher pay
scales" (Advisory Commission on Intergovernmental Relations,
Metropolitan Fiscal Disparities, op. cit., p. 67).

In 1957, when Galbraith was writing *The Affluent Society,* the per capita educational expenditures were already substantially larger in the suburbs of the large metropolitan areas of the Northeast and Midwest than in the central cities of the same regions. Since then the disparities in this respect have grown more shocking, amounting in some cases to almost double that spent in the inner cities. On noneducational expenditures, the situation was the reverse: In 1957 the areas outside the cities were paying $61 less per capita for these purposes than the central cities; by 1964–1965, the gap had widened to $81. This is a remarkable condition: The outer areas of our metropolises represent the nation's heaviest concentration of high-income residents, but the central cities with their high welfare rolls and other costly municipal services have the heaviest burden of expenditure for these purposes.

As a consequence, it is not surprising to find that the citizens of the central cities pay higher relative taxes than the suburbanites. In 1965 central city residents paid 7 percent of their income in taxes to local governments, while the suburbanites paid 5.4 percent.[80] Still, more ominously, the tax base of the central cities is shrinking, as industry and the well-to-do move to suburbia. In short, as has been said, the central cities have the problems, and other jurisdictions of government, usually the suburbs, have the resources.

The dynamics of metropolitan growth were not related by Galbraith to the emerging problem of social imbalance. Yet, from the historical perspective of the present, it is now evident that the spread of suburbia and the deepening plight of the "dark ghetto" were causally interrelated. The converging crises of race relations and of the city were accelerated significantly by these developments. "Separate but equal" in northern and midwestern regions of the nation was magnifying another "dependence effect" between whites and blacks which was of long standing. Kenneth Clark alludes to this dependent relationship in these words: ". . . The dark ghetto's invisible walls have been erected by the white society, by those who have power, both to confine those who have no power and to perpetuate their powerlessness. The dark ghettos are social, political, educational, and—above all—economic colonies. Their in-

[80] *Ibid.,* pp. 77–79. Rather than alleviating the social imbalance, state aid to localities contributes relatively to it. Cf. A. K. Campbell and S. Sacks, *Metropolitan America: Fiscal Patterns and Governmental Systems* (New York: The Free Press, 1967), p. 184.

habitants are subject peoples, victims of the greed, cruelty, insensitivity, guilt and fear of their masters."[81]

Rather than maintain the existing degree of social inequality, perverse policies of the national and local government after 1945 worsened the condition and opportunities of the ghetto residents and aggravated what has come to be called "institutionalized racism." Clark expresses it this way: "The suburbs drain the economy of the city—through subsidized transportation, housing development, and the like. The economy of the ghetto is drained and is not replenished."[82] Others have pointed to highway building in suburbia and the neglect of mass transit in the central cities; FHA policies guaranteeing mortgages for middle-class suburbanites and denying them to the poor in the central cities as bad risks; discriminatory employment practices and national policies regarding inflation and employment that hit the "exaggerated Americans" (the blacks) hardest. And, finally and not least, there have been social welfare practices that have perpetuated poverty rather than serving to eliminate it. In fairness to Galbraith, it must be said that he strongly urged public investment to counteract the deterioration of the urban slums and its people; but his analysis of social imbalance at the local level was too broad and general to pinpoint the more specific causes of ghetto blight.

By stressing the environmental causes of poverty, Galbraith called the nation's attention to dimensions of poverty other than low income. Poverty is now seen more clearly as involving not only insufficiency of income, but lack of freedom and absence of choice as well.[83] In writing of what he termed "the political economy of poverty," Galbraith also suggested the peculiar plight of the poor as an inarticulate minority in an otherwise affluent society. Social imbalance in the city was thus implicitly ascribed by him to the political dependence of the disadvantaged and to the lack of a balance in political power terms between the people of the ghetto and the ruling whites of the central cities and of suburbia. But, as we have argued above, this dynamic "de-

[81] K. B. Clark, *Dark Ghetto* (New York: Harper and Row, 1965), p. 11.

[82] *Ibid.*, p. 29.

[83] See, on this, S. M. Miller and F. Riesman, *Social Class and Social Policy* (New York: Basic Books, 1968), Chapter 1; also W. K. Tabb, *The Political Economy of the Black Ghetto* (New York: W. W. Norton, 1970), Chapter 5.

pendence effect" was not clearly delineated by Galbraith or made an integral part of his diagnosis of social imbalance.

"THE TYRANNY OF SMALL DECISIONS"

A standard reply of critics of Galbraith's exposition of the dependence effect and of the resulting alleged decline of consumer sovereignty has been to assert that a man should have the right and freedom to make his own errors of choice. Learning from his experience, he might thus become a wiser consumer. As illustration of this point of view, consider the following bit of conventional wisdom from the monthly bank letter quoted earlier:

> . . . When people spend their money they are casting ballots for what ought to be produced. They all make mistakes, as government does in procurement, but they may be a bit more careful because, after all, the money they are spending is their own. Moreover, the mistakes of individuals are small mistakes, never the billion-dollar variety.
>
> Tens of thousands in graduating classes this month, going out in the world, inevitably will make mistakes and profit thereby. This is an essential part of education, building wise and responsible citizens. As we all should know, the best remembered lessons are those learned in the school of experience.[84]

This avuncular advice has the reassuring tone of the homely wisdom of Poor Richard, but how well does it serve as a guide in the complex context of modern economic life? Let us examine these ideas from the Galbraithian standpoint and then from that of modern welfare economics.

Galbraith would, of course, reject the point of view expressed in this quotation. As we have seen, he attacked the orthodox theory of consumer demand as being invalid because it assumes the independence of wants from the process of satisfying them. Because of the urgency of production (GNP fetishism) and Mad Avenue's "demonic virtuosity in persuasion," the consumer is not completely a free agent in his market choices. From this Galbraith boldly draws his conclusion in welfare economic terms: Consumers may

<hr>

[84] *First National City Bank Monthly Letter*, June 1960, p. 66.

be collectively worse off at an all-round higher level of production than at a lower one. In his words: ". . . Wants thus come to depend on output. In technical terms, it can no longer be assumed that welfare is greater at an all-round higher level of production than at a lower one. It may be the same. The higher level of production has, merely, a higher level of want creation necessitating a higher level of want satisfaction."[85]

Galbraith's assault on the conventional theory of consumer demand and the welfare implications he draws from it were crucial to the whole enterprise of his essay. Though dazzlingly bold and sharp in its insights, it is questionable whether it convinced most of the "diligent readers" to whom it was addressed. In the first place, given our cultural heritage, this is a difficult proposition for modern Americans to accept—bigger has always meant better in the past. Second, it will be noted that the critique is stated in aggregative terms; the individual reader may be inclined to think that he is smarter and more astute as a consumer than his fellows. Third, Galbraith's argument involves a negative proof; a GNP that includes goods or services the want for which was contrived *may not* be as beneficial from a welfare standpoint as a smaller GNP. But what proportion of the GNP which is objected to is "contaminated" by contrived wants? Galbraith does not say. Furthermore, his analysis has the character of an *argumentum ad ignorantiam* and consequently is not fully convincing. Curiously, though he is a specialist in industrial organization, Galbraith did not choose to analyze consumer choice in microeconomic terms, but dealt with the subject in broad-brush fashion, stressing the anomalies of social imbalance.

Galbraith makes his case against the accepted view with characteristic force and remarkable graphicness. But perhaps it has suffered from being regarded as the argument of a brilliant dialectician who, as the saying has it, could argue the leg off a donkey. Many have marveled at his rhetoric, admire his iconoclasm, hail him as a pioneer, but then express reservations about his conclusions or policy recommendations. In these circumstances it may be helpful to consider the "backward art of spending money" from the standpoint of modern welfare economics. For Galbraith is not alone in believing that some untoward economic consequences flow from the untrammeled choices of

---

[85] *The Affluent Society,* 2nd ed. revised, p. 152.

the individual consumer.[86] Our excursion into this complex but important field of economics will be brief but, we hope, instructive.[87]

A market economy allocates resources on the basis of a host of smaller individual decisions made by consumers and businessmen which vary in size, in scope, and in their time dimension. Economists have traditionally been concerned with appraising the allocative efficiency of these choices, particularly with respect to how the cumulation or adding up of these individual decisions contributes to optimal economic results.

Welfare economists have spent considerable analytical effort in explaining why individual consumer decisions may not add up collectively to an economic optimum. Three cases may be noted:

1. Market imperfections, such as consumer ignorance or monopoly, may cause the total allocative result to be less than optimal. Galbraith's emphasis on the dependence effect, as practiced by oligopolists with substantial market power, might justify placing his theory of social imbalance mainly in this category.

2. Market failures,[88] such as those encountered even in perfectly competitive markets, where optimum allocative results may not be achieved because of so-called externalities (external economies or diseconomies, the uncompensated human and social costs of business enterprise, social benefits incapable of being appropriated privately, and internally increasing returns).

3. Consumer sovereignty has been challenged also on noneconomic grounds (for example, political or esthetic considerations); these are matters normally considered to be beyond the competence of economists. Galbraith's analysis includes some of the elements in (2) above, but he does not make explicit use of the concept of externalities.

[86] For example, Professor Lekachman in a recent article writes: ". . . The mechanism of consumer choice is so radically defective that we are compelled against our wishes to consume some items (not necessarily purchased by ourselves) and deprived of the opportunity to choose others which we might prefer" (R. Lekachman, "The Poverty of Affluence," *Commentary*, March 1970, pp. 39–44).

[87] In presenting these ideas, we have drawn heavily on the provocative article by A. F. Kahn, "The Tyranny of Small Decisions; Market Failures, Imperfections, and the Limits of Economics," *Kyklos*, volume XIX, fasc. 1, 23–47 (1966).

[88] On this, see, e.g., F. M. Bator, "The Anatomy of Market Failure," *Quarterly Journal of Economics*, August 1958, pp. 351–379.

Professor Kahn has suggested a fourth explanatory element, which he terms the "tyranny of small decisions," although he admits that the latter usually manifests itself in one or another of the three familiar categories. His phrase implies that the totality of a number of small decisions may not produce optimal efficiency, "merely because the decisive determinations are individually too 'small.' . . . It suggests that if one hundred consumers choose option x, and this causes the market to make decision X (where X equals 100x), it is not necessarily true that those same consumers would have voted for that outcome if that large decision had ever been presented for their explicit consideration. If this is true, *the consumer can be victimized by the narrowness of the contexts in which he exercises his sovereignty.*"[89]

As illustration of the situation, consider this question which the late Morris R. Cohen used to pose in his City College philosophy classes: "Suppose, seventy-five years ago, some being from outer space had made us this proposition: 'I know how to make a means of transportation that could in effect put 200 horses at the disposal of each of you. It would permit you to travel about, alone or in small groups, at 60 to 80 miles an hour. I offer you this knowledge; the price is 40,000 lives per year.' "[90]

The "big decision" Cohen asked his classes to make may be interpreted to be of the all-or-nothing variety, such as a collective political body might make, rather than a host of individual yeses or noes. Such an approach would constitute a rejection of the standards of modern welfare economics.

Another view may be that Cohen implied that individual consumers in such a situation may make the wrong decisions. If they had known the risks, they might have decided otherwise. So interpreted, this would be a simple case of market imperfection—inadequate knowledge.

Kahn points out that individual consumers, in purchasing automobiles, may generate excessive public (external) costs for others, particularly if below some level of purchases there are no risks of traffic jams or air pollution, but once a threshold of these are exceeded, these external costs grow disproportionately.

[89] Kahn, *op. cit.,* p. 24.
[90] *Ibid.,* pp. 29–30. Since Cohen first posed his question, the toll of traffic deaths on the highways has risen. In 1970, it was approximately 55,000 deaths per year.

Likewise, emulation in the purchase of automobiles or other private goods may impose what the British economist A. C. Pigou regarded as an external cost of consumption—envy—and a possible form of market failure.[91] An example might be the first girl who wears a mini in her neighborhood; soon numerous other females, envious of the masculine attraction so created, may be forced to follow suit. This is a familiar phenomenon that Veblen had in mind when he spoke of invention as being the mother of necessity.

Individual purchases, made in the context of a given way of life and alternatives, may cumulate until they diminish the very possibility of free choice. This process may feed on itself and become irreversible because alternatives become unprofitable and are abandoned (e.g., in the case of automobiles, the railroads, and other forms of mass transit). Under these conditions, concludes Kahn, "it may take a major, discrete step, breaking the market-dominated spiral of history, to offer consumers the full range of economically feasible alternatives required for rational choice."[92]

Another manifestation of the tyranny of small decisions may be what J. M. Clark called "product inflation." By this term he referred to the possibility that competition, especially in highly concentrated industries, may primarily involve "cost-inflating and largely specious quality improvements."[93] In citing this instance of the tyranny of small decisions, Kahn employs more technical terms than Galbraith, but the significance and outcome, so far as public welfare is concerned, are the same. Spurious quality variations may generate "external diseconomies of consumption—envy"—"My tail fin is bigger than yours," and so on —and thus serve to undermine the optimality of the market outcome. Second, such quality "improvements" may contribute to the process of want creation (contrivance)— what was once called the "annual model racket" creates dissatisfaction with what we have.

In Kahn's view, product inflation derives not from market failure, technically defined, but from the imperfectly competitive markets in which consumers in the first place are not given the proper small choices. "They [con-

[91] A. C. Pigou, *The Economics of Welfare* (4th ed., London: Macmillan, 1960), p. 191, as quoted in *ibid.*, p. 31.

[92] Kahn, *op. cit.*, p. 33.

[93] *Ibid.*, p. 39. See also J. M. Clark, *Competition as a Dynamic Process* (Washington, D.C.: Brookings Institution, 1961), pp. 252–257.

sumers] are often not offered a choice between unchanged and changed models at a price differential fully reflecting the cost-saving made possible by sticking to the former. . . ."[94] Thus "these two effects can involve households in a self-defeating spiral of model changes, each at one and the same time creating dissatisfaction and (temporarily) removing it, at a cost that buyers might well deem excessive if the question were ever put to them on something other than a piece-meal, family-by-family, year-to-year basis. . . ."[95]

Kahn qualifies this last conclusion somewhat, saying we can't be sure whether consumers would necessarily have it any other way because they may consider the changes as improvements and enjoy the process of buying and discarding for itself. Generally, however, Kahn sees Americans, as does Galbraith, on the "squirrel wheel" of contrived consumption, but thinks perhaps that they have become addicted to it. Kahn's examination of the affluent society from the perspective of welfare economics leads him to conclusions supportive of Galbraith's in many ways. The major difference is that he reaches them from a broad analysis of microeconomics; in probing the deficiencies of the market mechanism, he stresses the unanticipated consequences of even "rational" consumer sovereignty in an excessively narrow context. His emphasis on the process by which the individual consumer may be victimized may be more persuasive than Galbraith's stress on want contrivance and Madison Avenue "bamboozlement."

As we can see from this brief summary of Kahn's analysis, and from Galbraith's as well, the assumptions that are being challenged by these economists go back to the very foundations of classical economics, to Lockean and Smithean individualism. And if Kahn is correct, the fallacy involved in the conventional theory resembles that which Keynes detected in the Ricardian thought about saving— the paradox of thrift. If the totality of consumer decisions is not as beneficial to the individual and to society from a welfare standpoint as they are when made individually, it is conceivable that we may come to speak of the "paradox of consumer demand." Such a transformation in economic thinking, though it has long been in the making, may come to be ranked in importance, as Strachey predicted, with the Keynesian revolution.

[94] Kahn, *op. cit.*, p. 42.
[95] *Ibid.*, p. 40.

THE EXTENT OF POVERTY

Galbraith's treatment of poverty in the original edition of his book was one of its most criticized features. Some of this criticism has been unfair and stupid, but in some ways he unnecessarily exposed himself on this important subject. He had written, as of 1958, that with a weekly industrial wage of $80 and a $3960 median family income, "it [poverty] can no longer be presented as a universal or massive affliction. It is more nearly an afterthought."[96]

One of the first to attack him on this matter was Leon Keyserling, a lawyer-economist who had been a chairman of the Council of Economic Advisers under President Truman.[97] He rightly pointed out that the statistics supporting the idea that poverty was no longer a massive affliction were limited to those families with annual incomes below $1000. Galbraith had used the latter figure to delineate what he called "the hard core of the very poor." He had said that only 1 American family in 13 had an annual income of less than that amount. He had not intended to imply that all receiving above that amount were affluent. Keyserling cited figures to show that in 1957 we had more than 19 million family units with annual incomes below $4000. And, in addition, as of that same year there were almost 20 million families, or about 45 percent of the total, with annual incomes between $4000 and $7500. Galbraith left himself open to criticism by not explicitly considering those who, while not within the hard core of poverty, still suffered economic deprivation. Keyserling, noting that another Harvard economist saw satiety approaching, sarcastically remarked that evidently poverty was not massive in Widener Library. Another critic suggested that Galbraith was something of an ascetic, perhaps because he was a farm boy like Veblen, and they both "cast a cold eye on the gross, corpulent, consumer society in which they found themselves."[98]

Keyserling differed squarely with Galbraith on the remedy for poverty. Whereas the latter was ready to employ the sales tax to provide the income for public investment to abolish poverty, Keyserling argued that public services

[96] *The Affluent Society*, 1958, p. 323.
[97] L. Keyserling, "Eggheads and Politics," *New Republic*, October 27, 1958, p. 13.
[98] S. Thernstrom, "The Myth of American Affluence," *Commentary*, October 1969, p. 76.

could not be expanded in the absence of economic growth. "To raise public services," he wrote, "we must raise expenditures (federal, state, and local) to an annual rate by 1964 of *about $33 billion, or 38 per cent, above the recent annual rate.* To attempt to do this primarily by a redistribution of expenditures—from private consumption to public needs—rather than through high economic growth, defies history and reason."[99]

In 1962 Michael Harrington published *The Other America,* a powerful and moving book, in which he claimed that there were between 40 and 50 million poor people in the nation. It is notable that Harrington was not as critical as others had been of Galbraith on poverty. He said that the Harvard professor had underestimated the problem, but he also had been one of the first writers to describe the new, invisible poverty. Indeed, in Harrington's view, Galbraith's achievement had been considerable. "He was one of the first to understand that there are enough poor people in the United States to constitute a subculture of misery, but not enough of them to challenge the conscience and the imagination of the nation."[100]

In that same year Walter W. Heller, former chairman of the CEA under Presidents Kennedy and Johnson and a respected professional economist, had some worthwhile comments to make on the controversy. He noted that in 1961 nearly a third of American spending units had incomes of less than $4000 and over a half had less than $8000 a year. Furthermore, he pointed out, according to the U.S. Census Bureau at that time, almost one-fifth of American housing units were substandard. Given these facts, said Heller, "even in the United States in the 1960's, affluence lies in the eye of the beholder."[101]

In 1969, in the introduction to the revised edition of *The Affluent Society,* Galbraith sought to explain why he was so badly misunderstood or misread on the subject of poverty. He said, in effect, that his preoccupation with private affluence and its baneful effects had led him to push consideration of poverty to the latter part of his book where, he suspected, some did not read what he had to say.

[99] Keyserling, *New Republic, op. cit.,* p. 16. (Italics in original.) On the dispute between Galbraith and Keyserling, see R. Lekachman, "Liberals and the U.S. Economy," *New Leader,* January 26, 1959, pp. 4–6.

[100] M. Harrington, *The Other America: Poverty in the United States* (Baltimore, Md.: Penguin Books, 1963), p. 19.

[101] W. Heller, "Time for a Keynes," *New Republic,* October 20, 1962, p. 42.

He claimed that rather than neglecting poverty, his treatment had directed attention to "the continuing scandal of great deprivation amidst the great wealth of the United States." It is noticeable, however, that in the revised edition Galbraith took some pains to delete certain passages and to insert new material. He dropped completely the remark that poverty was "more nearly an afterthought." He revised his statistics about those with less than $1000 a year, and substituted more defensible figures, showing that poverty could vary with the size of the family and other factors. He paid more attention to the poverty of the ghetto and less to the rural variety. Curiously, however, and in seeming contradiction with the new emphasis he gives to poverty in the revised edition, he retained the closing quotation from Prime Minister Pitt, "Poverty is no disgrace but it is damned annoying." Turning this about, Galbraith says, "In the contemporary United States, it is not annoying but it is a disgrace."[102] We find it difficult to understand how poverty can be regarded as not annoying either from the standpoint of the individuals or families who suffer it or from that of the nation.

In this introduction Galbraith also dealt with another criticism which he says was a common Keynesian reaction. Why, said his critics, worry about social imbalance, when so many Americans have an income of less than so much and can hardly be considered affluent? He felt that such an argument showed obtuseness, because to postpone the question of how we should use our wealth until everyone or nearly everyone reached a seemingly decent minimum would be to postpone it forever for the simple reason that the desired minimum will rise with the increase in wealth. And, says Galbraith, since social imbalance is a major cause of chronic poverty, the critics were asking that we postpone the consideration of the causes of poverty until no one was poor.

SOME UNANTICIPATED CONSEQUENCES OF *The Affluent Society*

In writing *The Affluent Society,* Galbraith in some respects played the role of the little boy in Andersen's story who declared that the emperor was naked. He described a

---

[102] *The Affluent Society,* 2nd ed., p. 296.

society which in its pursuit of private affluence was destroying the common wealth and welfare of the nation. Yet, curiously, there were millions of Americans who never read Galbraith's book, but having heard of the phrase, concluded that they were not affluent. The resentment so generated has been the subject of several articles that have dealt with these unanticipated consequences of Galbraith's best-seller.

Thus Professor Stephan Thernstrom in a recent periodical essay contends that "the myth of American affluence has become the new conventional wisdom, and it constitutes a formidable obstacle to understanding our present condition."[103] He concedes that the central point of Galbraith's book was a sound one, namely, that there was an appalling lack of social imbalance in the American economy. While this book, along with Michael Harrington's, alerted President Kennedy to the problems of the poor and thus contributed to the passage of the Economic Opportunity Act of 1964, it helped to create the myth of American affluence. ". . . Whatever the author's intent, the book directed attention away from the economic deprivation which was still commonplace in the United States and provided the well-to-do with an intellectually respectable vantage point from which to criticize the materialistic strivings of the vulgar masses rather than the American social order itself."[104] With the rediscovery of poverty and the deepening racial crisis, the Galbraithian mythology has undergone significant modification, but the assumption of affluence persists. "It continues," says Thernstrom, "to influence popular perceptions of the nature of our society, and impedes the formation of political alignments which might bring about constructive social change."

In elaboration of his view, Thernstrom argues that the myth of American affluence which Galbraith helped to create reflected "the dominant political and social tendencies of the Age of Eisenhower." Republican speech-writers pictured a nation without substantial poverty and moving toward greater equality of income distribution. There was talk of "people's capitalism" and of "the twentieth century capitalist revolution." Even the Democrats joined in the paean to the new prosperity. Arthur Schlesinger announced that the successes of the Roosevelt and Truman years out-

[103] S. Thernstrom, "The Myth of American Affluence," *Commentary*, October 1969, pp. 74–78.
[104] *Ibid.*, p. 75.

moded "quantitative liberalism," and that the task of liberalism should now be one of improving the quality of American life. *"The Affluent Society,"* writes Thernstrom, "bears the marks of this cultural climate and indeed was a prime source of the new perspective. . . ."[105] The real villain of Galbraith's work, he says, was not economic deprivation, but conspicuous consumption. Galbraith's polemic against the latter, as with Veblen's earlier critique, was easily converted to snobbish and self-serving ends.

> . . . The notion that the ordinary American had more than enough income to meet his "real" needs but was being brainwashed by Madison Avenue to believe that he needed costly and ugly inessentials—a mauve and cerise air-conditioned, power-steered, and power-braked automobile was Galbraith's example—became an article of faith in cultivated circles in the Age of Eisenhower. Often the loudest complaints against tailfins were voiced by people whose own Spartan mode of transportation was a Porsche.
> Few of those who mouthed the clichés about American affluence felt *themselves* to be blessed with excessive income. The assumption was that others were not sufficiently spiritual to make proper use of their undue affluence.[106]

With the new awareness of the massiveness of economic deprivation in the United States, the notion that virtually all Americans are affluent enough to satisfy their "real" needs is heard no more; another version of the myth of affluence is still with us. "This is the myth of the affluent worker and the trade-union Establishment." For the older myth, Thernstrom contends, we have substituted a more sophisticated one that, apart from the underclass of the very poor, there are the affluent which include even "the most menial white-collar employees and the organized blue-collar workers." Some of the affluent middle-class liberals are so anxious to help the poor that they are willing to do so via measures such as "community control" which have no effect on the rich themselves. Those living on the wages provided by most unionized blue-collar or menial white-collar jobs grow bitter when others assume that poverty shades into comfortable affluence at the $3000 or $4000 line or, even more galling, believe that economic deprivation is confined largely to Negroes. Thernstrom states that it is not surprising that many such whites are fearful, defensive, and even punitive toward blacks who seem to

---

[105] *Ibid.,* p. 75.
[106] *Ibid.,* p. 76. (Italics in original.)

threaten them, with the support of upper-middle-class liberals.

The racism of many of the craft unions, Thernstrom correctly points out, stems from the scarcity psychology of workers who have known unemployment in the past. The intellectuals of the left, he insists, "must broaden their concern to embrace not only the very poor, but those who, through painful struggle, have inched a short rung or two up the slippery ladder of success."[107]

We have summarized this critique of "American affluence" because it illustrates so well the confusion that has arisen from the ambiguity in the use of the word "affluence." Galbraith used the term, without a modifier, to refer to the nation's productive capacity to eliminate poverty. The phrase "private affluence," on the other hand, was not used by him to refer to a given level of money income, but to unbalanced expenditure on private goods relative to the level of public expenditure in a community or in the nation. Less frequently he used the adjective "affluent" to mean merely prosperous.

Books, like our children, often have a destiny other than their makers envision or desire. Galbraith's title may well have an influence other than that he intended, as Thernstrom demonstrates. Galbraith wrote his book believing that the normal rate of economic growth would provide a prospect of increasing private income for those above the poverty line. But if in a period of lagging economic growth and substantial unemployment, its message comes to be popularly interpreted in a rather different fashion, this will only demonstrate ironically the truth of another favorite Galbraithian principle, namely, the unusual power of circumstances over the reception of ideas.

[107] *Ibid.*, p. 78.

6 *The New*

Industrial State

THE HOUSE THAT GALBRAITH BUILT

Galbraith's major third work, *The New Industrial State,* was published in the late spring of 1967 and immediately went on the best-seller lists. He had summarized the book in six Reith lectures over the British Broadcasting Corporation before its appearance; it thereby drew the critical fire of G. C. Allen and others even before its American debut.[1] Galbraith had been working on this book for about two years when he was appointed ambassador to India by President Kennedy in 1961. "With some misgiving," he later wrote, "I put the manuscript away in the vault of the bank. Only men of considerable vanity write books; consistently therewith, I worried lest the world were exchanging an irreplaceable author for a more easily purchaseable diplomat. . . ."[2]

Before this appointment was made known there had been some newspaper speculation that Kennedy might name Galbraith to the U.S. Senate. In fact, Galbraith asked the President whether he would not be more useful in that august body, where he might bring some decency back to Massachusetts Democratic politics. The President replied that he would be better employed in India "by a factor of five to one."[3] Ten days after the Inaugural, according to J. M. Burns, the President told him that he was glad that

[1] *The Listener and BBC Television Review,* Lecture I, Nov. 17, 1966, pp. 711–714; II, Nov. 24, 1966, pp. 755–758; III, Dec. 1, 1966, pp. 793–795, 812; IV, Dec. 8, 1966, pp. 841–843, 853; V, Dec. 15, 1966, pp. 881–884; VI, Dec. 22, 1966, pp. 915–918.

[2] *The New Industrial State,* p. viii.

[3] J. K. Galbraith, *Ambassador's Journal* (Boston: Houghton Mifflin, 1969), pp. 1–2.

Galbraith was going to India. "Otherwise, he would have him expounding a far too radical position."[4]

Upon his return from the ambassadorial post after the tragic death of the President, Galbraith resumed work on his book. Actually, he says, he largely discarded the earlier manuscript because he had reached a better view of the problem. In 1960 he had told a reporter that it had been "a very tough book to write," but that he thought that he had "finally broken its back."[5] It will be worth our while to explore the reasons for the difficulties he encountered in composing this work.

In his foreword to the volume, Galbraith emphasizes that in its origins his book has a close connection to *The Affluent Society*. ". . . It stands in relation to that book as a house to a window. This is the structure; the earlier book allowed the first glimpse inside." Possibly part of the trouble lay in the fact that *The New Industrial State* has a duality of themes. As he had explained in the interview cited above, he was seeking to develop a general, unified theory of large-scale organization in industry. This interest is reflected in his analysis of the so-called convergent tendencies of industrial societies and in their reliance on roughly similar designs for organization and planning.[6] The other theme which is more closely related to *The Affluent Society* involves further analysis of the causes of social imbalance in the United States. Galbraith does not forewarn his readers of the existence of these dual themes; he seeks to reconcile and accommodate one to the other, but in so doing he may have obscured other relationships.

It is necessary for the reader to approach *The New Industrial State* with some degree of scientific sophistication. In particular, we shall take note of its conceptual framework or analytical structure and compare it with that of *The Affluent Society*. Galbraith in the book under review offers his readers a theory of the functioning of the modern industrial system and its relationship to consumers, unions, the state, and what he calls the educational and scientific estate. Now, a theory, we know, is not a neutral entity; it is a way of perceiving reality; it orders observations such as may be made to test its validity. "A theory is composed of both systematic and doctrinal elements, which may be

[4] J. M. Burns, "Personal History," *Saturday Review,* December 20, 1969, p. 27.
[5] *Newsweek,* August 8, 1960, p. 77.
[6] See *The New Industrial State,* esp. Chapter IX and pp. 389–392.

imbedded in its language, logical tools, concepts, empirical relationships, and normative considerations. Together these determine the quality of a theory and pattern its descriptions. . . ."[7] By the analytical structure of a theory we refer to "those aspects of concrete phenomena which are delineated and included within it." Empirical structure refers to "the shapes and regularities that characterize the real world and the actual boundaries of phenomena."[8] Any given theory is bounded by a combination of its analytical and empirical structures. (The boundaries of a theory are the limits imposed on observation by its assumptions.) It will be useful to employ these concepts in our exposition of the ideas of *The New Industrial State.*

In this book Galbraith treats the dynamics of the American industrial system in a manner reminiscent of the great tradition of political economy; it is a *tour d'horizon* of economic change in the last seventy years done in broad strokes. The emphasis is on the rapidly changing institutions of the industrial system, rather than on the historic culture and its accompanying ideology as was the case in *The Affluent Society.*

The "industrial system," as Galbraith employs the phrase, refers to the "few hundred technically dynamic, massively capitalized and highly organized corporations in our economy." In his opening chapter he skillfully treats these giant, mature companies as the major agents of change in contemporary industrial society. The new relationship of the state to the economy, the further growth of mass advertising, the retardation in the expansion of the trade unions, and the phenomenal increase in the scale of higher education in the United States are examined in relation to these dynamic organizations and current technological change. He insists that these changes must be seen not in isolation from each other, but rather in terms of their close interdependence. In its effects on the American economy "this matrix of change has been more than the sum of its parts."[9]

In a manner very similar to Veblen, Galbraith contends that modern technology requires the mature corporation and the planning that it has developed to avoid market risks and make profits. Thus whatever the formal ideological billing of our economic system, it is "in substantial

[7] S. Krupp, *Pattern in Organization Analysis: A Critical Analysis* (Philadelphia: Chilton, 1961), p. 3.
[8] *Ibid.*, pp. 57–61.
[9] *The New Industrial State*, p. 4.

part" a planned economy. Boldly announcing his theme, Galbraith states that one of his conclusions will be that there is a broad convergence of industrial systems. "The imperatives of technology and organization, not the images of ideology, are what determine the shape of economic society. . . ."[10] He states too what some would term the "normative structure" of his analysis (what ought to be) when he says that this convergence is, on the whole, fortunate, regardless of what ideologists on both sides of the fence might think. But the good fortune is not unqualified, because "the subordination of belief to industrial necessity and convenience is not in accordance with the greatest vision of man. Nor is it entirely safe. . . ."[11]

Displaying his interdisciplinary proclivity, he asserts that "the boundaries of a subject matter are conventional and artificial; none should use them as an excuse for excluding the important." Thus he warns his reader that in his later chapters he will turn to the effects of economic change on social and political behavior. He sees the nation falling into a comfortable servitude to the machine that we have created to serve us, and he will propose the general lines of our emancipation.

He makes it clear too that his study is concerned primarily with the large, mature corporations—the heartland of the modern economy—and not with the thousands of small, traditional proprietors or entrepreneurial corporations. Relatively speaking, the latter lack the capital, advanced technology, complex organization, and other features which we have come to associate with modern enterprise. The two parts of the American economy, he says, are very different and in no way more significant than in the motivation to effort itself. Profits have a different role as an incentive in these contrasting sectors. Galbraith, it is evident, regards our economy as being substantially a dual one, made up of the largest corporations—what he terms the "industrial system" —on the one hand, and the remaining host of small enterprises. The industrial system is the dominant feature of the New Industrial State; this is "the house" that Galbraith proceeds to describe in the following chapters. Close scrutiny of Galbraith's early chapters is very important because in them he lays down the ground plan (the basic concepts) of the analytical structure which he erects.

[10] *The New Industrial State*, p. 7.
[11] *Ibid.*

THE IMPERATIVES OF TECHNOLOGY

Like Adam Smith, Galbraith knows the expository value of a good illustration. Instead of using the famous Smithian pins, he demonstrates what he terms the "imperatives of technology" by contrasting the production processes employed in making the first Ford automobile with those used in manufacturing the 1964 Mustang. Technology, he asserts, forces the division and subdivision of any task into its component parts. He regards technology not as a given, static factor in the economic process, but as a powerful, dynamic force, "having an initiative of its own." Technological specialization is not dependent, as in Smith's *Wealth of Nations,* on the extent of the market. Rather the technological division of labor is carried to any particular degree because only in that way can organized knowledge be brought to bear on performance. Technology, it is important to note, is treated as if it were a primary, autonomous force in its own right.[12]

Galbraith's treatment of technology differs from that of Joseph Schumpeter. It is not conceived as manifesting itself in a "perennial gale of creative destruction," visible in the changes brought about by interindustry competition. Technology is not seen as developing in a competitive industrial context or in relation to military need. The imperatives of technology are described in terms of six major consequences of technological specialization:

1. A lengthening span of time separates the beginning and completion of a task. For example, the first Ford was assembled in a "very slight" period of time, whereas the Mustang from its conception to completed car required three and one-half years.

2. With a more complex technology and specialized knowledge, there is need for more financial capital in the production process.

[12] Galbraith later characteristically qualifies the primacy he gives to technology in these words: "In examining the intricate complex of economic change, technology, having an initiative of its own, is the logical point at which to break in. But technology not only causes change, it is a response to change. Though it forces specialization, it is also the result of specialization. Though it requires extensive organization it is also the result of organizaton . . ." (*The New Industrial State,* p. 20). The average reader is likely to be impressed with the first strong affirmative statements and miss the significance of the qualifications.

3. Modern technology requires an inflexible commitment of physical capital (tools and equipment) to the particular task as it was initially defined.

4. Technology demands specialized manpower not only for production, but to guide and plan output and its distribution.

5. An inevitable concomitant of specialization is organization, because without coordination of their efforts, the work of the many specialists will be wasted.

6. Planning is necessary because of the time and capital that must be committed, the inflexibility of this commitment, the need for large organization, and the difficulties of achieving adequate performance under conditions of advanced technology.

INDUSTRIAL PLANNING

Galbraith presents his reader with a brief history of planning, noting that until the end of World War II or shortly thereafter, it was only a "moderately evocative" word in the United States. (Those who remember the controversies over New Deal planning will be inclined to doubt this.) It was only with the coming of the Cold War that the word acquired ideological overtones. With the lengthening of time between the beginning of production and sale, the greater capital commitment, and the attendant risk, the modern firm must exercise control over what is supplied— the market is too unreliable—"it must replace the market with planning." From the perspective of the industrial firm, "planning consists in foreseeing the actions required between the initiation of production and its completion and preparing for the accomplishment of these actions." Galbraith observes that national economic planning is generally viewed by the economist or political scientist as replacing prices and the market mechanism with an authoritative determination of what will be produced and consumed and at what price. Rather than being contradictory or inconsistent, says Galbraith, these two kinds of planning are "inextricably associated."

The uncertainties of the market require its replacement by an authoritative determination of prices and the amounts to be disposed of at these prices. This can be done in three ways: (1) the market can be superseded; (2) it can be controlled by sellers or buyers; (3) it can be suspended for definite periods by the use of long-term contracts. Supersession of the market is most often accomplished by vertical integration—the planning unit takes over the source of supply or the distribution process. (Galbraith ignores reliance on the market even by highly integrated firms such as General Motors; he takes no notice of partial or "tapered" integration which allows the big firm the advantages of both the market and planning.)

Market control is better accomplished by the large firm, large in relation to the particular market. Size, he flatly says, enables GM to set the prices for autos and the rest of the products it produces; the fact that it is one of few sellers in many of its markets facilitates this control. Advertising and product design further enable large firms to stabilize the demand for their products and thus control them. Market uncertainty can also be eliminated by the use of long-term contracts. Similarly, outside the industrial system, in agriculture, for example, the government intervenes to fix prices and thus suspends the operation of the market. The procurement contracts of military suppliers and space contractors are likewise cited as examples of planning replacing the market with all its associated vagaries.

Galbraith draws two conclusions from this bit of analysis: (1) industrial planning is in "unabashed alliance" with size; (2) the enemy of the market is not ideology, but the engineer. In the light of this interpretation, "The modern large corporation and the modern apparatus of socialist planning are variant accommodations to the same need."

The planning of the large corporation extends to its supply of capital. Pointing to the trend toward internal financing, Galbraith notes that in 1965 American corporations raised only one-third of their capital requirements in the capital market. The rest was internally generated from undistributed profits or depreciation funds. Next, in something of a historical digression, Galbraith surveys the shifting locus of power in Western society. He contends that power over the productive enterprise and indirectly over society at large has shifted from Land to Capital and now to the Technostructure, the relatively scarce technical elite who alone are capable of managing gigantic organizations. "Power," he writes, "goes to the factor of production which is hardest to obtain or hardest to replace. In precise language it adheres to the one that has the greatest inelasticity of supply at the margin."[13]

[13] *Ibid.*, p. 56.

Max Weber, the German sociologist, predicted at the beginning of this century that modern man was destined to live in "the iron cage of bureaucracy." Galbraith prefers his neologism, "technostructure," to the connotations of bureaucracy. One reason, perhaps, is that he sees the advantages of group decision-making rather than reliance on the unaided individual. Committees permit the pooling and testing of information. Another, more basic difference is that Galbraith believes that the technostructure is more powerful and indispensable in decision-making than top management. The technostructure consists of the numerous specialists who collect, digest, and aid in the collective decision-making process. It is this organization, Galbraith insists, not the managers, who decide. The effective power of decision in the modern, mature corporation is lodged deeply in the technical, planning staff of specialists. Group decision-making has replaced the classic entrepreneur, Schumpeter's hero.[14]

Turning to the corporation, Galbraith reiterates the idea that the most obvious requirement of effective planning is size. Economists have for long quarreled over the reasons for the emergence of large corporations, some holding that they far exceeded any possible economies of scale in the firm, others that they have a justification other than monopoly. Galbraith says his analysis allows both parties to the dispute to be right, but, in addition, it explains what others have failed to explain. "The size of General Motors is in the service not of monopoly or the economies of scale but of planning. And for this planning—control of supply, control of demand, provision of capital, minimization of risk —there is no clear upper limit to the desirable size. It could be that the bigger the better. . . ."[15]

In Galbraith's view, the corporation has prospered and grown large because it accommodates itself admirably to the needs of the technostructure. The corporation is vulnerable to intervention by external authority which, being uninformed, is likely to be arbitrary. The corporate form gives the technostructure a high degree of autonomy, that is, protection from meddling by the state and from intervention by stockholders. The latter results from the familiar

[14] For a book which sees the emergent tendency which Galbraith describes as an accomplished fact, see W. C. Bennis and P. E. Slater, *The Temporary Society* (New York: Harper and Row, 1968), Chapter 1. See also A. Toffler, *Future Shock* (New York: Random House, 1970).
[15] *The New Industrial State*, p. 76.

separation of control from ownership in the large corporation; internal financing and relative stability of corporate earnings, he thinks, have contributed to the autonomy of the technostructure. In the industrial system, he believes, we no longer have a profit-and-loss economy. The organized technostructure is able to protect its profits by planning. As support for this, he cites the United States Steel Corporation, which has not had losses for a quarter of a century. Stockholders in steel corporations who for years have been earning less on their investment than they could obtain from a savings bank will not be exactly convinced by Galbraith's example.

Galbraith next philosophizes about the relation of the entrepreneur to the technostructure. The great entrepreneur, he says, must be compared in life with the male *Apis mellifera*—he dies almost with the act of conception. The point is that the founder of an enterprise frequently brings into existence an organization which requires managerial skills he does not possess. "What the entrepreneur created, only a group of men sharing specialized information could ultimately operate." In a day of automation, linear programming, and capital budgeting, one has to see this happen, to appreciate the poignancy of the situation.

Passing over Galbraith's digression on socialism for the nonce, we consider next his analysis of the goals of the technostructure. In an admirably clear summary of price theory, he argues that belief in the regulatory role of the market requires a parallel belief that the participating firms will always seek to maximize their profits. This ancient assumption of economic theory must be explored before there can be any realistic examination of the goals of the technostructure. His previous analysis had pointed to the conclusion that rather than being controlled by the market the modern firm has made the market subordinate to its planning. Prices, costs, revenues are decided not by the market but by the planning decisions of the firm. Is the goal of these decisions still the greatest amount of profits? While a flow of earnings is still necessary for the technostructure, the market is no longer specifying and enforcing that goal. Profit maximization—the only goal that is consistent with the rule of the market—is accordingly not necessary.

Yet Galbraith observes that conservatives and liberals alike maintain the postulate of profit maximization. The fear that rose in the 1930s that a few top managers would aggrandize themselves at the expense of the stockholders did not materialize. There is no great danger of this because the small stockholdings of top management and the remarkably effective code of the technostructure bars such behavior. "The danger of abuse through personal profit maximization disappeared as power passed into the technostructure." Yet in the conventional view, the technostructure is believed to pursue maximum profits in the interest of the anonymous mass of stockholders. There is no reason to believe *a priori,* says Galbraith, that the technostructure will maximize the return to capital. It is more likely to maximize its success as an organization.

In recent years many corporate leaders have proclaimed a doctrine of social responsibility, abandoning the commitment to profit maximization. Galbraith thinks that it is wrong to dismiss these assertions about corporate trusteeship as "an exercise in competitive banality." They are significant because they reflect the underlying reality that the modern corporation has the power to shape society. But the statements of the corporate statesmen and their public relations offices do not reveal the real purposes of this power. Most of what is dispensed by these men, as many have suspected, is hot air. Their power is used to achieve the deeper interests or goals of the technostructure.

In seeking to understand these interests and goals, Galbraith turns to the literature of organizational behavior and cleverly summarizes its findings and relates them to the motivating system of large corporate enterprise. He analyzes four major motivations—compulsion, pecuniary compensation, identification, and adaptation—contending that the last two have become more important in the behavior of the inner circles of the technostructure. Identification involves "the voluntary exchange of one's goals for the preferable ones of the organization"; adaptation means "the association with the organization in the hope of influencing its goals to accord more closely with one's own."

From this sociopsychological analysis Galbraith formulates a basic principle of consistency; there must be consistency in the goals of the society, the organization, and the individual. This, he proclaims, is "a deeply interconnected matrix." And from this it follows, he says, that "if we know how individuals are motivated, we will know how organizations are motivated and also the reverse."[16] (This proposition, as stated, will not be acceptable to those social psychologists for whom group behavior is an entity in itself.) From this principle of consistency Galbraith

[16] *Ibid.,* p. 159.

concludes that "the goals of the mature corporation will be a reflection of the goals of the members of the technostructure. And the goals of the society will tend to be those of the corporation."[17] Furthermore, the social purpose of the society becomes by a process of adaptation what serves the goals of the members of the technostructure. To be more specific, expansion in the output of goods becomes a social purpose because it is in accord with the goals of the technostructure. The gospel of economic growth—namely, that social progress is identical with a rising standard of living—has consequently the character of a faith.

Galbraith's emphasis on this symmetry in motivation and the goals of organizations and individuals will be objected to by some on the ground that he neglects the effects of primary socialization in producing the "bigger and better" mentality. Erich Fromm's concept of dynamic adaptation might be mentioned in this connection.[18] Galbraith's stress on role socialization in the organization ignores the earlier influences of the home, the peer group, and the mass media in shaping values. Something of this nature is reflected in the late David M. Wright's contention that Galbraith has the cart before the horse: "Growth is not something imposed on us by a corporate elite, but an expression of the deepest aspirations of our culture."[19] Galbraith might reply that his worry is that the corporate system is reinforcing individualistic tendencies and giving the pursuit of status and private affluence a pathological urgency. In any case, having made his point, he covers himself with the qualification, "Society also has goals, stemming from the needs which are unassociated with its major productive mechanism, and which it imposes on the mature corporation. As elsewhere I argue only for a two-way process. The mature corporation imposes social attitudes as it also responds to social attitudes. . . ."[20] However useful this remark may be from a polemical standpoint, analytically it still leaves us in the dark as to where the balance falls between the two socializing influences. Moreover, Galbraith's qualification implies perhaps that society's goals, derived from its cultural legacy, serve to counteract the attitudes the corpora-

[17] *Ibid.,* p. 161.
[18] E. Fromm, *Escape from Freedom* (New York: Rinehart, 1941), Appendix. See also D. Riesman et al., *The Lonely Crowd* (New Haven: Yale University Press, 1950).
[19] "To Hell with It All," *The Intercollegiate Review,* November/December 1967, pp. 49 ff.
[20] *The New Industrial State,* p. 165.

tion engenders, when in fact it may be reinforcing them.

Galbraith turns next to the goals of the industrial system as distinct from those of the technostructure. He argues that the mature corporation puts secure minimum earnings ahead of maximum profits. As an organization it seeks its own survival first, and autonomy from outside interference as a means of assuring it. It avoids maximum return because that objective invites increased risk of loss. It preaches against government interference in business because this protects its autonomy.

Having assured its survival, the technostructure seeks maximum growth as measured in sales. Such a goal is entirely consistent with its interests: Expansion of output conduces to expansion of the technostructure; it means more jobs and promotions. In accordance with the principle of consistency, growth as a goal acquires the character of a strong social purpose. Galbraith goes so far as to say, "The acceptance of economic growth as a social goal coincides closely with the rise to power of the mature corporation and the technostructure."[21]

Intimately related to growth as a goal of the technostructure is technological virtuosity. Innovation and technological progress mean jobs and promotions for technologists. And thanks to the process of adaptation, there is little difficulty in convincing the broader society that technological advance is in the public interest. Achievements in space are inherently more meritorious than help to the poor, because the former generates more technological opportunities, more jobs for the technologists. However, once the prime goals of the technostructure are assured, there is room for other objectives, especially if they improve the corporate image and are not in conflict with the higher objectives. So, Galbraith can say, "What has been called the 'social corporation' is a logical manifestation of the mature corporation and the motivations of its members."[22]

PRICES IN THE INDUSTRIAL SYSTEM

In this part of the book Galbraith has great fun in showing the inconsistencies in the work of some of his fellow economists who demonstrate theoretically that the detailed performance of oligopolistic industries is bad, but later admit that the aggregate performance of the economy

21 *Ibid.,* p. 174.
22 *Ibid.,* p. 177.

(e.g., the overall growth of productivity) is excellent. The criticism is an old one with him; he made essentially the same points in his *American Capitalism* (1952). In brief, his position is that oligopoly theory leads to conclusions which cannot be reconciled with empirical studies.

As Galbraith interprets price theory, oligopoly is an imperfect form of monopoly. But this presents a very uncomfortable dilemma for those who make public policy concerning business. With oligopoly as pervasive in the economy as it is, you simply can't indict and prosecute the whole industrial sector. The solution has been to ignore oligopoly for all practical purposes. While we have legal condemnation of monopoly, there is a *de facto* acceptance of it in its slightly imperfect form as oligopoly. In practice, this has meant that the law exempts the market power of the strong, while pouncing on those who would be strong "like a tiger." The fact is, says Galbraith, that our anachronistic antitrust laws are "sadly at odds with reality"; they attack the symbols of market power and leave the substance.

The contradictions between price theory that condemns oligopoly as inefficient but applauds its performance as efficient disappear when price control is seen in the full context of industrial planning and in relation to the goals of the technostructure. The control of prices insures the security of the technostructure and serves the goal of growth. In addition, it provides a stable numerator for planning decisions. In view of these functions, it is hardly surprising that it enjoys a *de facto* exemption from the antitrust laws. In short, to use a favorite Galbraithian term, price control in the industrial system is organic—it serves the most fundamental goals of the technostructure. In this light, "the antitrust laws, in seeking to preserve the market, are an anachronism in the larger world of industrial planning."[23] Galbraith predicts that there will be many in business and in academia who will defend these laws, but circumstance will be on the other side. Eventually the laws will be accommodated to the reality.

THE MANAGEMENT OF
SPECIFIC DEMAND

By specific demand Galbraith means the demand for individual products. By demand management he means

[23] *Ibid.,* p. 197.

more than advertising and salesmanship. It refers in his usage to "product design, model change, packaging and even performance. . . ."[24] In treating this subject in the book we are reviewing, Galbraith employs an analytical structure which is markedly different from that in his *American Capitalism* and in *The Affluent Society*. In the former he dealt with advertising in a more conventional way, stressing the competitive differentiation of product and so on, and concluding that "our proliferation of selling activity is the counterpart of comparative opulence. . . . It may be waste but it is waste that exists because the community is too well off to care."[25] In *The Affluent Society* he also treated advertising in a competitive context and in relation to demand theory and modern want creation. The phenomenon of social imbalance is attributed in part to this competitive touting of private goods relative to the persuasion that is undertaken for public goods. In *The New Industrial State*, on the other hand, salesmanship and advertising are pictured as having an organic role in the industrial system; they are now related to the planning process. The purpose of demand management, Galbraith flatly says, is to insure that people buy what is produced. The general effect of such effort in the broadest sense is "to shift the locus of decision in the purchase of goods from the consumer where it is beyond control to the firm where it is subject to control." Such demand management need not be perfect to be functional for the purposes of the corporate planners. It is only necessary to keep the exercise of consumer discretion within workable limits—that is, to stabilize it. The costly failure of the Edsel, in Galbraith's mind, was the exception which proved the rule of the general efficacy of demand management.

As for those nonconformists who claim immunity from the artful persuasion of Madison Avenue, it must be pointed out that it is improbable that enough people will ever assert their individuality as to endanger the effectiveness of demand management. Moreover, the relentless advertising of goods maintains the propensity to consume that is so necessary for the industrial system. "Advertising and its related arts thus help to develop the kind of man the goals of the industrial system require—one that reliably

[24] *Ibid.,* p. 203.
[25] *American Capitalism,* p. 102.

spends his income and works reliably because he is always in need for more."[26]

Under these conditions the accepted economic doctrine of consumer sovereignty no longer holds. The unilateral control of the producer by the consumer—what Galbraith calls the accepted sequence—is increasingly an inadequate description of reality; it is replaced by the revised sequence, under which the producer manages consumer behavior and shapes the attitudes of those he serves. However, the revised sequence has not completely replaced the accepted sequence; the latter still persists outside the limits of the industrial system. Indeed, the consumer occasionally can resist the persuasion of the large corporation. ". . . The accepted and revised sequences exist side by side in the manner of a reversible chemical reaction."[27] So long as people believe in consumer sovereignty, we have a doctrine that celebrates individuality and thus provides a cloak for organization. Possibly "people need to believe that they are unmanaged if they are to be managed effectively."

THE REGULATION OF
AGGREGATE DEMAND

The control of individual prices is insufficient to assure the stable operation of the industrial system. There must be provision as well of adequate total demand; this need has become so urgent that it may be said that regulation of aggregate demand is an organic requirement of the industrial system.

In the United States the regulation of demand became recognized public policy in the thirties, in response to its advocacy by Keynesian economists, but it was staunchly opposed by many entrepreneurial corporations. The latter had much less need for such regulation than the large corporations. The big firms with their advanced technology and heavy capital investment needed this stabilization of aggregate demand to facilitate their planning and to protect the technostructure. The smaller corporations, having a simpler technology and less capital, had no compelling need for such planning. But the mature corporations and their respective technostructures early supported the new eco-

[26] *The New Industrial State*, p. 210.
[27] *Ibid.*, p. 213.

nomics. Since then the industrial system has come to look with favor on heavy military expenditures because they not only serve to maintain aggregate demand, but provide underwriting for advanced technology and aid in corporate planning. The revised sequence works also in the public sector—"defense expenditures in their present magnitude are, in part, an accommodation to the needs of the industrial system and the technostructure."[28]

Reviewing the changing nature of employment, Galbraith discusses the relative decline of the blue-collar workers in the American labor force. He observes the concomitant rise in the need for those with higher educational qualifications to fill white-collar jobs and do the myriad tasks of the technostructure. Education, he believes, has become the difference that divides; the divisions in politics reflect the gulf between the intellectuals and the educated generally, and those less fortunate in this respect.

CONTROL OF THE WAGE-PRICE SPIRAL

Galbraith next turns to a policy with which he has been increasingly identified—the advocacy of wage-price controls to check inflation. He argues that maintenance of a high level of demand makes prices and wages inherently unstable in the industrial system. So long as aggregate demand is regulated to provide full employment, and no other measures are taken to counteract the trend, the spiral of wage and price increases is an organic feature of that system. But an "incomes policy" is difficult to enact in peacetime in the United States because it lacks ideological sanction. Nevertheless such a system is inevitable; no other advanced nation has been able to dispense with such regulation. The United States will not be an exception.

THE INDUSTRIAL SYSTEM AND THE UNIONS

Galbraith uses two chapters to analyze the impact of the industrial system on the trade unions. Noting their

[28] *Ibid.*, p. 317.

loss of membership in the post-World War II years, he states that this is not a temporary setback, but the earlier stages of a permanent decline. He finds that with the acceptance of trade unions, industrial relations have improved because the interests of the larger corporations and labor are "concordant." The interconnected structural changes that have brought the industrial system into being have changed the function of the union and subtracted from its role. The mature corporations are less opposed to unions than the entrepreneurial companies; they more readily concede them their demands in the service of a good corporate image. Very often this is possible because they can pass the wage increases on in the form of higher prices to the consumer. The change in the labor force to more white-collar workers and fewer blue-collar men has worked to the disadvantage of unions. The white-collar workers have proved harder to organize, partly because they identify more easily with the technostructure. Finally, full employment and general economic affluence reduce the power and appeal of trade unionism. ". . . It was the accommodation of the state to needs of the industrial system that the labor movement most sought. It was the thing most designed to make unions less needed."[29]

Tho induotrial oyotom hao ohorn tho uniono of oomo of their functions and greatly diminished them as a social force, but they will not disappear or become completely unimportant. The reason for this is that they still perform a number of important functions for the industrial system: (1) Their rules and grievance machinery reduce the feeling of arbitrary and unjust treatment by the employer; (2) in various ways they help prevent the alienation of the worker or, expressed differently, remove barriers to identification with the corporate employer; (3) they aid in accommodating the workers to technological and other changes; (4) they cooperate with and second the pressures of the technostructure for higher tariffs or lucrative government procurement contracts; (5) more important, the standardization of wage costs under union contracts assists price control and planning by industry; (6) finally, the stabilization of wages during a trade agreement reduces government interference and tends to keep wage increases within the amounts that can be paid from productivity gains.

In general, Galbraith no longer regards the trade union

[29] *Ibid.,* p. 270. Galbraith does not consider the question whether workers will turn to unions to protect themselves from the inflation generated by full employment and the related wage-price spiral.

as a major countervailing force to the large corporations; rather it has been domesticated and made a part of the Establishment. In his words, "The industrial system has now largely encompassed the labor movement. It has dissolved some of its most important functions; it has greatly narrowed its area of action; and it has bent its residual operations very largely to its own needs."[30]

THE EDUCATIONAL AND
SCIENTIFIC ESTATE

With the relative decline of the unions, a new group—the educators and research scientists—gains in power in the industrial system. They are closely related to the scientists and engineers within the technostructure and with "civil servants, journalists, writers and artists outside." Adapting a phrase of Professor Don K. Price, Galbraith terms this large group the "educational and scientific estate." Its influence derives mainly from its rapid growth in numbers and consequent political potential, its access to scientific innovation, and its singular role in social innovation.

The relationship of this new technical elite to the industrial system is significantly different from that which existed in the era of the entrepreneurial corporation. In the earlier stage, as Veblen showed so well, the innovative, often radical ideas of the men of higher learning often clashed with the money and power of the captains of industry.[31] Under the dispensation of the technostructure, there has been a radical transformation between the corporate managers and the educational and scientific estate. Motivationally, neither group is now so attuned exclusively to pecuniary considerations. They are both interested in social goals, but not necessarily the same ones. The educational and scientific estate is no longer small in number or wholly impecunious; the technostructure has become heavily dependent on it for its trained manpower. The proposals for social innovation of the former are now not so threatening to the corporate managers; the costs of social reform may be passed on to the consumers or back to stockholders. Furthermore, social in-

[30] *Ibid.,* p. 281.
[31] T. Veblen, *The Higher Learning in America* (Stanford: Academic Reprints, 1954).

novation no longer connotes revolution; for that matter, the academics no longer engage in revolutionary talk. Just how closely the educational and scientific estate will identify with the goals of the industrial system is difficult to say, because the former is not homogeneous in its composition. One source of conflict is very likely, regarding the management of individual behavior. The economy requires for its success a considerable amount of "organized public bamboozlement"—raucous advertising and the like—and this effort is viewed with disdain by the educational and scientific estate and the larger intellectual community. The educational and scientific estate is also in potential competition and conflict with the technostructure concerning their respective relations to the state. The members of the technostructure are hampered in politics by their relation to the large corporation; while they have considerable influence in public life, their organizations cannot back them in the political arena.

The technical elite, on the other hand, are not restrained politically by their organizational ties. While growing in numbers, this group lacks a sense of its own identity and has been subordinate in the past to entrepreneurial power. "Yet it is possible that the educational and scientific estate requires only a strongly creative political hand to become a decisive instrument of political power. . . ."[32]

THE INDUSTRIAL SYSTEM AND
THE STATE

The industrial system needs educated manpower, provided in the main by government, as well as the research carried on with the aid of government subsidy. It requires regulation of aggregate demand and such stabilization of prices and wages as the state provides. It is evident that the relationship between the technostructure and the state is very different from that between the state and the older forms of entrepreneurial enterprise. Indeed, "in notable re-

[32] *The New Industrial State*, pp. 294–295. It is interesting to note that Heilbroner sees science conquering in the future as an idea rather than a political force. The contest, he thinks, is between the charismatic powers of science and the limitations of the capitalist imagination. See R. L. Heilbroner, *The Limits of American Capitalism* (New York: Harper & Row, Torchbook Edition, 1967), pp. 98–100, 125, 129, 132–133.

spects the mature corporation is an arm of the state. And the state, in important matters, is an instrument of the industrial system."[33]

The modes of relationship of the entrepreneurial and of the mature corporation to the state differ fundamentally. The entrepreneurial corporation's connection to government was primarily pecuniary and highly unstable. Well-heeled entrepreneurs could and did purchase votes and legislators, in some cases controlling entire company towns and the legislatures of great states. There was a fear in the nineteenth century and the early years of the twentieth that such entrepreneurial corporations would dominate the nation.

These relationships began to change in a marked way in the thirties, during the era of the New Deal. In that period the rising power of the federal government and of unions was opposed not so much by the mature corporations as by the surviving entrepreneurs. The fact is that much government activity has a different effect on the entrepreneurial corporation as compared with the large, mature corporation. "What is damaging to the first is benign for the second." The entrepreneurs did not need as much qualified manpower, a large public sector, or control of aggregate demand; the development of these institutional functions reflected more the accommodation of the state to the necessities of the large corporations.

While the technostructure of the mature corporations cannot exercise much pecuniary influence over politics, its influence on the state is much greater than that of the entrepreneurial corporation. Its members can identify with the goals of the state and adapt the latter's objectives to its own. These processes of identification and adaptation are seen most clearly in the field of weapons procurement; the "industrial-military complex" is a reality, not so much because of deliberate conspiracy or even of similar social backgrounds, as C. W. Mills contended, but because of the shared goals of the industrial and military participants. In other words, the revised sequence operates also in the field of public procurement—the producer influences what the state purchases—but the relationship is complex and not one-way; there is a two-way flow of influence.

Turning to the Cold War, Galbraith holds that foreign policy in the post-World War II era has been based on an imagery which derives in part from the needs of the industrial system. Military spending has the great value of under-

[33] *Ibid.,* p. 296.

writing advanced technology, subsidizing research that is transferable to the private sector, and providing relatively riskless projects to counterbalance the risks of civilian production. Instead of emphasizing the tendencies to industrial convergence between the Communist countries and our economy, there is a strong tendency to exaggerate the elements of implacable conflict and of a unified Communist conspiracy against the West. The educational and scientific estate has grown increasingly skeptical and critical of the imagery of the Cold War.

THE FUTURE OF THE
INDUSTRIAL SYSTEM

Our predicament, says Galbraith, is that we have been captured by the needs of the industrial system. ". . . It is the genius of the industrial system in that it makes the goals that reflect its needs—efficient production of goods, a steady expansion in their output, a steady expansion in their consumption, a powerful preference for goods over leisure, an unqualified commitment to technological change, autonomy for the technostructure, an adequate supply of trained and educated manpower—coordinate with social virtue and human enlightenment. . . ."[34] In recent years there has been much questioning of our conventional goals, there has been evidence of alienation among our youth, and we have read the reports of various commissions which have explored the national purpose or purposes. Almost invariably, such reexamination resulted in "a strong affirmation of the goals that serve the industrial system." What are the means or mechanics of our emancipation from such domination?

First, there is the need for understanding of the forces that have "enthralled" us; second, we must clearly perceive the dimensions of life which the industrial system does not or cannot serve; third, we must identify some political force which will promote the neglected dimensions of life. The industrial system tends to ignore those services which are not closely related to its own needs; there is, in particular, a "negative discrimination" against public services. The industrial system is, in fact, a cultural process with an ethos of its own. It is not oriented to aesthetic considerations—except to the extent that they yield economic advantage in

[34] *Ibid.*, p. 343.

the long run. The state, Galbraith holds, must assert the aesthetic priority, where there is a conflict between industrial and artistic goals. Becoming more the futurist or utopian, he says "the test of esthetic achievement is the one that, one day, the progressive community will apply."[35]

Our faith in the beneficent working of the market and the concurrent development of the industrial system have left large planning lacunae or gaps in our otherwise largely planned economy. Most notably, there are our "systems" of urban and suburban transport, residential housing, the conservation of natural resources, development of outdoor recreation, and forestry in the eastern United States; these are areas where the market has failed. It is very noticeable in this chapter that Galbraith does not emphasize the disruptive effect of the private planning carried out by the mature corporations. The task, as he sees it, is the easier one of filling in the gaps where the planning of the industrial system does not suffice.

Evaluating the prospects for work and leisure, he thinks that the industrial system with its expanded wants will lead men to consider meaningful work more important than leisure. For the emancipation of man from the industrial system, nothing is more strategic than education, higher education in particular. It can be the necessary force for skepticism, emancipation, and pluralism; the educator must exert his power on behalf of the entire human personality. He urges educators to assert the values and goals of educated men—"those that serve not the production of goods and associated planning but the intellectual and artistic development of man." This peroration in behalf of only intellectual and artistic men is somewhat paradoxical and inconsistent, after he has just finished arguing for the whole man and the need for farsighted planners. In any case, the political leadership in the reform of the industrial system must come from the educational and scientific estate. Scientists and artists must assume their responsibility in reshaping society. Economists are not the best guides in this endeavor; allowing for numerous exceptions, they are too prone to identify economic goals with the whole of life. "They are, in the main, the natural allies of the industrial system."

Like Karl Marx, Galbraith sees the industrial system creating its own gravediggers—the educational and scientific estate. "It [the industrial system] brings into existence, to

[35] *Ibid.,* p. 353.

serve its intellectual and scientific needs, the community that, hopefully, will reject its monopoly of social purpose." While Galbraith analyzes the prospects for our emancipation from the industrial system, he does not apparently view industrial man as having too much existential freedom. His area of decision is "exceedingly small." "It is part of the vanity of modern man that he can decide the character of his economic system. . . . He could, conceivably, decide whether or not he wishes to have a high level of industrialization. Thereafter the imperatives of organization, technology and planning operate similarly, and we have seen to a broadly similar result, on all societies. Given the decision to have modern industry, much of what happens is inevitable and the same."[36] These deterministic forces of industrialization can, however, be transcended by an educational and scientific estate conscious of dimensions of life other than the economic.

[36] *Ibid.*, p. 396.

7 Assent

and Dissent

GALBRAITH'S LATEST MODEL

The immediate response to Galbraith's new model of the American economy, as summarized in the last chapter, was overwhelmingly favorable. "Believe it or not," stated *Book Buyer's Guide* in the summer of 1967, "the most popular book in the country at this moment is *The New Industrial State*. The success of its predecessor, *The Affluent Society*, prepared book people for its success, but who would expect a highly intelligent book on economics to sweep the country?" The shorter reviews in newspapers and periodicals generally praised Galbraith's style for its lucidity, wit, and aphoristic wisdom. However much reviewers differed with his conclusions, they were inclined to agree that this was an important book.

As usual with Galbraith's books, comment ranged from high praise to sweeping condemnation. A. A. Berle expressed the belief that *"The New Industrial State* will make economic history."[1] Michael Harrington hailed it as "a book which must be ranked as one of the most significant works of social thought in this generation. . . ."[2] On the other hand, Professor George Stigler caustically queried whether Galbraith was a scholar seeking to understand the contemporary economy or "a gifted satirist seeking to penetrate our complacency and force us to re-examine long accepted views and using the long-accepted methods of exaggeration, caricature and gross omission appropriate to this jester role?" His answer was that Galbraith's book was an exasperating mixture of the two, with the proportion run-

[1] A. A. Berle, "Analyzing the Corporate Complex," *Saturday Review*, June 24, 1967, p. 29.
[2] M. Harrington, "Liberalism According to Galbraith," *Commentary*, October 1967, pp. 77 ff.

ning much too far toward the latter.[3] William R. Rickenbacker, reviewing the book for *Barron's,* found it "turgid,
dull, mechanically faulty, and downright perverse. The
diction is poor, the book is studded with flaws, and wrong
headed in the extreme. It is . . . a work of egregious ignorance."[4]

Robert Heilbroner was more moderate in his criticism,
asserting that the book was hard to deal with critically: "A
fundamental difficulty lies . . . in the level of abstraction of
the work, which hovers between a very generalized schema
and an empirical study, and is not quite either."[5]

But it was Irving Kristol, writing in *Fortune,* who perhaps
best expressed the significance of Galbraith's book. Noting
that in American history there has been a tradition of cultural and social criticism that looked with suspicion at the
nation's economic growth, he says that the effects of this
dissidence have been limited because the dissenters were
not economists. And when they engaged in economic analysis, it was usually amateurish, incompetent, or simply
cranky. He observes too that though we have had an up-
surge of academic radicalism during the past decade, no one
produced a really radical treatise to challenge the Keynesian
thinking of our time. Galbraith's latest work changed all
that:

> What is truly significant about this book is that, for the first
> time, it ingeniously combines the tradition of moral-social
> criticism with a professional and plausible economic analysis.
> In doing this, *The New Industrial State* goes beyond liberal
> reformism, beyond Marxist or even neo-Marxist socialism, and
> —the boldest leap of all—beyond economics itself. For Pro-
> fessor Galbraith raises the question of whether the American
> people actually want the particular kind of material progress
> their system delivers. His answer, which is negative, will be
> good tidings to the entire spectrum of dissenters—to the
> socialist squares and those who are far out, to individualists
> who despise "the power structure" and embryonic central
> planners. Professor Galbraith patiently explains to them all
> that they are right in attacking the system, though not always
> for the right reasons. It is predictable that his book will be-
> come one of their sacred texts.[6]

[3] G. J. Stigler, "Galbraith's New Book: A Few Problems," *Wall
Street Journal,* June 26, 1967, p. 16.

[4] W. F. Rickenbacker, "Galbraith on Business: Unoriginal and
Wrong," *Barron's,* October 2, 1967, p. 10.

[5] R. L. Heilbroner, "Capitalism without Tears," *New York Review of Books,* June 29, 1967, pp. 16 ff.

[6] I. Kristol, "Professor Galbraith's 'New Industrial State,'" *Fortune,* July 1967, pp. 90 ff.

Kristol's intuition on this latter point, if we may call it that, was strikingly borne out three years later by the publication of Charles A. Reich's *The Greening of America*.[7] This influential and widely read best-seller by a Yale law professor explicitly cited Galbraith's book as providing the factual foundation for part of its severely critical analysis and condemnation of the American corporate state. Not all dissenters from the American establishment, however, have regarded it as reverentially as Reich.

THE VIEW FROM ABROAD

Galbraith's book stirred reactions in foreign intellectual circles as well as domestic. The British especially, perhaps because of the advance publicity which it received from his Reith lectures over the BBC Home Service in the fall of 1966, took critical note of it. The respected welfare economist Professor E. J. Mishan, of the London School of Economics and Political Science, reviewed it briefly in the *New Statesman*.[8] To him, Galbraith's book "might well have carried a subtitle, the third blast of the trumpet against the monstrous regiment of economists—the first two blasts being *The Concept of Countervailing Power* [sic] and *The Affluent Society*. . . . This [blast] contains much of the essential message of the previous two." Otherwise he had nothing very striking, provocative, or original to say about the book.

The review in *The Economist* was likewise rather commonplace in its short remarks. It made one penetrating observation, however, that deserves quotation:

> The really interesting question for social and economic research should be: why in some countries (such as America and Japan) does this striving for greater corporate sales become the main motive force of the technostructure, while in some other countries (including Britain) the ruling motive in big corporations, both nationalized and private, is much more likely to be the obvious one, namely the cosy desire of the non-profit-making technostructure for minimum disturbance and a quiet life.

Professor Galbraith does not probe this question. . . .[9]

[7] New York: Random House, 1970.
[8] E. J. Mishan, "What's Wrong with Economics?", *New Statesman,* October 27, 1967, pp. 555–556.
[9] *The Economist,* September 9, 1967, p. 894.

This point of criticism deserves further consideration; we shall return to it in the following chapter.

The most extended foreign commentary on Galbraith's themes appeared in a paper written by George C. Allen, emeritus professor of political economy at the University of London. Subtitled "A Rejoinder to Galbraith's Reith Lectures," this was published in March 1967, a few months before *The New Industrial State* itself appeared. A second edition, containing a postscript on the book proper, was published in 1969.[10]

Professor Allen, a distinguished student of industrial organization, has given us one of the most discriminating and temperate analyses of this book. He acknowledges at the outset that Galbraith almost invariably asks the right questions, but finds that sometimes his answers "fail to carry conviction." He states that Galbraith's expository methods violate certain principles of rational discussion. Though a speaker may rightly seek to be challenging, he argues that he is never justified in "presenting an idiosyncratic interpretation of orthodox doctrine in order to give force to his own arguments. It is not permissible to set up Aunt Sallies" (what we would in American parlance call strawmen). He faults Galbraith on two counts in this respect. First, he advances views as if they were novel and heretical, though they have been accepted as commonplaces by many economists for several decades. Second, by concentrating on certain important trends in Western economies and neglecting others, he presents an incomplete and even distorted image of these economies and of their functioning.

After summarizing the main themes in Galbraith's lectures, Allen goes on to admit that many of Professor Galbraith's assertions about the "industrial system" can be accepted "without demur." Included in this category are the phenomenon of separation of ownership and control, the futility of choice between doctrinaire individualism and socialism, and even the decline of the consumer's sovereignty. On the last of these, he calls attention, interestingly enough, to a rather neglected passage from a work of Joseph Schumpeter, once Galbraith's colleague at Harvard, who wrote in 1911: "Innovations in the economic system do not as a rule take place in such a way that first new wants arise spontaneously in consumers and then the productive apparatus swings around through their pressure. . . . It is . . . the

[10] G. C. Allen, *Economic Fact and Fantasy,* Occasional Paper 14, 2nd ed. (London: The Institute of Economic Affairs, 1969).

producer who as a rule initiates economic change, and consumers are educated by him if necessary; they are, as it were, taught to want new things, or things which differ in some respect or other from those which they have been in the habit of using."[11]

Though Galbraith is thoroughly familiar with Schumpeter's writings and has quoted from them frequently, he has never cited the relevance of this passage to his analysis of the "revised sequence." Allen admits that Galbraith's impatience with irrelevant theorizing about perfect and imperfect competition has justification, but this is hardly a reason for slighting the dangers of monopoly for social welfare and admitting the vital function of competition ("as sensibly defined") for economic progress.

Galbraith's emphasis on the rise of the giant industrial company and the expansion of the state's economic functions is an acceptable proposition, but "when he goes beyond this point in deploying his argument it is more difficult to agree with him. He has established a solid foundation, but his super-structure seems to me in many respects unsound. In particular, his assertions about the relations of the modern industrial concern to the market are so sweeping and extreme as to render them invalid. . . ."[12] We shall consider this point in more detail below.

Allen differs on other matters with Galbraith, such as ownership and control in industrial firms and the role of top management in their operation, the desirability and effectiveness of antimonopoly policy, and the autonomy of management in state-owned enterprise. On this last, on the basis of his study of British industry, he confidently states that Galbraith is "clearly wrong" and "naïve" to believe that the managers of nationalized industries can enjoy the same measure of freedom as the directors of a large private corporation.

In his postscript dealing with the text of *The New Industrial State*, Allen admits that at first glance the developments in Great Britain in the two years since he wrote the original version would seem to lend plausibility to Galbraith's ideas. The mergers and the growing centralization of decision-making and the resort to planning procedures are in line with his predictions, he says; the Labour government's sup-

[11] *Ibid.*, p. 10, citing J. A. Schumpeter, *The Theory of Economic Development* (Cambridge, Mass.: Harvard University Press, 1934), p. 65.
[12] *Ibid.*, p. 11.

port of its prices and incomes policy, thus endangering its trade union support, lends credence to Galbraith's stress on the imperatives which shape policy, despite their inconsistency with ancient ideologies. Allen shows how many of these plans, public and private, have missed their mark and often aggravated the seriousness of problems; Galbraith, he admits, would reply that the failures do not condemn planning as such, but only specific plans. The Britisher insists that the forces of competition have continued unceasingly to assert themselves in the world steel market, in aircraft manufacture, in synthetic fibers, and in petroleum, disproving the ability of giant concerns to "bind the future."

Allen's critique of Galbraith's lectures and book is powerful and judicious in many ways. However, in the author's opinion he misses the crucial distinction which Galbraith makes between the industrial system and the rest of the economy and does not fully comprehend the thrust of Galbraith's argument when he says that he (Galbraith) relies on the state to preserve our threatened spiritual and esthetic values.[13] So much for some of the foreign reactions to Galbraith's "latest blast."

In reviewing the general criticisms that have been made of *The New Industrial State,* we shall here consider them not in the chronological order of their publication, but in more topical fashion, following the sequence of Galbraith's subjects in his book. This approach, it is hoped, will enable the reader to obtain a more systematic, critical understanding of the volume. It will also permit us to add our own comment and evaluation of the criticism at appropriate points.

THE IMPERATIVES OF TECHNOLOGY

Early in his book Galbraith attributes the scale of the nation's mature corporations to what he terms the "imperatives of technology." His reasoning on this matter was forthrightly challenged by Professor Walter Adams of Michigan State University shortly afterward.[14] Adams wrote:

Galbraith's contention that corporate giantism dominates American industry requires no adumbration. On that there is

[13] *Ibid.,* p. 32.
[14] W. Adams, "A Blueprint for Technocracy," *Science,* August 1967, pp. 532–533.

consensus. But Galbraith fails to prove that this dominance is the inevitable response to technological imperatives and hence beyond our control. Specifically, he offers little evidence to demonstrate that Brobdingnagian size is the prerequisite for and the guarantor of (i) operational efficiency, (ii) invention, innovation, and technological progress, and (iii) effective planning in the public interest.

Insisting that the unit of technological efficiency is the plant, not the firm, Adams argues that there is no justification for the dinosaur proportions of some of our present-day corporate giants. Citing empirical studies by John M. Blair which show that technological trends may be making plants of smaller size optimally efficient, Adams contends that Galbraith's reasoning ignores these tendencies.[15] He refers to the study by Professor J. S. Bain, which concludes that our multiplant firms have gone beyond the size that is optimal for efficiency.[16] Adams notes too that while Galbraith acknowledges the validity of Bain's findings, he justifies the size of a General Motors in terms of its ability to plan. Adams argues that if (corporate) size has to be justified in terms of ability to plan, "then it must be justified on grounds other than efficiency."

Adams denies also that there is a strict correlation between corporate size and technological progressiveness (innovation). He cites studies showing the large number of inventions which have originated with independent inventors and the relative few that have come from large concerns; he points to the heavy subsidy of research by these large firms by the federal government and the poor record of the giant steel companies in this respect.[17]

Rejecting the argument of economic inevitability and the imperatives of technology, Adams acknowledges that Galbraith is "an eminently civilized and literate political economist. He focuses attention on real problems and vital issues. His questions are invariably to the point. But his answers are sometimes wrong." He eloquently writes:

[15] Antitrust and Monopoly Subcommittee, Committee on the Judiciary, U.S. Senate, *Economic Concentration* (1965), Part 4, pp. 1541–1551.
[16] J. S. Bain, "Economies of Scale, Concentration and the Condition of Entry in Twenty Manufacturing Industries," *American Economic Review,* March 1954, pp. 15–39. See also his *Barriers to New Competition* (Cambridge, Mass.: Harvard University Press, 1965).
[17] J. Jewkes, D. Sawyers, R. Stillerman, *The Sources of Invention* (New York: St. Martins, 1959), Chapter 4.

Industrial gigantism in America is not the product of spontaneous generation, natural selection, or technological inevitability. It is often the end-result of unwise, man-made, discriminatory, privilege-creating governmental action. Defense contracts, R & D support, patent policy, tax privileges, stockpiling arrangements, tariffs, subsidies, and the like have far from a neutral effect on our industrial structure. In controlling these variables, the policy maker has greater freedom and flexibility than is commonly supposed; the potential for promoting competition and dispersing industrial power is both real and practicable.[18]

In answering this type of liberal argument, Galbraith would admit that his mature corporations have benefited handsomely from governmental largesse and support. In fact, he would say that he has shown in *The New Industrial State* how governmental policies have been bent to the needs of the evolving corporate system, first, by crass pecuniary influence (graft and outright bribery) and, second, more efficiently by the more subtle accommodation of the state to the requirements of the mature corporations. Rather than ignoring these facts, Galbraith would say that he has provided something of a theoretical explanation of them. Moving from the defensive to the offensive, he would attack the orthodox view that the economies of the large firm are small and inconsequential. He would cite argument and evidence that in some industries the big firms can better survive the risks of market fluctuations than their smaller rivals, can carry full lines of product, achieve savings by vertical integration, gain access to more product innovations from research conducted under their own auspices, make economies in advertising and in distribution generally, and benefit from superior administrative and entrepreneurial skills. Galbraith is not alone in believing that in the dynamic, uncertain world of modern business as opposed to the static models of neoclassical theory, major firm economies exist and are socially beneficial.[19] The denial or minimization of these economies of the large firm is often a rationalization of a cherished public policy rather than a conclusion firmly established by the relevant facts.

[18] Adams, *op. cit.*, p. 533.
[19] R. E. Low, *Modern Economic Organization* (Homewood, Ill.: Richard D. Irwin, 1970), pp. 155–174; W. Z. Hirsch, "Technological Progress and Micro-Economic Theory," *American Economic Review*, May 1969, pp. 36–43; O. E. Williamson, "Allocative Efficiency and the Limits of Antitrust," in *ibid.*, pp. 115–116.

THE NATURE AND LIMITS OF
INDUSTRIAL PLANNING

Galbraith's concept of planning and, in particular, his contention that our economic system is "in substantial part a planned economy" elicited considerable criticism on the ground that his treatment of the subject is ambiguous, to use the most charitable characterization. Those who reject his thinking on this subject generally go on to challenge his view that the Soviet and the Western economic systems exhibit a "measurable convergence to the same form of planning."[20]

Irving Kristol has expressed his objections to Galbraith's treatment of planning in a provocative, persuasive way. He writes:

. . . But it is one thing to say that corporations plan for their future growth (as they do) or that the U.S. Government plans for full employment (as it does). It is quite another thing to take the sum of all these plans as adding up to a "planned economy" (as Galbraith does). A homely analogy can make the distinction clear. A man who plays poker with due regard to the odds, to his financial resources, to the level of expertness of the other players, etc., is in a sense "planning" his game, in a way that someone whose decisions are impulsive is not. But assembling a group of expert and prudent poker players does not result in a "planned" poker game. To achieve that end, the house would have to rig the game according to its particular intentions—and it is this latter condition that a "planned economy," as commonly understood, approximates. The purpose of corporate planning in the U.S. today is to define and weigh the risks that will be taken. The purpose of central planning in the Soviet Union today is unrelated to risk taking and wholly dependent on what outcome has been predetermined by the central authorities. The difference is anything but negligible.[21]

Professor J. E. Meade of Cambridge University challenges Galbraith on this matter in even more cogent fashion.[22] He points out that in describing corporate planning

---

[20] *The New Industrial State*, p. 108.
[21] *Fortune*, July 1967, p. 195.
[22] J. E. Meade, "Is 'The New Industrial State' Inevitable?", *Economic Journal*, June 1968, p. 377. K. De Schweinitz also criticized Galbraith's "antipodal characterization of planning and the market, coupled with an exaggerated emphasis on the manufacturing sector, leads to an unwarranted minimization of the role of the market in the organization of economic life . . ." ("Who Decides—Economics and Politics," *Public Administration Review*, January/February 1968, p. 88).

Galbraith fails to explain "why and by what mechanism these individual plans can be expected to build up into a coherent whole." He asks, for example, what happens if all the steel-using industries plan production of products made from steel which require more (or less) steel than the steel industry's planned output? The government's maintenance of aggregate demand at full employment will not solve this problem.

"In short, if all individual plans are to be simultaneously fulfilled they must in the first instance be consistent. But Professor Galbraith never considers this problem. It is a strange oversight in a modern professional economist—to overlook the problem of general, as contrasted with particular equilibrium."[23]

Meade also believes that Galbraith fails to see that use of the price mechanism (as distinct from the market mechanism) is indispensable as a signaling device to indicate to producers and consumers what is and what is not scarce. The planned socialist societies, he contends, are not overlooking the functional usefulness of the price mechanism. Galbraith seemingly acknowledged the validity of Meade's criticism on this point in a later statement: "Professor Meade . . . has rightly taxed me with failing to make clear the very great difference between planning within the market framework and planning that embraces the market. . . ."[24]

In justice to Galbraith, it must be pointed out that Meade believes that there is much truth in many of his contentions. He writes:

> Nevertheless, when one has cast aside all of Professor Galbraith's exaggerations there remains a very important core of truth in his assertions. The large modern industrial corporation does cover an important sector of the economy and

[23] *Ibid.,* p. 378.
[24] J. K. Galbraith, "Professor Gordon on 'The Close of the Galbraithian System,'" *Journal of Political Economy,* July/Aug. 1969, pp. 494–503. While this book was in galley, a second, revised and updated edition of *The New Industrial State* appeared. Galbraith acknowledges that this "on the whole, is a light revision." After a brief review of what he regards as minor criticisms, he considers more sympathetically the point made by Professor Meade quoted in the paragraph above. He states in this connection that "The notion of planning as put forward in the first edition was not satisfactory. . . ." (*The New Industrial State,* second edition, revised. Boston: Houghton Mifflin Co., 1971, p. xx.) While conceding this error in the Introduction, Galbraith made no changes in the body of the book's text on this matter. See also "Galbraith Corrects Galbraith's Errors," The *New York Times,* Aug 25, 1971, p. 39.

its management does call for a new dimension of planning; its control has without question passed from its legal owners to its technostructure, which does not have the same direct interest in maximizing profit; the technostructure does attempt through advertisement and other sales techniques to create, mould and close contracts with, and influence over, government programmes for the procurement of complicated industrial products, in particular in connection with armaments. . . .[25]

Professor Scott Gordon of Indiana University has a similar complaint to make about Galbraith's treatment of corporate planning.[26] He notes that Galbraith does not invoke the concept of countervailing power to explain, say, the price of automotive steel where two technostructures confront each other. This shortcoming points to what he regards as the "main defect of Galbraith's conception."

He deals with the organization of the individual firm, but he says nothing about the organization of the *economy*. How is the economy organized into a coherent system? By means of what mechanism or procedure are the activities of the "five or six hundred firms" that constitute "the heart and soul of the modern U.S. economy" . . . made to mesh? Galbraith rejects the market mechanism of traditional economies, but he offers no answer of his own to these fundamental questions. *The New Industrial State* fails to present a coherent picture of what it sets out to describe, the organization of the American economy. It seems to me that Galbraith slips from the proposition that the firm plans to the proposition that the economy is planned, without realizing that such statements possess only a verbal similarity. His view of the forces making for a convergence of Soviet-type and capitalistic economies is marked by similar elision.[27]

How much validity do these criticisms of Galbraith's work have? By way of an answer we wish to interject at this point some reflections of our own on *The New Industrial State,* particularly on its treatment of corporate planning. We would call attention especially to the difference in Galbraith's analysis of corporate behavior in that book and in *The Affluent Society.* In the latter he pictured the corporate oligopolies as being engaged in aggressive competitive efforts to promote their respective products by advertising and consumer financing. This competitive pushing of private goods as contrasted with public services was stressed as

[25] J. E. Meade, *op. cit.,* p. 381.
[26] S. Gordon, "The Close of the Galbraithian System," *Journal of Political Economy,* August 1968, pp. 635–644.
[27] *Ibid.,* p. 640.

a cause of social imbalance. In *The New Industrial State,* on the other hand, he minimizes the rivalry and competition among the mature corporations in our oligopolized industries. He emphasizes instead the management of consumer demand in accordance with the objective of corporate planning. He contends that "out of this effort, from firms that are fully able to play the game, comes a crude equilibrating process which accords to each participant a reasonably reliable share of the market."[28] Though he mentions the fiasco of the Edsel as being the exception that proved the rule of the general efficacy of corporate planning, he does not consider interindustry competition which has frequently brought about substantial shifts in demand, despite all the efforts of corporate planners. We refer to well-known developments in such industries as transportation, packaging, nonferrous metals and entertainment (e.g., the competition between motion pictures and television.)[29]

Professor Allen regards this matter of interindustry competition as "the most vulnerable part of Galbraith's case, namely, his assertions about the relations of large firms to the market."[30] Galbraith cites the continuity of giant concerns and the fact that very few of them in a recent period suffered losses. Allen says this argument is not supported by the available statistical evidence for Great Britain (which he cites in an appendix). What Galbraith might have contended more plausibly is that the large concerns have often succeeded in stabilizing their profits, relative to the record of smaller firms. Allen insists that Galbraith does not discuss the important possibility that in this era of diversification the markets of large firms are liable to attack by other giants hitherto engaged in other industries. "It is odd that Professor Galbraith did not see the inconsistency between his two propositions, first, that the main purpose of giant firms is to make themselves larger, and, second, that once they have achieved a great size their security is assured. In practice the path of expansion pursued by one giant usually leads sooner or later into the territories of other giants and

---

[28] *The New Industrial State,* p. 206.
[29] For illustration, see W. Adams (Ed.), *The Structure of American Industry* (4th ed., New York: Macmillan, 1971), pp. 328 ff. Galbraith himself inadvertently admits the force of this type of competition later in his book: ". . . Over a longer period, of course, the resisting unions have been outflanked by competitive change—as the anthracite miners were outflanked by oil and the railroad brotherhood by automobiles, trucks, and planes" (*The New Industrial State,* p. 267, footnote 3).
[30] Allen, *Economic Fact and Fantasy,* p. 17.

in this way established positions are constantly being challenged."[31]

A recent American study of diversification strongly supports Galbraith's interpretation.[32] It shows that diversification by large firms in the years 1960–1965 did not significantly erode structural monopoly. "Cross-industry entry by large firms is at its weakest in such tight oligopoly areas as chemicals, metals, petroleum, transportation equipment, machinery, electrical equipment, and cigarettes. It reaches substantial proportions precisely in those groups (apparel, lumber products, and furniture) whose structure . . . is already competitive."[33] Schumpeter's creative destruction, on the basis of this analysis, tends to destroy the weak rather than the strong.

We obtain some clarification of Galbraith's concept of planning from a paper read by him to the American Economic Association in 1969. In it he says that the most meaningful distinction between a market and a planned economy depends on the degree of accommodation to producer or consumer choice. "The more responsive the producer must be to consumer choice, the more it is a market economy. The greater his power to establish prices and to persuade, command or otherwise arrange the consumer response at these prices, the more it is a planned economy." Intervention by the state is not decisive in determining whether a planned economy exists or not; it changes, he says, only its nature, extent, or efficiency. "In everyday language, planning means the systematic exercise of foresight."[34]

It will be noted that Galbraith employs the conception of planning found in "everyday language." He does not refer to the economic concept which stresses the need to integrate and coordinate the planning activities of subordinate entities if there is to be a planned economy.

As we have suggested above, Galbraith incorporated two main themes in *The New Industrial State* which were poten-

---

[31] *Ibid.,* p. 21.

[32] C. H. Berry, "Corporate Bigness and Diversification in Manufacturing," *Ohio State Law Journal,* Summer 1967, pp. 402–426.

[33] W. G. Shepherd, *Market Power and Economic Welfare* (New York: Random House, 1970), pp. 142–143.

[34] J. K. Galbraith, "Economics as a System of Belief," *American Economic Review,* May 1970, p. 472, footnote 13. In *American Capitalism,* Galbraith, it would seem, entertained a different conception of planning: "A minimum requirement of planning, for an economy where competition is no longer assumed to regulate prices, would be systematic price regulation by the state" (p. 59).

tially in conflict, depending on how he treated them. The "window" on private affluence and social imbalance which he opened up in *The Affluent Society* provided a glimpse of the interior of the larger "house" which became the former book. The theme of social imbalance could have been developed as a consequence of the nonprice rivalry of corporate oligopolies that were prone to cooperate on price. But the second theme, the convergence between industrial systems, required an emphasis on the common element of planning. In elaborating this idea, Galbraith emphasized the management aspect of advertising and played down its competitive, disruptive effects on market stability. The difference in treatment followed in part from the focus or perspective of the two books: *The Affluent Society* looked at social imbalance from a broad social viewpoint. In *The New Industrial State,* on the other hand, these matters were apprehended more from the standpoint of the technostructure and the alleged imperatives of technology and organization. It is important to see, however, that the analytical structure of the latter book had, so to speak, its own internal imperatives. They tended to impose "boundaries" on the empirical realities that Galbraith had conceptualized in rather different fashion in the earlier book. What we are saying in effect, to return to Galbraith's own metaphor, is that he is a clever literary architect: The "window" of *The Affluent Society* was made to fit (at least, superficially) into the structure of the larger, later "house," *The New Industrial State.*

The portent of an all-embracing industrial state with its monopoly of social purpose which Galbraith delineates is a forbidding one. Many economists are critical about the technostructure's definition of the public interest under any such system of corporate planning. They recall the cartel-like restrictions of the corporate planners under the New Deal's National Industrial Recovery Act.[35] It is in this light

[35] On this, see the definitive study of E. W. Hawley, *The New Deal and the Problem of Monopoly: A Study in Economic Ambivalence* (Princeton, N.J.: Princeton University Press, 1966). On corporate planning and the public interest, see M. W. Watkins, review of *The New Industrial State,* in *The Antitrust Bulletin,* Spring 1968, p. 281; also W. Adams, "A Blueprint for Technocracy," *Science,* August 1967, pp. 523–533. Galbraith-versus-Adams on this question reads like a rerun of an old exchange between Professors A. F. Burns and F. A. Fetter; see A. F. Burns, *The Decline of Competition* (New York: McGraw-Hill, 1936), and F. A. Fetter, "Planning for Totalitarian Monopoly," *Journal of Political Economy,* XLV (1937), pp. 95–110.

that Professor Meade asks, "Is the New Industrial State inevitable?" As he points out in the article cited, Galbraith has presented an economic determinist view of our destiny under industrialism. Some of the factual questions we have raised about his description of the setting of corporate planning should lead us to recognize that the imperatives he alleges are inexorably and seductively leading us toward industrial servitude may be in part the result of the way he has conceptualized the modern economic process. Our destiny is shaped neither by stars nor by ineluctable economic forces; much depends on our will and our consciousness of where we are and where we are moving. Galbraith's book, in dramatically portraying the powerful economic forces that shape our common lives, performs a valuable service; but an image which exaggerates the power of corporate giantism can alienate and stultify the will to structure and reform our society closer to a nobler and more humane vision. This is a subject to which we shall return in the concluding chapter.

THE TECHNOSTRUCTURE AND
ITS MOTIVATION

It is generally agreed that Galbraith's conception of corporate management derives from the classic work of A. A. Berle and G. C. Means, *The Modern Corporation and Private Property,* which vividly described the phenomenon of separation of ownership and management in the large corporation more than thirty years ago.[36] But Galbraith goes beyond this pioneer effort to present the corporation as a primary social institution. Drawing on modern organizational theory and studies, he analyzes once again the corporation as an adaptive rather than as a profit-optimizing organization. He relates the human interactions within the firm to its market and economic behavior generally. The managerial bureaucracy is shown to be "a coherent social psychological system with motives and preferences of its own."

Galbraith, it will be noted, avoids use of the term "bureaucracy" with its connotations of red tape, inefficiency, and organizational pathology. He uses the more positive term, technostructure, to describe the group which makes

[36] New York: Macmillan, 1932.

the strategic decisions. He claims, as we have seen, that the effective power of decision is lodged deeply in the technical staff of specialists. This, says Heilbroner, is one of the central contentions of his book—"that the strategic group within the economic system has shifted from the possessors of wealth to the possessors of collective expertise."[37]

Heilbroner believes that Galbraith treats this tendency "as if it were already an accomplished fact, and this is doubtful. . . . In even the most mature corporations, there is still a final level of decision-making power that is lodged firmly at the top, and this top upon examination often turns out to be a small group of stockholding interests or their representative." Galbraith, this critic holds, "hides distinctions of power behind the undifferentiated screen of the technostructure."[38]

It is significant that some of the most eminent and respected students of organizational behavior discern the tendency toward sharing of decision-making with lower echelons of the corporate structure. But they see this phenomenon primarily in science-oriented industries, whereas Galbraith describes it as a general trend.[39]

Galbraith's attack on the conventional assumption of profit maximization is considered in a rather acerbic exchange of views with Professor Robert M. Solow of M.I.T. Professor Robin Marris, a native Britisher, now in this country and author of *A Theory of Managerial Capitalism*, later joined in this controversy, siding in the main with Galbraith.[40] Solow opened the debate with an article entitled "The New Industrial State or Son of Affluence," written in a breezy style. It contained some personal references which Galbraith apparently resented, judging from his reaction. He summarized *The New Industrial State* and, among other criticisms, found fault with Galbraith's theory of corporate behavior. He compared the latter's model with that

[37] R. L. Heilbroner, *op. cit.*, p. 18.

[38] *Ibid.* For a similar view, see L. S. Silk, "Business Power, Today and Tomorrow," in *Perspectives on Business, Daedalus,* Winter 1969, pp. 181–182; also Allen, *op. cit.*, pp. 19–20.

[39] W. C. Bennis and P. E. Slater, *The Temporary Society*, (New York: Harper and Row, 1968), *passim.* See the interesting opening chapter entitled "Beyond Bureaucracy."

[40] R. M. Solow, "The New Industrial State or Son of Affluence," *The Public Interest,* Fall 1967, pp. 100–108; J. K. Galbraith, "A Review of a Review," *The Public Interest,* Fall 1967, pp. 109–118; "A Rejoinder," *ibid.,* pp. 118–119; R. Marris, "Galbraith, Solow and the Truth about Corporations," *The Public Interest,* Spring 1968, pp. 37–46; R. M. Solow, "The Truth Further Defined," *The Public Interest,* Spring 1968, pp. 47–52.

of William Baumol (who had stressed sales maximization with a profit constraint) and Marris. "Marris' theory," Solow wrote, "is very much like Galbraith's, only much more closely reasoned. . . . But Marris is more careful, and comes closer to the conventional view, because he is fully aware, as Galbraith apparently is not, of an important discipline in the capital market. . . ."[41] Solow refers to the possibility of a merger bid or a take-over of a company that too freely sacrifices profit to growth. He admits that the very largest corporations are not subject to this kind of threat. "But quite good-sized ones are."

Galbraith, in expounding his position on profit maximization, had argued that a company which was maximizing profit would have no incentive to pass on a wage increase in the form of higher prices to consumers. Since corporations often do this, Galbraith reasoned, they must not be maximizing profits in the first place. Solow commented rather caustically that Galbraith's argument involved "a sophomore error." Galbraith's reply to this criticism was as follows: ". . . I am accused of being indifferent to dangers that by his admission do not exist for the large firms with which I am excessively concerned. In point of fact I considered the problem at length. The danger of involuntary takeover is negligible in the management calculations of the large firm and diminishes with growth and dispersal of stock ownership." Galbraith does not offer any factual evidence to bolster this assertion, a shortcoming which many complain of in their evaluation of *The New Industrial State.*

Marris, in seeking to resolve the differences between these two verbal sluggers, concludes that Solow was "disingenuous" and that "Galbraith had left out vital elements and laid himself open to legitimate attack." Despite the discipline of the capital market, the real-world system, he says, behaves very differently from that implied in the conventional model; on the other hand, he felt that Galbraith, in failing to meet the argument that profits are needed for growth, had not explained why there could be divergence between the technostructure's preference for growth and the conventional theory's emphasis on stockholders' interest in maximum return.

Galbraith, in answering Solow, returns to the fundamental point of the self-interest of the technostructure. ". . . If the technostructure—the autonomous and collegial

[41] Solow, "The New Industrial State or Son of Affluence," p. 106.

guiding authority of the corporation—maximizes profits, it maximizes them in the first instance at least for others, for the owners. If it maximizes growth, it maximizes opportunity for, among other things, advancement, promotion and pecuniary return for itself. That people should so pursue their own interest is not implausible. Professor Solow, as he elsewhere makes clear, does not think it so."[42]

This debate was marked by a considerable amount of personal references and sarcasm in which Galbraith more than proved himself equal to his critic in polemic. Solow claimed that in his jibes he was joking, but Galbraith evidently took umbrage at his mention of "sophomore error," "child's play," and so on, and proceeded to give this particular critic a lecture in the rules of scientific discourse. At the end, the M.I.T. professor assumed a more decorous tone and said in reply to Galbraith's well-placed jabs and assertion that he was defending establishment economics, "I shall try to roll gracefully with the punch, and if I cannot, well, then *Après moi, la sociologie.*"[43]

GALBRAITH AND THE SOCIAL CORPORATION

In his book Galbraith contends that it is an error to dismiss the mature corporation's pursuit of social goals. The "social corporation," in his mind, is a logical manifestation of the mature corporation and the motivation of its leaders. Michael Harrington is one of those who is skeptical of an evolution of the corporate conscience.[44] He sees "a persistence of an atavistic egotism in the semi-collectivised enterprises of a semi-directed economy." He argues that there are several reasons for this: (1) The business heritage with its self-interested conviction that private greed is socially virtuous; (2) the commercial ethos of American society; (3) "reactionary Keynesianism" (public expenditure for military purposes) tends to preserve the traditional vices of the corporate regime. In general, he thinks

[42] J. K. Galbraith, "A Review of a Review," *The Public Interest, op. cit.,* p. 114.

[43] R. M. Solow, "A Rejoinder," *The Public Interest, op. cit.,* p. 119.

[44] M. Harrington, "Liberalism According to Galbraith," *Commentary,* October 1967, p. 81.

that the motivation of the technostructure is more complex than Galbraith's analysis suggests.

ECONOMIC PLANNING AND
ANTITRUST

Galbraith's long-standing criticism of antitrust as a public policy was clearly expressed in *The New Industrial State*. His opinion on this subject was reviewed in an unusual way a few days after that book was published. A subcommittee of the United States Senate, no less, held a symposium, in effect, on the question, "Are planning and regulation replacing competition in the new industrial state?"[45] As a member of the Senate's Select Committee on Small Business, Senator Wayne Morse had previously introduced into the *Congressional Record* one of the Reith lectures Galbraith had delivered in the fall of 1966. Three days after the publication of *The New Industrial State,* Galbraith and three eminent scholars (Dr. Donald F. Turner, Assistant Attorney General in charge of the Antitrust Division; Dr. Willard F. Mueller, chief economist of the Federal Trade Commission; and Professor Walter Adams of the economics department of Michigan State University) assembled to discuss the above question before two subcommittees of the Senate. Few authors have enjoyed the benefit of a "live" book review from a Senate committee; Galbraith, of course, is one of the exceptions.

Galbraith led off in the presentation, suavely maintaining in his usual fashion that the trend to great corporate size was immutable, given our commitment to economic development, and that the present antitrust laws were a charade. The latter element, he went on to argue, lies in the fact that if a firm is already large it is substantially immune under those laws. Rather than being a threat to big business, they constituted a façade behind which it operates with greater impunity. He conceded that the antitrust laws which restrain or prevent unfair trade practices—naked aggression—are serviceable, but only in the most marginal way do they affect the structure of industry. Citing the market power which the other participants had condemned in their published work, he challenged them to ask for "all-

---

[45] Subcommittees of the Select Committee on Small Business, U.S. Senate, 90th Congress, 1st Session, *Planning, Regulation and Competition* (Washington, D.C.: U.S. Government Printing Office, 1967).

out dissolution proceedings" against General Motors and a roster of other corporate giants. Only such an onslaught, he declared, would legitimize the objections to his position. If such a crusade is not to be launched, then his colleagues in the seminar had no alternative but to agree with him. The antitrust laws are simply part of American folklore; we should allow them quietly to atrophy.

Incidentally, one of the most competent younger specialists on industrial organization, Professor William G. Shepherd, supports Galbraith in part on this point. He writes: ". . . Since about 1952, antitrust has largely abandoned attempts to make changes in established (market) structure, even where structural monopoly would appear to warrant it. Prime examples of potential candidates for action are automobiles, steel, and the vertical tie between Western Electric and the Bell operating subsystems. Though one would be unduly harsh to call it a 'charade,' antitrust policy has now largely acquiesced in, and therefore ratified, existing market structures. . . ."[46]

Professor Adams in his remarks attacked the technological imperatives alleged to necessitate bigness, challenged the record of the corporate giants on research and innovation, and pointed to the shabby performance of oligopoly planning in a variety of industries since World War II. What was needed was not mere enforcement of the antitrust laws, but a total integrated policy—on all levels of government—of promoting competition. "The disciplining force of competition," he concluded, "is superior to industrial planning—by the private or public monopolist, the benevolent or authoritarian bureaucrat. . . ."[47]

The next participant to challenge Galbraith's ideas whom he spoke of as "the Goliath of the economics profession" was Dr. Mueller of the Federal Trade Commission. Although he too praised the artistry with which Galbraith had put new and old ideas into "a new and bigger package," he contended that he had failed to muster the evidence to sustain his thesis. As to the technological imperatives alleged to necessitate corporate bigness, recent studies show that productive efficiency requires high concentration in only a small, and declining, share of all manufacturing industries. Nor does similar research support the idea that large size is necessary for inventive or innovative activity; quite the

[46] W. G. Shepherd, *Market Power and Economic Welfare, An Introduction* (New York: Random House, 1970), p. 166.

[47] Subcommittees of the Select Committee on Small Business, *op. cit.*, p. 16.

reverse is the case, in fact. The chief pillar of his thesis, therefore, rests upon an inadequate empirical foundation, on "sands of fancy rather than rocks of evidence."

Galbraith asserts that because the market has perished we must be saved, said Mueller, by an extension of extra-market planning. Here, again, Galbraith ignored mounting evidence, some of it gathered by Mueller himself, which shows a broad decline in economic concentration in the producer goods industries over the years 1947 to 1963. Mueller admitted that concentration has been rising in the consumer goods industries in the postwar years—a tendency favorable to Galbraith's views, but this was not due to technological imperatives.

Contradicting Galbraith's statistics on economic concentration, Mueller insisted that modern technology has not made obsolete our competitive, market economy. "Galbraith, like Gertrude Stein, has trouble with shades of difference." All oligopolies are not alike; they are not as concentrated as Galbraith suggests. In fact, in the larger part of American manufacturing industry, market forces severely limit the discretionary pricing power of firms.

In thinking that antitrust is a charade, Galbraith shows that he hasn't done his "homework." Rather than attacking the midgets, antimerger activity has been primarily aimed at the largest industrial companies; over 60 percent of the largest (those with over a billion dollars of assets) were served antimerger complaints in the years 1947–1963. It is true, however, that antitrust cannot easily destroy deeply entrenched power. Finally, Galbraith exaggerates the role of the state in the planning process and minimizes the coordinating function of the market.

In his statement, Dr. Turner of the Antitrust Division conceded that the government was relatively inactive in dealing with the existing excessive market power. But such a policy is justifiable to the extent that such business size reflects economies of scale, initial competitive superiority, or does not rest on exclusionary behavior of any kind. Galbraith exaggerates the extent of the oligopolistic sector of the economy; it does not dominate the latter, but comprises 20–25 percent of the national income. Even if we can do nothing about existing concentration, the antitrust laws preserve the opportunity for declining concentration by weakening patent and other restrictions on new entry and new products.

Here, again, Professor Shepherd seems to find reason to

agree with Galbraith about the likelihood of growth reducing concentration. He says, "As for growth as a strong solvent of structure, the evidence for it is so far very weak indeed. It apparently has not significantly eroded concentration in the United States or Britain. It offers only an uncertain and slight prospect of reducing structural monopoly in the future."[48]

In the exchange that followed the formal presentations, Galbraith noted that the others had argued issues other than the ones he offered. He stressed the need to attack "the great concentrated core of American industry" which has market power, to undertake a "demerger" process. Yet he asserted that he had not heard a single word from the others as to how we are going to break up existing corporate concentrations "other than Professor Adams' oratory, incantation and prayer, all of which are excellent but of dubious operative value. . . ."[49] Rather than living under such illusions, we have to learn to live with great organizations; more positively, this means, according to Galbraith, that the government must have, as a durable policy, a system of wage and price restraint. On the whole, Galbraith came off well in this part of the seminar; he skillfully concentrated on the weakest aspect of the opposition case and rejected all other means of undermining market power (short of dissolution) as evasions of the main issue.

His opponents assaulted him on the assumption that he was defending the economic efficiency of the large firm. But he rejected this, saying, "I do not want to seem to be associated with the efficiency or technological virtuosity of the large firm as something I am morally for." All that he was contending for was that the large firm enjoys an advantage; "whether this advantage is good or not, whether it is something which we want or not, is a question from which I remove myself both morally and emotionally. . . ." His opponents did not press him to reconcile this statement with the fearful prospect that he draws toward the close of *The New Industrial State* of a nation in deep servitude to corporate power with respect to both the ends and means of life.

Galbraith's weakness on the factual side of the subject of antitrust led him to overlook points in his favor. On one occasion he conceded, as he said, "the accuracy of every

[48] W. G. Shepherd, *Market Power and Economic Welfare, op. cit.,* pp. 20, 179.
[49] Subcommittees of the Select Committee on Small Business, *op. cit.,* p. 33.

one of those dreary studies, including—here I enthusiastically confess fault—the several that I have not read. . . ."[50] Legal victories, in merger cases, according to a recent study, often have a Pyrrhic character.[51] Unless effective relief follows the court triumph, "the government," as Justice Jackson once said, "has won a lawsuit and lost a cause." In the study cited, it is shown that in a sample of 39 of the 81 antimerger cases filed by the government between 1950 and 1964, 21 relief orders were unsuccessful and 8 deficient. Antitrust, as Galbraith has argued, makes work for lawyers, but its economic consequences often fall short of expectations because of faulty relief and compliance.

DEMAND MANAGEMENT AND THE
REVISED SEQUENCE

The idea that producers largely create the demand for their own products is one of the central themes of *The New Industrial State*. Yet, say several of Galbraith's critics, he fails to provide systematic evidence for this crucial proposition. Scott Gordon writes, for example, that "it would be easy to challenge Galbraith to show empirical support for his view that the techniques of demand management he speaks of are effective in altering the allocation of income between savings and aggregate consumption or among broad consumption categories. . . ."[52]

Galbraith's general position involves the notion that human wants are cultural phenomena and advertising is a powerful force in mass culture. On this question, Gordon, for one, admits that "Galbraith is not to be faulted on this fundamental point or on his view that great consequences for economic theory spring therefrom. . . ." Where the production system is a large part of the culture and is able to mold the wants it satisfies, how, says Gordon, do we establish a solid foundation for economic analysis and the determination of economic efficiency? Galbraith is of little help in this regard because he does not explore the important issues raised by his own approach. His writings in general are much concerned with the influence of culture, in-

---

[50] *Ibid.,* p. 32.
[51] K. G. Elzinga, "The Antimerger Law: Pyrrhic Victories," *The Journal of Law and Economics,* April 1969, pp. 43 ff.
[52] S. Gordon, *op. cit.,* p. 641.

cluding advertising, on consumer behavior. Galbraith, like Alfred Marshall, sees that economic activities affect wants, but he does not examine this complex subject in the depth and with the scholarly care that it requires.

Professor Stigler in a more critical vein questions the efficacy of "Svengali-like advertising" and argues that Madison Avenue does not hypnotize consumers into brand slavery.[53] If large firms can shape demand, he says, the Pennsylvania Railroad would have stopped the automobile industry in 1910. (Refutation by example is no more persuasive than Galbraith's casual empiricism.)

In his answer to Gordon, Galbraith replied that since *The New Industrial State* was a book of some breadth, there was, of necessity, some sacrifice of depth and of scholarly detail. Galbraith again demonstrated his skill in argumentation in this exchange. Gordon had criticized him on the ground of scholarly deficiency, saying in one place, "By any test except the rigorous one of scholarship, he is a highly successful author." In his rejoinder, Galbraith pointed out Gordon's own violations of the canons of criticism, calling attention to his use of loaded words, *ad hominem* arguments without persuasive support from the facts, and employment of careless and superficial interpretations of an author's position in order better to attack it. As illustration of the latter, Galbraith compares his description of demand management (with its qualification that "the consumer can still reject persuasion," even under the industrial system) with statements such as this from Gordon: "The consumer enters the Galbraithian picture of the American economy as a puppet of the production system—his function is to purchase whatever the technostructure has decided to produce in the quantities and at the prices set by the technostructure's plan."[54] Galbraith questions whether the latter statement represents scholarly rigor. He insists that the system he has described does operate subject to restraints; the individual firm can affect the position of the demand function for its products, it can stabilize (note the word) the market response, but these efforts encounter similar efforts of other firms—"a process I have sketched although far from fully described—and against the increasing market resistance of the consumers and the increasing

[53] G. Stigler, *op. cit.*, p. 16. See also, for criticism of this type, H. Demsetz, "The Technostructure, Forty-Six Years Later," *Yale Law Journal*, March 1968, p. 815.
[54] Gordon, *op. cit.*, p. 640.

cost (as Professor Gordon rightly observes) of a given increment of sales. . . ."[55]

The American scholar is chastised; in the process, it is indicated that the British do these things better—Professor Meade's remarks are "a model for temperate scholarly debate." At the close of his reply to Professor Gordon, Galbraith, repeating his conception of partial producer sovereignty, makes a significant concession when he says, "I would be one of the first, or anyhow one of the many, to agree that my argument leaves much to be decided. But it surely helps if we have learned to look in the right places or in the right direction."[56]

An interesting and important comment on the effects of advertising *à la* Galbraith has recently been made by one of his colleagues at Harvard, Professor Richard Caves.[57] He points out that one implication of Galbraith's model of the inner workings of the large corporation is that the latter foregoes potential profits latent in its market position in order to avoid uncertainty, and that such action has important allocative effects on the economy. Caves describes the various patterns of market conduct employed by large firms to avoid uncertainty, and the shifts and transformations in risk that they sometimes make. Then, in a footnote, he adds: "With this suggestion I necessarily part company with Galbraith's proposition that giant corporations succeed in fending off all uncertainties, in which case no shifting would be necessary. . . ."[58] He reminds us that Galbraith's conception of the prowess of the large corporation in de-

[55] J. K. Galbraith, "Professor Gordon on 'The Close of the Galbraithian System,'" *Journal of Political Economy, op. cit.,* p. 501. The "sketch" would seem to have left some readers with the simple notion that the large corporations absolutely control demand. Note this statement from Professor Reich's *The Greening of America* (New York: Random House, 1970). "But the more important fact is that producers largely create their own demand for products. This is the central thesis of Galbraith's *The New Industrial State,* and it is hard to see how it can be disputed. Corporations decide what they want to produce, and they convince people that they want it, thus fashioning their own market. What we now produce and consume, the way we use our resources, the plans we make for the future use of our resources, are therefore not directed by what the people want . . ." (p. 102).

[56] Galbraith, "Professor Gordon on 'The Close, etc.,'" *op. cit.,* p. 503.

[57] R. E. Caves, "Uncertainty, Market Structure and Performance: Galbraith as Conventional Wisdom," in J. W. Markham and G. F. Papanek (Eds.), *Industrial Organization and Economic Development* (Boston: Houghton Mifflin, 1970), pp. 283–302.

[58] *Ibid.,* p. 289, footnote 15.

mand management refers to the long run, not to the short run.

Galbraith's admission that his "sketch" of the process of demand management leaves much still to be decided is rather damaging, considering how much of the structure of *The New Industrial State* rests on this proposition. He stated that in writing this book, as he embarked upon each section, he made the usual canvass of the literature to see what he had missed in more casual reading. One is puzzled that he did not see fit to consider at least Professor Bain's empirical work *Barriers to New Competition*[59] because of its obvious relation to the effects of advertising on the stability of market shares. There are also other books and journal articles that he overlooked that are relevant to his hypothesis. Telser, for example, in a much-cited 1964 article reached a conclusion that runs contrary to Galbraith's reasoning about advertising: "There is little empirical support for an inverse association between advertising and competition despite some plausible theoretical theorizing to the contrary."[60] While *The New Industrial State* was in press, other articles of importance on this subject appeared and since 1967 there have been many more.[61]

A valuable insight into Galbraith's methods and purposes in writing *The New Industrial State* is to be gained from a paper he read to the American Economic Association late in 1969.[62] In it he stated that "*the* theme [our italics], explicit or implicit," of that book and of its predecessor, *The Affluent Society,* was "the surrender of the sovereignty of the individual to the producer or producing organization. . . ." In attacking the conventional belief in consumer and citizen sovereignty, he points out, he was faced with a

[59] Cambridge: Harvard University Press, 1956. He had cited in another connection an earlier article by this author, J. S. Bain, "Economics of Scale, Concentration and the Condition of Entry in Twenty Manufacturing Industries," *The American Economic Review,* March 1954, pp. 15–39.

[60] L. G. Telser, "Advertising and Competition," *Journal of Political Economy,* December 1964, p. 558.

[61] See, e.g., P. Doyle, "Economic Aspects of Advertising: A Survey," *Economic Journal,* September 1968, pp. 570–602; W. S. Comanor and T. A. Wilson, "Advertising Market Structure and Performance," *The Review of Economics and Statistics,* November 1967, pp. 423–439; L. G. Telser, "Some Aspects of the Economics of Advertising," *Journal of Business,* April 1968, pp. 166–173; I. Horowitz, "Advertising and Uncertainty," *The Journal of Industrial Economics,* April 1970, pp. 151–160.

[62] J. K. Galbraith, "Economics as a System of Belief," *American Economic Review,* Papers and Proceedings, May 1970, pp. 469–484.

peculiar problem of persuasion. "A scientific proposition is refuted by proof to the contrary. Belief, especially if it is playing a functionally protective role in society, is by no means so vulnerable. . . ." The economics profession, he argues, has a vested interest in the larger framework of assumptions in which it operates and on which its structure of knowledge is erected. To attack such a framework of assumptions from within the discipline is consequently a perilous business. Therefore another strategy of persuasion is called for:

> . . . The alternative is to engage a larger public and thus, as it were, force the issue on the discipline. For, if the assumptions being attacked are vulnerable—if they are incongruous with reality—the public intuition will be responsive. So will be that of the social radical. And if enough support can be enlisted, the old framework can be broken. The use of this technique naturally incurs a certain measure of professional discomfort. It bypasses the system by which ideas and innovations are submitted for professional scrutiny and winnowing before being passed along to students and the lay public. And it similarly renders nugatory the process by which intellectual vested interest is protected. To the legitimate rebuke for the first is added the more personal discontent inspired by the second.[63]

In the light of these remarks, I think it can be said that Galbraith did not attempt in *The New Industrial State* to argue the case for producer sovereignty in detail, as an alternative hypothesis, but rather, as he states in the paper previously cited, "to assume it (though less comprehensively) as consumer sovereignty is now assumed. . . ."[64] In other words, in this book he did not advance a hypothesis concerning demand management (the revised sequence) and seek to test it systematically and empirically. Instead he assumed producer sovereignty, described its techniques of demand management, and examined economic reality from that vantage point. The resulting essay in social theory concerned itself with much more than the role of advertising in the industrial system; its very breadth prevented him from closely studying the latter process. It was helpful, as he said in his reply to Professor Gordon, to persuade his fellow economists to look in the right places and in the right direction.

But there is a weakness in this defense of his procedure. Galbraith had admitted in his book and in the reply to Gor-

[63] *Ibid.,* p. 471.
[64] *Ibid.,* p. 475.

don that producer sovereignty was not absolute, but only partial.[65] If one starts from an assumption of partial producer sovereignty so far as demand management is concerned, the inevitable question arises, how partial is corporate control of consumer demand? And how do corporations cope with the consequences of that partiality of control, that is, with uncertainty? To treat the matter only in long-run terms is not altogether satisfactory, because if we do not know what happens in the short run, how confident can we be in our analysis of the long run which, after all, is simply a cumulation of a number of shorter periods? I take it that it was his dissatisfaction with this aspect of the argument of *The New Industrial State* that led Professor Caves to refer to "Galbraith as the Conventional Wisdom."[66]

THE REGULATION OF AGGREGATE

DEMAND

One of the most interesting of Galbraith's contentions in the book under review is the idea that Keynesian fiscal policy after World War II came to have the strong support of the mature corporations and of their technostructures. In this view, the entrepreneurial corporations and their leaders, having less of a functional need for such demand stabilization, were unalterably opposed to the regulation of aggregate demand. This interpretation of the progress of the Keynesian revolution and of the political support for it has met with strong dissent from Professor Meade of Cambridge University.[67] He writes of Professor Galbraith's "strange aberration" in attributing this important policy development to the growth of the technostructure. He thinks that it is "surely a mistaken view" to suggest that stabilizing fiscal policy was opposed to the interests of the old-time entrepreneurs. The adoption of modern fiscal policy, he asserts, had no practical relation to the replacement of the "captains of industry" by the professional technostructure.

It is difficult to say whether Professor Meade has

[65] *The New Industrial State*, p. 213; J. K. Galbraith, "Professor Gordon on 'The Close of the Galbraithian System,' " *op. cit.*, p. 502.
[66] Caves, *op. cit.*, p. 283.
[67] J. E. Meade, "Is 'The New Industrial State' Inevitable?", *Economic Journal*, June 1968, p. 380.

reached his conclusion on this matter from British experience more than American. From the standpoint of the latter alone, there would seem to be considerable evidence for Galbraith's position. To cite just a few bits of information on this, we may note that the Committee for Economic Development, a body more representative of the corporate technostructure than any other, took the lead in supporting a moderate Keynesian policy in this country.[68] Or, again, in 1964, at the time of the famous tax cut, the smaller businessmen took the conventional stance, while the managers of the large corporations approved federal fiscal action to underwrite mass consumption.[69]

Similarly, it is hard to agree with Professor H. Demsetz, who criticizes Galbraith for being so conventional in his acceptance of Keynesianism.[70] He feels, at least, that he should have presented the dissenting view, especially the alternative of a Friedmanite monetary policy. Actually, Demsetz ignores the fact that Galbraith is no longer an unqualified Keynesian. Indeed, he now believes that the economics associated with the brilliant Britisher has become part of the conventional wisdom.

LABOR IN THE INDUSTRIAL SYSTEM

Galbraith's speculations about the role of organized labor in the industrial system, his prediction of a "permanent decline" and the reduction of unions as a social force have not gone without criticism, particularly from those to the left of him ideologically. Michael Harrington, for one, regretfully remarks that Galbraith has abandoned a significant portion of his theory of countervailing power. On the contrary, he (Harrington) envisions unions as making an important contribution in the political struggle for an alternative to the new industrial state.[71]

[68] On this, see K. Schriftgiesser, *Business Comes of Age: The Story of the C.E.D. and Its Impact upon the Economic Policies of the United States, 1942–60* (New York: Harper and Row, 1960).

[69] Particularly instructive on this subject is H. Rowen, *The Free Enterprisers: Kennedy, Johnson and the Business Establishment* (New York: G. P. Putnam, 1964); also D. Bazelon, *Power in America: The Politics of the New Class* (New York: New American Library, 1967).

[70] H. Demsetz, "The Technostructure, Forty-Six Years Later," *Yale Law Journal,* March 1968, pp. 802–817.

[71] Harrington, "Liberalism According to Galbraith," *op. cit.,* p. 82.

A British socialist, Ralph Miliband, dissents much more forcefully from these Galbraithian perspectives on the future of unionism. He ridicules "the happy industrial family which Professor Galbraith has conjured up; where, but fifteen short years ago, there were large reserves of countervailing power, there is now unalienated integration. . . ."[72]

On white-collar employment in relation to the industrial system, Professor William G. Shepherd of the University of Michigan has assembled data which cast doubt on the so-called corporate conscience, particularly in relation to Jewish and black discrimination in employment. His correlation analysis of the relationship between corporate concentration and Negro employment as officials, managers, and professionals suggests that "the degree of monopoly does affect minority group hiring as an independent factor." "Generally speaking," he concludes, "it is in competitive and nonprofit agencies that employment tends to be relatively nondiscriminatory, and not in firms with market power. Evidently, firms with market power, which *could* enact nondiscriminatory employment policies, cannot normally be relied on to do so voluntarily."[73]

On the whole, Galbraith's survey of the impact of the industrial system on labor unions shows real insight into the limitations of what Reich calls Consciousness II as it operates in the labor field. But his analysis, though it recognizes its inapplicability to the nonindustrial sector of the economy, neglects perhaps the broader cultural forces influencing labor and the political dynamics associated with a more progressive labor leadership than now dominates the American scene.

THE INDUSTRIAL SYSTEM

AND THE STATE

Surprisingly, critics of *The New Industrial State* have had relatively little to say about Galbraith's conception of the relationship of the industrial system and the technostructure to the state. Before considering what criticism there

[72] R. Miliband, "Professor Galbraith and American Capitalism," *The Socialist Register* (London: Merlin Press, 1968), reprinted in D. Mermelstein (Ed.), *Economics: Mainstream Readings and Radical Critiques* (New York: Random House, 1970), p. 541.

[73] W. G. Shepherd, *Market Power and Economic Welfare* (New York: Random House, 1970), pp. 88–92, 213–220 (quoting p. 220).

is, we should note that there are several formulations in *The New Industrial State* of the emergent relationship between the corporate economy and the state. There is Galbraith's statement, for example, that "in notable respects the mature corporation is an arm of the state and the state, in important matters, is an instrument of the industrial system."[74] In another place, he remarks that "the abhorrent association of public and private organizations is normal." And toward the end of his book, in writing about the future of the industrial system, he states, ". . . Increasingly, it will be recognized that the mature corporation, as it develops, becomes part of the larger administrative complex associated with the state. In time the line between the two will disappear."[75]

Galbraith's treatment of the industrial system and the state takes the form of a contrast between the entrepreneurial and the mature corporation. Recognizing that his generalizations on this subject were "abstractions," he offered defense procurement as the clearest manifestation of this process. But in contending that the state underwrites industrial planning with long-term contracts for large capital outlays and advanced technology, he indicated that this relationship was not limited to the defense agency; it is illustrated also, he stated, by NASA, the Atomic Energy Commission, the Civil Aeronautics Board, and other governmental agencies. He added, "There are few mature corporations which do not have this relationship with the modern state."[76] However, he did not provide much quantitative measure of such relationships.

This phase of Galbraith's analysis has been forthrightly challenged by Murray L. Weidenbaum, a specialist in the economics of national defense.[77] He argues that the line between all the mature corporations and the state is not disappearing; this tendency is limited to the defense sector of the economy. Agreeing in part with Galbraith, he admits that "in a sense, the close, continuing relationship between the Department of Defense and its major suppliers is resulting in a convergence between public and private

[74] *The New Industrial State*, p. 296. In "Economics as a System of Belief," *op. cit.*, p. 478, Galbraith approximates the Leninist formulation: "The state as here envisaged comes close to being the executive committee of the large producing organization—of the technostructure. . . ."

[75] *The New Industrial State*, p. 393.

[76] *Ibid.*, p. 315.

[77] M. L. Weidenbaum, "Arms and the American Economy: A Domestic Convergence Hypothesis," *American Economic Review*, May 1968, pp. 428–437.

activities in an important branch of the American economy." But Galbraith, he says, does not differentiate enough between the major defense contractors, and the other large mature corporations. "The corporate giants of American industry do not dominate the government markets." In 1965 "the 27 corporations with assets of one billion dollars or over received only 25% of the defense contracts going to the top 100 companies. . . . In contrast, the 30 companies with assets in the $250–999 million range received 58% of the contracts, the largest share of any group."[78] He points out also with regard to the possible disappearance of the line between the mature corporations and the state that "the stock market, at least, seems to distinguish increasingly clearly between the government-oriented and commercially-oriented corporations."

In defense of Galbraith's position on this question, one should note that the defense and space industries occupied the role of a leading sector in the expansion of the American economy during the postwar years; as such they could be regarded, as Galbraith undoubtedly regards them, as establishing a paradigm of the new relationship of the state to the economy.[79] Furthermore, many of the defense-oriented companies were already diversifying and have gone forward in this direction; such a development would seem to justify the view that the defense contractors are more than simply a branch of the American economy.

Galbraith's theory of the state, expressed or implied, in *The New Industrial State* differs significantly from that presented in his *American Capitalism*. In the latter the state was pictured as something of a neutral umpire balancing the different countervailing groups of the society. Now this pluralist model is apparently abandoned, and in its place there is substituted a more elitist view of power with respect to both the technostructure and the educational and scientific estate.

Galbraith recognizes the dangers to liberty "as the in-

[78] M. L. Weidenbaum, *The Modern Public Sector, New Ways of Doing the Government's Business* (New York: Basic Books, 1969), p. 34. For data which point to conclusions similar to Weidenbaum's, see W. L. Baldwin, *The Structure of the Defense Market, 1955–1964* (Durham, N.C.: Duke University Press, 1967).

[79] On the place of these industries in the postwar economy, see H. L. Nieburg, "Social Control of Innovation," *American Economic Review,* May 1968, p. 669; also H. G. Vatter, *The American Economy in the 1950's* (New York: W. W. Norton, 1963); also S. Melman, *Pentagon Capitalism, The Political Economy of War* (New York: McGraw-Hill, 1970).

dustrial system evolves into a penumbra of the state. . . ."
He points to the recent conflicts between the state and intellectuals in Soviet-type economies. And he adds: "The instinct which warns of dangers in this association of economic and public power is sound. It comes close to being
the subject of this book. . . ."[80] At least one critic of his
volume felt, in the light of these statements, that the treatment of the merger of economic and political power was
altogether too skimpy and superficial. The dangers alluded
to were too little analyzed.[81] Galbraith's answer to this complaint is to be found in his text; he states quite clearly that
he is "less interested in telling where the industrial system
is going than in providing materials for consideration of
where it has arrived."[82]

As Galbraith describes it, the industrial system accommodates men to its needs, subverts the trade union, bends
education to its requirements, adapts the state to its functioning, and, worst of all, threatens the community with its
monopoly of social purpose. Economic liberals, rejecting
his deterministic diagnosis of the allegedly inexorable forces
that are leading us to such corporate domination, reply that
they have long argued that economic concentration begets
political concentration of power. In their view, Galbraith's
analysis not only slights the economic inadequacies of the
mature corporations, but having done so, then suddenly,
toward its conclusion, raises the terrible prospect of a loss
of personal liberty and of that variety of life of which
Keynes wrote so tellingly in *The General Theory*.[83]

The reply of one such liberal to the prospectus of the
new industrial state was unequivocal:

[80] *The New Industrial State*, p. 397.
[81] A. S. Miller, "Government and the Corporations," *The New
Republic*, July 8, 1967, pp. 26–28.
[82] *The New Industrial State*, p. 324.
[83] "But, above all, individualism, if it can be purged of its defects
and abuses, is the best safeguard of personal liberty in the sense
that, compared with any other system, it greatly widens the field
for the exercise of personal choice. It is also the best safeguard of
the variety of life, which emerges precisely from this extended field
of personal choice, and the loss of which is the greatest of all the
losses of the homogeneous or totalitarian state. For this variety pre-
serves the traditions which embody the most secure and successful
choices of former generations; it colours the present with the diversification of its fancy; and being the handmaid of experiment as
well as of tradition and of fancy, it is the most powerful instrument
to better the future." J. M. Keynes, *The General Theory of Employment, Interest and Money* (New York: Harcourt, Brace, 1936),
p. 380.

Here is a blueprint for technocracy, private socialism, and the corporate state. The keystone of the new power structure is the giant corporation, freed from all traditional checks and balances, and subject only to the countervailing power of the intellectual in politics. Happily, this blueprint need not cause undue alarm: first, because Galbraith's analysis rests on an empirically unsubstantiated premise; and second, even if this analysis were correct, there would be more attractive public policy alternatives than Galbraith suggests.[84]

Our "worldly philosopher" from Harvard would reply to this liberal attack by noting its use of scare words and shibboleths, some of them of rather ancient vintage. He would agree that the traditional checks on corporate power have lost a good deal of their effectiveness, but would call attention to others which he describes in his book. As for the intellectual in politics, he could call attention to his disclaimer that his remarks on that subject were offered in as definitive a mood as his earlier analysis. Finally, he would probably suggest that the alternative public policies Professor Adams alludes to have been far from successful in checking economic concentration in the past.

Liberal doubts about the wisdom of enlarging the role of the state are expressed too by the Britisher G. C. Allen:

Galbraith may be right in foreseeing a growing centralization of authority, but we need not accept it as inevitable. One may agree with him that this centralization, together with the exacting claims of economic growth, will threaten spiritual and esthetic values. But one may dissent from his view that we can confidently call on the state to preserve them. The state can help to maintain an environment where initiative is widely diffused and it can do something to ensure that the concentration of power is limited to those spheres where it is proper to the proper conduct of a complex modern economy. But it does not follow that the state should assume responsibility for a vast multitude of particular decisions. Can we really rely on the "coarse thumb and the finger" of the bureaucrat to mould the good society? . . .[85]

Galbraith's response to Allen's points would, I suspect, stress that the British economist persists in seeing a dichot-

---

[84] W. Adams, Opening Statement before the U.S. Senate Small Business Committee, press release, June 29, 1967, p. 2 (mimeographed). For a similar view of Galbraith as an ideological defender of monopoly capitalism, see R. Fitch, "A Galbraith Reappraisal: The Ideologue as Gadfly," *Ramparts,* May 1968, pp. 73–84. (Published also as a pamphlet under that title by the Radical Education Project.)

[85] Allen, *Economic Fact and Fantasy, op. cit.,* p. 32.

omous relationship between enterprise and the state, whereas he sees and foresees a diffusion of authority and responsibility. He would admit that there is "an uncomfortably collectivist and monolithic aspect" about the present structure of the industrial state. But the remedy for this, he states, is a skepticism and systematic questioning of the goals impressed by the industrial system and, secondly, a political pluralism representing a broader constituency than the reigning technostructure and its allies. It is easy to confuse Galbraith's advocacy of such short-term measures as price and wage control to contain inflation with his later argument for a more comprehensive planning guided by a reformed technostructure.

Marxist criticism of Galbraith's analysis of the relationship between the industrial system and the state emphasizes the limitations of his accommodation theory in explaining the imperialist thrust of American capitalism. Thus Harry Magdoff cites the passage in which Galbraith asserts that the industrial system has become identified with weapons competition because this is the area where "the largest amount of money to support planning was available with the fewest questions asked."[86] Magdoff notes that the reader's attention is thus directed to military orders as the source of corporate identification with foreign policy.

> But by the same token, the examination of any other interest of the industrial system . . . in U.S. pacification and control of foreign lands is eliminated. The avoidance of such an issue seems quite strange in a book devoted to proving the vital need of the giant corporations to control their sources of raw materials and to achieve persistent growth of sales. One would imagine that if control over sources of supply is an imperative for the corporation, then the latter might have more than a vague curiosity about the stability and security of their foreign properties from which life-giving raw materials come. . . .
>
> Perhaps, then, there is more than a mild interest by the corporate organizations in U.S. foreign policy and its military complement as a convenience in sustaining a comfortable business environment. In Galbraith's analysis, though, the irrationality of the cold war and militarism is an unfortunate accompaniment to the rational need of industry for government support of domestic markets; as such, it is unrelated to the persistent needs for business expansion and control.[87]

[86] H. Magdoff, "Rationalizing the Irrational," *The Nation,* September 18, 1967, pp. 246–248.
[87] *Ibid.,* p. 247.

Adequate comment on this criticism would take us far afield; suffice it to say that the conceptual framework of *The New Industrial State* does not extend to an analysis of the class structure in the United States and its possible relation to foreign policy. That, it may be contended, is a serious weakness, but it probably derives from the more modest purpose of the author.

Other socialist commentators have been more sweeping in their condemnation of Galbraith for his rejection of the Marxist faith and its accompanying economic analysis. Thus, Ralph Miliband, a British writer, ridicules his faith in the educational and scientific estate as "a decisive instrument of political power," and asks, "political power for what?"[88]

> Professor Galbraith has no serious answer to that question. For all the verbal iconoclasm, and the seeming dismissal of "conventional wisdom" and orthodox economics, there is too much here of apologetics and obfuscation, too little genuine probing, too ready an acceptance of the "logic" of the system, too cramped a view of its contradictions, too much underlying intellectual and political timidity, notwithstanding the self-conscious *enfant terrible* posturings, for Professor Galbraith to speak seriously to the American condition, or to those who seriously seek to change it. For such people, *The New Industrial State* has little to offer, either by way of diagnosis, or of prescription. What it does offer is a further demonstration of the limitations, both in diagnosis and prescription, of a type of liberalism which constitutes not an alternative but a variant of that conservatism which Professor Galbraith claims to condemn.[89]

Comment on this diatribe would be superfluous; it must be evident that the life of the Galbraithian type of liberal is, indeed, not an easy one, caught as he inevitably is between the crossfire from the left and the right.

The social philosophy toward which the industrial system and "the socialization of the mature corporation" might lead is, to state it mildly, not a subject on which all are agreed. To some, Galbraith's plea for political involvement of the educational and scientific estate sounds like "the fighting words of democratic liberalism." To others, as we have just seen, they are indistinguishable from the most standpat conservatism. To still others, they suggest an ob-

[88] R. Miliband, *The Socialist Register* (London: Merlin Press, 1968).

[89] Miliband, "Professor Galbraith and American Capitalism," *op. cit.*, p. 542.

noxious elitism. One economist has written: "Galbraith is a Tory radical. He wants the people to recognize that the elite are the elite. And then he wants the elite to decide what the good life really is."[90] Galbraith has been called everything from a Puritan to "an upper-class aristocrat." What are his basic values and what is distinctive about his vision of the American economy and society? These fundamental questions are the subject of our concluding chapter.

[90] "The Implications of the Industrial State," *Business Week,* July 8, 1967, p. 77.

8 The Galbraithian

Vision of the Economic

Process

THE EVOLUTIONARY ECONOMICS
OF J. K. GALBRAITH

One of the master economists of this century, the late Joseph A. Schumpeter, once a colleague of Galbraith's at Harvard, was in the habit of talking about a research worker's "vision." By this term he meant that "mixture of perceptions and prescientific analysis" which shapes and influences the theoretical model or the empirical research that an economist produces.[1] Schumpeter contended that the initial vision of the social phenomena was the source of ideological bias in an economist's work, but that ordinarily that bias was destroyed in the course of subsequent scientific analysis. In relation to this concept, in this chapter we shall explore the Galbraithian vision of the economic process and consider some of its sources and consequences.

In doing this, we encounter one difficulty at the very outset that reminds us of an ancient joke in economics. It is the one about there being five economists in a room, but six opinions. Some of Galbraith's critics would assert that he has not had one vision, but several, in the post-World War II years. For example, they would call attention to the fact that in *American Capitalism* he described a pluralistic economy of countervailing powers and argued that our growing wealth was a solvent for mistakes and for what

[1] J. A. Schumpeter, "Science and Ideology," *American Economic Review*, March 1949, p. 350. Schumpeter emphasized in this Presidential address to the AEA that "ideologies are not simply lies; they are truthful statements about what a man thinks he sees . . ." (p. 349).

might have been grave social strains.[2] In *The Affluent Society* and more particularly in *The New Industrial State* he portrayed an increasingly monolithic economy and insisted that our mounting private affluence was aggravating social strains and imbalance. Confused by these conflicting images, his critics might humorously exclaim, "Will the *real* Professor Galbraith please stand up?"

Galbraith's answer to such charges of inconsistency has been to say that if the facts of American economic life have changed, he at least has been flexible and open-minded enough to change with them; he then gets in a "dig" about his critics' making a virtue of their fixed ideas. Indeed, in this matter it can be maintained that the evolution of Galbraith's ideas has in some respects reflected the swift and almost revolutionary changes in the nation's economy and culture. Galbraith would characteristically admit that he has been ahead of the intellectual procession, but even from his viewpoint there are encouraging signs, as we shall see, that others are scurrying to catch up with some of his ideas. Irving Kristol, one of his critics, frankly concedes that "the spirit of the age is obviously sympathetic to Galbraith's emphasis on 'questions that are beyond the reach of economics—the beauty, dignity, pleasure and durability of life.' "[3] And Professor Gordon, another critic, points out that "Galbraith's ideas have become important elements in the contemporary popular culture of American social thought."[4]

"Galbraith," Gordon states, "has chosen to write *sub specie temporis,* and has done so with consummate skill, but it is clear that he hopes his books will prove to be *sub specie aeternitatis.* How do they seem to rank in that great contest?"

He answers his own question in the following terms:

> It is always hazardous to declare what the Muses will in time decree; the history of economic thought is filled with many surprises. But it seems quite certain to this reviewer that Galbraith's work will not be the foundation of a new school of economics and that its impact on social thought in general is unlikely to outlast the immediate consciousness of the author's contemporaries. But immortality has many circles, and Galbraith's name is now firmly fixed on the high middle

[2] *American Capitalism,* p. 113.
[3] Kristol, *Fortune,* July 1967, p. 195.
[4] Gordon, "The Close of the Galbraithian System," *op. cit.,* p. 636.

ranges where dwell the spirits of the effective gadflies of an age. . . .[5]

Whether one regards Galbraith as an immortal or as an economic ignoramus, a genius or merely an academic gadfly, there is a need to understand the sources of his vision or visions, or as he would express it, the provenance of his philosophy. To that we now turn.

THE INTELLECTUAL BACKGROUND
OF GALBRAITHIAN ECONOMICS

Schumpeter, in writing about the origins of economists' visions, observes that "in practice . . . we hardly ever start from scratch so that the prescientific act of vision is not entirely our own. We start from the work of our predecessors or contemporaries or else from the ideas that float around us in the public mind. In this case our vision will also contain at least some of the results of previous scientific analysis. . . ."[6] To what extent can we detect parts of the foundations and of the building blocks that went into the Galbraithian edifice in the work of his predecessors?

This is a somewhat delicate and difficult subject because, apart from the inherent pitfalls in tracing the lineage of a thought, there is the fact that some of Galbraith's critics have complained that he has not properly acknowledged his intellectual indebtedness to others. To be specific, and, I hope, not tactless, M. W. Watkins in particular complains that he has not done so with respect to T. B. Veblen, J. M. Clark, and E. H. Chamberlin, "the three pillars upon which Galbraith bases his critique of the modern industrial system."[7] Professor Stigler also wishes, in connection with *The New Industrial State*, that Galbraith had "spared a word of thanks to Thorstein Veblen's books, especially *The Engineers and the Price System.*"[8]

In his verbal encounter with Professor Solow and in other places, Galbraith sought to put to rest these charges of a "spurious claim to novelty." In the addendum to *The*

[5] *Ibid.,* p. 644.
[6] Schumpeter, *op. cit.,* p. 350.
[7] Watkins, *The Antitrust Bulletin,* Spring, 1968, p. 274.
[8] Stigler, *Wall Street Journal,* June 26, 1967, p. 16.

New Industrial State, he acknowledged that he had drawn on specialists' work, both quantitative and qualitative, "at every stage" of his composition, but he obviously annoyed some economists by ridiculing the degree to which professional specialization has been carried. He had mentioned that at the University of California a quarter of a century ago there were specialists not on economic theory, but "prune economists" and citrus fruit specialists. These were useful men, he says, highly respected by the growers, but they would have been less useful if they had diversified to artichokes.[9]

As to his reliance on Veblen, Galbraith answers that his work has a different focus from that of his able predecessor in iconoclasm. The latter was concerned with the manner in which the owners sabotaged the industry of the engineers and technicians; the owners were too much in control. Whereas, in his view, the technostructure has a much freer hand in the management of the mature corporations. Still, some of his critics see a general resemblance in the common emphasis on planning and note Galbraith's employment of some of Veblen's apt phrases.[10]

Regarding Chamberlin, Watkins should certainly recall that Galbraith has for long regarded the work of Chamberlin and Joan Robinson as having failed in the positive analysis of oligopoly, though he grants that they introduced important refinements in some concepts. Nevertheless, in his view Chamberlin and Robinson merely "substituted a new set of frustrations for the old ones."[11] J. M. Clark's work has apparently not impressed Galbraith as it has some economists (including the author), because he sees it as concerned mainly with the maintenance of competition.

As we have noted earlier, Galbraith's approach is in the tradition of the institutional school. He has long been restless with the conventional corpus of so-called price theory and has sought to formulate an economics that had more realism and relevance to contemporary industrial realities. At the University of California, he studied under economists of this more heterodox persuasion, and at Harvard he was

[9] *The New Industrial State,* p. 402.

[10] See, *e.g.,* M. W. Watkins, Review of *The New Industrial State, The Antitrust Bulletin,* Spring, 1968, pp. 269–281. Watkins notes that Veblen designated industries composed of mature corporations as "the modern industrial system." (See T. B. Veblen, *The Engineers and the Price System,* New York: Viking Press, p. 69.)

[11] J. K. Galbraith, "Monopoly and the Concentration of Economic Power," in H. S. Ellis (Ed.), *A Survey of Contemporary Economics* (Philadelphia: Blakiston, 1948), p. 103.

thoroughly familiar with the outlook of Dean Edward S. Mason, who had written, "The theory of oligopoly has been aptly described as a ticket of admission to institutional economics."[12]

Galbraith has been a holder of that kind of ticket for a long while. As such he has been very well acquainted not only with the work of Veblen and other institutionalists, but also with that of such social scientists as R. H. Tawney, A. A. Berle, Jr., G. C. Means, A. R. Burns, R. A. Gordon, and others who could be mentioned. Others, such as J. A. Schumpeter, J. M. Keynes, and A. H. Hansen, all of whom had keen insights about the institutional structure of the modern economy, have also influenced the development of Galbraith's thought—but then, what contemporary economist of any worth has not been affected by them?

This question points up the difficulty of tracing the heritage of the Galbraithian vision. Like many others, he has been conversant with the publications of these economists, but out of his reading and independent thought he has formulated a distinctive picture of the economic process. Some of his critics, however, do not credit him with much originality. For example, one student of his books writes, "There can be no doubt that Hansen was a prophet of affluence before Galbraith and that in some respects he made out a better case. But he did not elaborate to the extent that Galbraith did, and of course his rhetoric was not as startling."[13]

The close reader of Galbraith's books can discern many elements and even phrases that suggest the work of his predecessors, both of those whose ideas he seems to have found congenial and of those he found wanting. If we wish to engage in that sort of exploration, I would call attention especially to Tawney's *The Acquisitive Society* and A. R. Burns's *The Decline of Competition* for their relevance to some of the themes of *The New Industrial State*. But, for that matter, one might in justice mention as well Edward Bellamy's novel, *Looking Backward!* The point is that so many of the ideas in question have been in the public domain for so long that it is fairly fruitless, except for very academic purposes, to pursue this sort of investigation. The professionals know the intellectual history of these themes

[12] E. S. Mason, "Price and Production Policies of Large-Scale Enterprise," *American Economic Review, Proceedings,* March 1939, pp. 64–65.

[13] A. M. Sievers, *Revolution, Evolution, and the Economic Order* (Englewood Cliffs, N.J.: Prentice-Hall, 1962), p. 120.

and are very capable of tracing their different forms and nuances. As for acknowledgment of intellectual debts, that is mainly a matter of Galbraith's conscience; at last reports, he had not taken to sackcloth and ashes.

Let us return to our central concern in this subject. Is Galbraith's image of the modern economy wholly a matter of rhetorical differentiation of product? Is there nothing different and distinctive, in a substantive sense, in his work? In the following section we consider some of the distinguishing features of his economic vision in its various manifestations and compare them briefly with conceptions formulated, for their times and in their own inimitable styles, by Veblen, Schumpeter, and Keynes.

THE EVOLVING GALBRAITHIAN VISION

In Chapter 2 it was made clear that the central conception of *American Capitalism* was the idea of countervailing power. We have noted too how the historical context of that book gave it a somewhat backward or retrospective orientation toward the accomplishments and philosophy of the New Deal. Yet, in formulating that particular concept, Galbraith was trying to overcome some of the limitations and deficiencies, as he saw them, of conventional microeconomic theory. He was also interested, it seems, in offering a new perspective on the antitrust laws in the light of his preferred "partial model." In a sense, he was seeking, shall we say, to salvage something out of what appeared to him to be an increasingly obsolete and ineffective public policy.

From this viewpoint, it can be maintained that there is a kinship between the ideas of *American Capitalism* and those later traced out in *The Affluent Society* and in *The New Industrial State*. In the first and third of these books especially, Galbraith was analyzing the economic process in terms of dynamic adaptation rather than as a state of static optimization. One of those who has perceptively noted the significance of Galbraith's work in this regard is Professor Almarin Phillips of the University of Pennsylvania. In an important recent essay, he explains that conventional economic analysis stresses the causal relationship between an industry's structure and conduct and its performance, but tends to ignore the "feedback" between the latter and the former categories.[14] He points out that when Galbraith introduced the notion of countervailing power, one response was to dismiss it as simply a verbal statement of the static theory of bilateral monopoly. But, he adds, "it is not that at all." What Galbraith has observed is that, when some groups in society—farmers and workers, for instance—find their rewards low relative to those perceived to flow from alternative behavioral arrangements, the low achievements cause them to search for new means to institute new modes of conduct, or to search for new organizational forms. The end of the process may be bilateral monopoly, but the process itself is a feedback from market performance to either conduct or structure. Galbraith, it seems, claimed too much concerning the social value of the process, but he was describing a system of dynamic adaptive response that was not a part of the then current body of static theory."[15]

Galbraith returned to his concern with the adaptive behavior of organized economic groups in *The Affluent Society* and in *The New Industrial State*. In the former essay, however, the emphasis was more on the cultural and ideological factors underlying social imbalance. The book had a topical character in that it partly reflected the economic state of the nation in the late 1950s. After this preface or "window," as he termed it, Galbraith delineated more fully the economic and social impact of the mature corporation in *The New Industrial State*. It is instructive to note what Galbraith emphasized as the dominant motif of these books in his retrospective remarks to his fellow economists, members of the American Economic Association, in December 1969. He did not stress social imbalance or the convergence thesis, but rather "the surrender of the sovereignty of the individual to the producer or producing organization," as the theme, explicit or implicit, of those two essays.[16] This, then, is the mature vision of the economic process that Galbraith advances—in a significant part of the economy, the ultimate accommodation by the consuming public and by Congress is to the producers, the armed services, and their supplying firms.

---

[14] A. Phillips, "Structure, Conduct and Performance—Performance, Conduct, and Structure?", in J. W. Markham and G. F. Papanek, *Industrial Organization and Economic Development, In Honor of E. S. Mason* (Boston: Houghton Mifflin, 1970), pp. 26–37.

[15] *Ibid.,* p. 32.

[16] J. K. Galbraith, "Economics as a System of Belief," *American Economic Review,* May 1970, p. 471, footnote 8.

As Galbraith insists, this vision of the economic process does differ from the conception that Thorstein Veblen developed. That dour outsider saw the conflict between industry and business with the latter tending to sabotage and suppress the productive potential of machine industry. Galbraith, writing at a much later stage in our industrial development, sees the technostructure in command of the large corporations, with the owners in a distinctly secondary role. Both, however, emphasize the technological imperatives that powerfully shape social behavior and propel us toward a planned economy.

In the past Galbraith has drawn upon some elements of Schumpeterian economics, but his conception of economic reality and of the future differs substantially from that of his conservative late colleague. Schumpeter was the philosopher of entrepreneurial capitalism, but he believed that the development of large-scale, bureaucratized enterprise was likely to bring about the obsolescence of the entrepreneurial function.[17] In analyzing innovation, he clearly saw that producers often initiate economic change and educate consumers to want new products. But he did not elaborate on this aspect of demand management and incorporate it into the dynamics of corporate planning, after the fashion of Galbraith. Further, he foresaw the decay of individualistic capitalistic civilization as the modern corporation socialized the bourgeois mind.

John Maynard Keynes's vision was that of economic stagnation brought about by the excess of capitalist saving in the face of declining investment opportunities. Though he first advanced this conception in his prophetic *Economic Consequences of the Peace* (1920), he did not implement it analytically until the circumstances of the world crisis in the 1930s led him to compose *The General Theory*. In some of his essays Keynes did anticipate a time when Western man would enjoy an age of leisure and abundance, but he apparently placed that development considerably farther in the future than did Galbraith. Like the latter, however, Keynes realized that the advent of such an age would entail major changes in social values. By way of comparison with Galbraith's remarks about the pursuit of self-realization by the New Class and his insistence on the need for aesthetic standards to replace or subordinate the pecuniary, consider

[17] The work that presents Schumpeter's views on these subjects is *Capitalism, Socialism and Democracy* (rev. ed. New York: Harper and Row, 1947).

the following remarkable passage from Keynes's *Essays in Persuasion:*

> When the accumulation of wealth is no longer of high social importance, there will be great changes in the code of morals. We shall be able to rid ourselves of many of the pseudo-moral principles which have hag-ridden us for two hundred years, by which we have exalted some of the most distasteful of human qualities into the position of the highest virtues. We shall be able to dare to assess the money-motive at its true value. The love of money as a possession—as distinguished from the love of money as a means to the enjoyments and realities of life—will be recognized for what it is, a somewhat disgusting morbidity, one of those semi-criminal, semi-pathological propensities which one hands over with a shudder to the specialists in mental disease.[18]

It is rather fashionable these days for some people, especially politicians, to proclaim their conversion to Keynesianism. But when we ponder the above quotation, we realize how far they still have to go to catch up with Keynes, let alone Galbraith.

It is evident that in challenging the conventional and accepted ideologies and offering his own vision of the economic process and where it is taking us, Galbraith is writing in the tradition of the "big thinkers." Yet, as Professor Solow has pointed out, "economists are determined little thinkers. . . ." They are engaged usually in making analyses and predictions of specific economic changes flowing from tax developments, wage increases, or the like. Solow goes on:

> . . . They are not likely to be much helped or hindered in these activities by Professor Galbraith's view of Whither We are Trending.
>
> Professor Galbraith makes an eloquent case for big-thinking, and he has a point. Little-thinking can easily degenerate into mini-thinking or even into hardly thinking at all. Even if it does not, too single-minded a focus on how the parts of the machine work may lead to a careful failure ever to ask whether the machine is pointed in the right direction. . . .[19]

In asking the big questions, Galbraith's work reminds us very much of the point of view that animated C. Wright Mills's *The Sociological Imagination.*[20] Mills, like Gal-

---

[18] New York: Harcourt Brace Jovanovich, Inc., 1932, p. 369.
[19] R. M. Solow, "The New Industrial State or Son of Affluence," *The Public Interest,* Fall 1967, p. 100.
[20] New York: Oxford University Press, 1959.

braith, was tired of what he called "abstracted empiricism" (i.e., minute studies, out of context, of trivialities) and pleaded for a liberation of the imagination of social scientists that would lead them to concern themselves with urgent public issues. "All social scientists," he wrote, "by the fact of their existence are involved in the struggle between enlightenment and obscurantism."

Similarly, Galbraith, in an unusually forthright speech to his fellow economists of the American Economic Association, urged them to repudiate the established doctrine of consumer sovereignty and to address themselves to the urgent and politically disturbing questions which are obscured from their professional vision by the neoclassical model of the economic process. In the past, he argues, economics has often served not as a science but as a supporting belief system that excluded ideas hostile or unsettling to the discipline or to an influential economic or political community. In a scolding and almost strident tone, he asks whether the discipline, "after years of comfortable coexistence with industrial and associated public bureaucracy," can make producer sovereignty a central preoccupation. It has a choice—it can remain with consumer sovereignty and be "comfortable, non-controversial, increasingly sophisticated in its models and increasingly, and perhaps even dramatically, unrelated to life." Or it can accept the implications of producer power and then it will be "contentious, politically perilous and for a long while, perhaps, intellectually inelegant in its models." But in compensation, it will be relevant to the most pressing concerns of the industrial society.

Answering his own rhetorical question, Galbraith says, "I have little doubt as to the choice. Among my generation it will be, in principle, for comfort and its associated refinements. We have had one revolution: Keynes was enough. . . . I say this will be choice in principle for it will not be so in fact. . . ." His ideas, he concludes, divorced from the circumstances of the existing great private and public organizations, would be nothing; but "reinforced by such circumstances they are ineluctable."[21]

Is Galbraith alone in holding this vision of the power of the great organizations in managing demand and adapting other institutions to their requirements? It would seem not. One of those who saw contemporary social reality in some

    [21] J. K. Galbraith, "Economics as a System of Belief," *American Economic Review*, May 1970, p. 478.

respects, though not all, as did Galbraith was the late C. W. Mills. He believed that all advanced industrial societies, capitalist or noncapitalist, are subject to many of the same dynamic forces. In his view, modern society is especially influenced by the process of rationalization; this is an instrumental approach to social organization which stresses technocratic efficiency, bureaucratic rule and standardization, and promotion on a meritocratic basis. Rationalization as it expresses itself in these forms is not the same thing as ordinary rationality. In the field of economics, Mills saw a process of increasing economic concentration and bureaucracy. In the military field, he described the rise of the modern military machine—"vast, bureaucratized, armed with the weapons of mass destruction." In politics, he pointed to governmental bureaucracy and the mass media as the modern means of manipulating people. According to Mills, this process of rationalization has only been resisted in society as a whole, at least in the capitalistic countries.[22]

Among economists, there are several who have essayed the formulation of a theory of managerial enterprise, but few, if any, who have sought to relate the large-scale corporation to other institutions with the boldness and imagination of Galbraith. One calls to mind the work of Oswald Knauth, R. M. Cyert and J. G. March, and Robin Marris. All these economists point to the need for a new theory of the firm and develop versions of the same,[23] but their ideas do not coincide exactly with Galbraith's. Perhaps the closest confirmation of the Galbraithian vision of the economy is found in the work of a young economist whose volume appeared a year after *The New Industrial State*. I refer to Professor Robert T. Averitt's *The Dual Economy: The Dynamics of American Industry Structure*.[24] This author treats the economy as composed of center and periphery firms, a distinction which corresponds closely with Galbraith's between the mature and the entrepreneurial corporation. He too describes the planning of the large corporation, its technological imperatives, and its close dependence on government. The similarity of his point of view to Gal-

[22] E. V. Schneider, "The Sociology of C. Wright Mills," in *C. Wright Mills and the Power Elite*, compiled by G. W. Domhof and H. B. Ballard (Boston: Beacon Press, 1958), pp. 15–16.

[23] O. Knauth, *Managerial Enterprise, Its Growth and Methods of Operation* (New York: W. W. Norton, 1948); R. M. Cyert and J. G. March, *A Behavioral Theory of the Firm* (Englewood Cliffs, N.J.: Prentice-Hall, 1963); R. Marris, *The Economic Theory of Managerial Capitalism* (New York: The Free Press, 1964).

[24] New York: W. W. Norton, 1968.

braith's on many subjects, though not on all, is striking and significant.

Galbraith is by no means alone in believing that the concept of consumer sovereignty needs to be replaced. In an influential essay written in 1958, Dean Edward S. Mason of Harvard remarked that "it becomes more and more difficult to prop up the wasting concept of consumer sovereignty." He added that "though this monarch is obviously on the way out, his successor is still to be found."[25] In writing *The New Industrial State,* Galbraith certainly had Mason's view in mind. He believes that he has found the heir apparent to the throne of consumer sovereignty; producer sovereignty, he vigorously contends, is a concept with a future.

THE AESTHETIC CRITERION
AND THE FUTURE

In *The New Industrial State,* it will be recalled, Galbraith briefly considers the relationship between the industrial system and aesthetic experience. Under the former, he says, art and beauty tend to be a neglected dimension of life because of a conflict of goals: what is aesthetically desirable usually runs counter to what is profitable and efficient, so, at best, aesthetic considerations are regarded as a constraint on profit-making. Further, aesthetic achievement, he asserts, is beyond the reach of the industrial system and of the technostructure that manages it.

A still more fundamental conflict derives from the fact that the industrial system depends on organization, but "artists do not come in teams." In any case, in the future the cultivation of the aesthetic dimension will necessitate a new and vital role for the state. Where industrial and aesthetic priorities clash, the state will have to favor the latter, but Galbraith thinks the technostructure will be handicapped in participating in such decisions by its inherent nature.

Generally, aesthetic goals can only be achieved at a cost to industrial expansion. But our accommodation to the needs of the industrial system is so profound that we hesitate to sacrifice an increase in gross national product for beauty.

[25] E. S. Mason, "The Apologetics of Managerialism," *Journal of Business of the University of Chicago,* January 1958, pp. 1–11.

Galbraith admits that while painting, sculpture, and music are outside the ambit of the industrial system, they do "reasonably well" on the patronage that it provides. But architecture and environmental design are another matter; they lie more within the jurisdiction of the state. In the future, the state will do more in behalf of the aesthetic dimension than it has in the past; such action will be regarded as "a high public responsibility." Galbraith adds, "It is worth hoping that the educational and scientific estate, as it grows in power, will encourage and enforce more exacting standards. . . ." He closes on the note that in the future the progressive community will apply the test of aesthetic achievement rather than that of production.

As we have seen, Galbraith has been ridiculed for daring to introduce aesthetic considerations into the practical, rational, hardheaded realm of economics. Professor Gordon laments that Galbraith's writing recalls "the bitter plaints of the Victorian romantics—Carlyle, Dickens, Ruskin and others—who looked upon the youthful face of industrialism and found it a monstrous evil. . . . A century ago Ruskin admonished, 'There is no wealth but life,' and Galbraith echoes, 'What counts is not the quantity of goods but the quality of life.' "

"It is a great and lyrical theme," says Gordon sarcastically, "one of the most emotive in romantic literature," but Galbraith's argument is "essentially wrongheaded." It is just conventional wisdom to believe that there is "an inherent conflict between the satisfaction of material wants and the needs of the cultivated spirit." Gordon continues:

> Material welfare and the "higher" humanism are complementary, not competing, things. The civilized sensibilities flourish where there is economic plenty; and the more the better, even when it is devoted in part to automobiles and television sets. The common man is not a noble primitive who has been spiritually pauperized and morally enslaved by material progress; he has in fact been freed and elevated by it. There is much more distance to go along this road, even in the "affluent society" of the United States.[26]

In his reply to this line of criticism Galbraith restricted himself to demonstrating the semantic devices that Gordon uses to damn him—use of loaded expressions, such as referring to his books as being in the realm of "contemporary popular culture." Galbraith complains too that he is

[26] S. Gordon, "The Close of the Galbraithian System," *Journal of Political Economy,* July/August, 1968, pp. 635–644.

made guilty by association with "Victorian romantics," flirting with "progressive ideas," and sympathizing with "the superior values of those youthful aesthetic ascetics who flock to the asphalt Waldens of Haight-Ashbury and Washington Square."

This type of rejoinder is good polemic, but it does not deal with the substance of Gordon's criticism. The latter's contention, for example, that there is no conflict between material welfare and humanism, is simply an abstract proposition that does not take account of the psychological compulsions and repressions that are commonly involved in the single-minded pursuit of material success. Long before Freud, Tocqueville wrote, "A man who raises himself by degrees to wealth and power, contracts in the course of this protracted labor, habits of prudence and restraint which he cannot afterward shake off. A man cannot enlarge his mind as he would his house. . . ."[27] If we wished, other commentators on American character and culture, such as David Riesman or Charles A. Reich, could be cited as showing the limitations and inhibitions which the pursuit of wealth in America has imposed on the appreciation and capacity for enjoying beauty and nature.[28]

From his brief remarks on aesthetics, one gains the impression that Galbraith regards the artistic dimension as providing a criterion of order for society. "Art," he states, "is one manifestation of order." Apparently, he sees the aesthetic principle providing us with a standard to bring harmony and beauty out of the unbalanced wasteland of private affluence. One wishes that he had stressed equally the role of art in helping man to transcend the familiar and the conventional.[29] Art is, above all, a form of play. In a cul-

---

[27] A. de Tocqueville, *Democracy in America* (Commager Edition, New York: Oxford University Press, 1947), p. 426.

[28] D. Riesman, R. Denney, and N. Glazer, *The Lonely Crowd* (New Haven: Yale University Press, 1950); C. A. Reich, *The Greening of America* (New York: Random House, 1970).

[29] On this, see E. Becker, *The Revolution in Psychiatry* (Glencoe, Ill.: The Free Press, 1964). Becker writes: "Conviction integrates our world by sealing us into the mold of the familiar. He [the creative artist] creates an aesthetic product that fuses the private and the public, the subject and the object, the symbolic and the material—but it does not imprison. On the contrary, it liberates us somewhat. It makes us secure in our present meanings, and also reveals a sliver of new possibilities. It shows the object all wrapped up in its appropriate rules, but it shows an object that is a little different than we expected to see . . ." (p. 238). Becker quotes John Dewey as saying that "the Aesthetic object shows that the perfect

ture still partially in the grip of the Puritan ethic with its emphasis on work and action, Galbraith might well have quoted Schiller in his *Letters on the Aesthetic Education of Man:* "Man only plays when in the full meaning of the word he is man, and he is only completely a man when he plays."[30]

Galbraith casts his analysis of aesthetics and economics more or less in sociological terms; he treats the incompatibilities between the social structure of industrialism and the individualism of the artist. In doing this, he perhaps slights the psychological potentialities of the technostructure in incorporating aesthetic considerations in its planning. A close observer of the American scene, Professor Walter Weisskopf of Roosevelt University, is more optimistic than Galbraith on this subject: "The affluent society has brought about, to a certain degree, an abandonment of purely economic goals and a certain satiation with consumers' goods. This manifests itself also in the increasing interest in the performing and the creative arts. All this is still in its infancy and not clearly understood in the Western countries; but the turning towards non-economic goals in private business administration and in public agencies, is already visible. . . ."[31] Weisskopf insists, however, that a fundamental reversal of values and the emergence of a world outlook are a necessary precondition for the further development of these tendencies. This is a subject that we shall consider further in the following section.

THE STRENGTH AND WEAKNESS OF GALBRAITH'S SOCIAL THEORY

At this point in our consideration of Galbraith's work, it will pay us to examine the architectural structure

---

union of ends and means is possible, and it does this by containing within itself the perfect matching of ends and means. Thereby, it embodies, in one moment for all to see, the vision that fulfillment is possible" (p. 233).

[30] Quoted by Norman O. Brown in his *Life against Death,* Wesleyan University Press, 1959, p. 33.

[31] W. A. Weisskopf, "Repression and the Dialectics of Industrial Civilization," *Review of Social Economy,* September 1965, p. 126; see also H. Taubman, "Rise in Business Aid to the Arts," *The New York Times,* February 10, 1971, p. 34.

of the edifice he has constructed. Galbraith begins *The New Industrial State* with an institutional economic analysis of the mature corporation and of the industrial system, and then extends his treatment to the even more complex relations of the latter to labor unions, the state, the educational and scientific estate, and the political future. In other words, he moves from the narrow sphere of industrial organization and economics to the broader and more unpredictable realm of social change and of political and social theory. Now, Galbraith, we have observed, is not the soul of modesty and caution; on the contrary, he inclines and prefers to be bold and challenging. Therefore, when he warns us that he is less certain of his diagnosis and prognosis, it is wise to take notice. Toward the end of Chapter 28 of *The New Industrial State* he tells the reader that he undertakes his analysis of the "more distant horizons" of the Cold War, of the planning lacunae, and of the future of the industrial system in "a much less definitive mood" than in the previous chapters. He frankly reiterates that he is "less interested in telling where the industrial system is going than in providing the materials for consideration of where it has arrived."

In appraising *The New Industrial State*, we must keep in mind that it was not offered by Galbraith as a technical contribution to the professional literature of industrial organization. It was written for a wider readership than economists would provide, yet it contains some features which make it superior to many academic treatments. To be specific, Galbraith's anatomy of the mature corporation goes beyond the theoretical framework of the microeconomics of the Chamberlin-Robinson tradition. The latter approach incorporated product differentiation (product innovation and advertising) and oligopoly into the static analysis inherited from neoclassic economics. In the 1930s this new economics was heralded as giving us a theory of the firm, but as Averitt and others have pointed out, it was in fact only "a theory of the product."[32] This theory did not describe the activities of the firm falling outside the market under analysis. It recognized the reduction in the number of firms that had taken place in many of our in-

[32] R. T. Averitt, *The Dual Economy, op. cit.,* p. 84. In 1948 Galbraith himself stated that "the analytical task would appear to have failed because oligopoly . . . has not yielded to the kit of tools long employed for analysis of the competitive market. . . ." H. S. Ellis (Ed.), *A Survey of Contemporary Economics* (Philadelphia: Blakiston, 1948), p. 127.

dustries in the twentieth century, but it took no account of the concomitant changes in the organizational structure of the large-scale firm (i.e., its increasingly bureaucratic character) or of its employment of "planning" and other techniques to cope with market uncertainties. For a popular presentation, Galbraith's theory of the firm has a realism and plausibility that is lacking in many textbooks.

From an overall perspective, the strength of Galbraith's vision of the economic process lies in the central place which it gives to the dynamic role of the large corporation and of the industrial system generally in the unrestrained technological evolution of Western society. Other economists have proposed adaptive theories of the firm, but few have related the larger dynamics of the industrial system to the rest of American society as vividly and lucidly as he. He describes a corporate system which strenuously seeks autonomy for its aims and activities, but which in its very thrust toward domination and control of its social environment threatens the independence of our other cherished institutions. In his view we have a society that prides itself on an ideology of separation of powers and the maintenance of pluralism and individual variety, yet that "master institution," the mature corporation and its associated powers, perversely and insidiously endangers the very foundations of freedom and of a viable "ecosystem."

It is a powerful functional analysis of what sociologists would term institutional dominance, but it embodies a serious misconception. In his insistence on the deterministic influence of the technological and organizational imperatives, Galbraith slights the influence of the deeper historical sociocultural forces that shape American life. It is true that in *The Affluent Society* he emphasized the ideological elements in our culture that underlie the vested interest in production and employment. In *The New Industrial State* he shows how sales growth and technological virtuosity serve the needs of the technostructure, but, aside from mention of social emulation, he does not relate the frenetic status-striving of the corporate elite to the nation's social class structure and to its basic value system. In other words, the success and achievement orientation of American culture is not causally related to the behavior of the technostructure.

Within the mature corporation, especially within the inner circle of the technostructure, Galbraith asserts that identification and adaptation become "increasingly plausible motivations"; they have a "clear run." Now, as an alternative to simple profit maximization, Galbraith's motivational analysis has considerable merit, but it is to be noted that his picture of organizational life in the big organizations leaves out the tensions, the conflicts, and the ambivalence which other students of the subject have described.[33]

In his portrait of the American worker Galbraith stresses identification, loyalty to the employer, and satisfaction with pecuniary compensation. In concentrating on the union as an institution and its relationship to the industrial system, he recognizes little of the alienation and cynicism among some groups of workers that others have noted.[34] Here, too, analysis of the values and attitudes of American workers in the context of a fast-changing culture might have produced different conclusions.

Essentially, the criticism we are making is that Galbraith's institutional analysis does not do justice to the cultural context in which the mature corporations and the industrial system operate. GNP fetishism and the pursuit of private affluence cannot be wholly attributed to the techno-structure's vested interest in production and growth and Madison Avenue's demonic skill in persuasion. The fact is, given the success and status orientation of our culture, most of the avid consumers of durable goods are already "sold" on the indispensability of such products for the good life even before the advertisers exert their promotional efforts. In a culture apparently lacking in other satisfactory means of establishing self-esteem, there are strong pressures for Americans to buy status symbols and thus establish their pecuniary repute. As Elton Mayo, in referring to R. H. Tawney's *The Acquisitive Society,* once wrote, it is not so much the sickness of an acquisitive society, but the acquisitiveness of a sick society.[35]

Galbraith's relative neglect of the element of culture in his analysis is illustrated in his discussion of the goals of the industrial system. In the course of his treatment, he makes the surprising statement that "the acceptance of economic growth as a social goal coincides closely with the rise to power of the mature corporation and the technostruc-

[33] See, e.g., R. Presthus, *The Organizational Society* (New York: A. A. Knopf, 1962), Chapters 8–10. Galbraith may have omitted this subject deliberately, believing that it had been covered adequately by other writers.

[34] See E. Chinoy, *Automobile Workers and the American Dream* (Garden City, N.Y.: Doubleday, 1955).

[35] E. Mayo, *The Human Problems of an Industrial Civilization* (New York: Macmillan, 1933), p. 153.

ture."[36] Perhaps I am misinterpreting what Galbraith means by "acceptance of economic growth *as a social goal*," but I find it hard to reconcile the general import of the sentence with my understanding of American history. From the days of Alexander Hamilton to those of Andrew Carnegie and Henry Ford I, there would seem to have been wide acceptance of the desirability of material progress for the nation. From Comte to Herbert Spencer, progress was not only an ideal to many nineteenth-century Europeans, it became almost a scientific law. Americans as a "people of plenty," to use David Potter's expression, were the most progress-intoxicated of all. The relative abundance of our economic environment contributed to optimism and the faith in progress. In this sense, "growthmanship" is a relatively old characteristic of the American way of life that much precedes the advent of the mature corporation.

Galbraith's concern with growth as a monopolizing, obsessive goal in American life needs to be explored from the perspective of a longer historical study of our culture. Gibson Winter offers a provocative hypothesis for such an inquiry. He suggests that the technological will to control emerged from our Puritan heritage and, as the obedient will under God, became a commitment to unlimited growth and exploitation.[37] But this is a much too complex subject to discuss further here.

THE ROLE OF THE EDUCATIONAL
AND SCIENTIFIC ESTATE

The nature of a social analysis influences what is regarded as an appropriate policy or remedy for a given situation. Thus a study which stresses institutional factors as opposed to cultural values is likely to result in a different prescription for solving society's ills. To illustrate, in *The Affluent Society* Galbraith urged the expanded use of the sales tax to redress social imbalance at the local level of government. This was a proposal for institutional change. Its implementation, however, depended on whether political power and the values and attitudes of people could be modified so as to make the suggestion feasible.

[36] *The New Industrial State*, p. 174.
[37] G. Winter, *Being Free, Reflections on America's Cultural Revolution* (New York: Macmillan, 1970), p. 124.

Similarly, by way of proposing a solution to the domination of American society by the industrial system, Galbraith in *The New Industrial State* calls on the educational and scientific estate to challenge the existing technostructure and assume responsibility for political action and leadership. Several critics have expressed their skepticism about the salvation to be found in this direction. Thus M. W. Watkins writes of his disappointment: "After such a masterful analysis of the untoward trend of things and of the stupendous risks involved in the management of the modern industrial system by a near-sighted, nose-grinding technostructure, one feels rather let down to find at the end no more than a euphemistic wish for the wakening of the somnolent intellectuals. . . ."[38] Watkins recalls that Veblen too looked for a reformation of the ills of the industrial system of his day by a revolution of the engineers; instead we got Herbert Hoover as President.

Kenneth E. Boulding, otherwise very sympathetic to Galbraith's social philosophy, complains that his reliance on the educational and scientific estate derives from his deficient social theory. According to Boulding, the educational and scientific estate is to a very large extent part of the technostructure; it is, therefore, futile to place much hope for reform in it. Boulding thinks that Galbraith does not properly understand the dynamics of what he (Boulding) calls the "integrative system"—that aspect of society which provides a basis of community and of love and trust among human beings. He believes that it is "the church rather than the universities which is the principal countervailing power, feeble as it may be, to the appalling potency of the merciless state and its corporate and labor allies. . . ."[39] Incidentally, Watkins also was puzzled by Galbraith's exclusion of the clergy from his educational and scientific estate. All that this suggests, to go no deeper, is that economists differ on the nature of our redeemer.

Another reviewer of Galbraith's work, in writing of his invocation of the scientific and educational estate, says simply that he wants "an elite to catch an elite." From our previous discussion it should be evident that Galbraith does not regard his fellow economists, for the most part, as the elite that is going to save us. Nevertheless, it is interesting in this connection to examine the reaction of the nation's

[38] M. W. Watkins, *The Antitrust Bulletin,* Spring 1968, p. 281.
[39] K. E. Boulding, "The Scientific-Military-Industrial Complex," *The Virginia Quarterly Review,* Autumn 1967, p. 677.

economists to *The Affluent Society,* as reported by public opinion pollster Elmo Roper in 1959.[40] This revealing study was based on a questionnaire sent to every fiftieth member of the American Economic Association as well as to a list of unattached prominent economists. It asked their reactions to twelve of Galbraith's theses.

A second group of businessmen-trustees were also questioned as to their opinions about social imbalance and other topics. These men were described by Roper as presiding over the corporations that produce the nation's "private goods" as well as serving as trustees over private colleges, universities, and foundations. Roper indicated his own conception of where power lies in American society by stating that if there is to be any alteration in the relative balance between private goods and public services during the next ten years (after 1959), "the opinions and attitudes of these men will, in large measure, determine its nature."

Perhaps to Galbraith's surprise, his fellow economists, by a hair's breadth, voted him more agreement than disagreement on his general point of view (41 percent to 38 percent). The businessmen-trustees (including, presumably, some of the nation's finest specimens of the technostructure) overwhelmingly disagreed with him. To Roper the central thesis of *The Affluent Society* was the contention that "our preoccupation with high production also promotes a continuing social imbalance in American life." On this proposition a bare majority of the economists "tended to agree" (52 percent), while only 13 percent of the businessmen-trustees did so. A heavy majority of the latter saw no social imbalance and opposed any action enlarging the sphere of government's influence.

While the general tone of the discussion of Galbraith's economics in this survey was moderate (most agreed with him on ends, but found reason to dispute his means), some violently denounced him, saying, for example, "This man would be welcome in the Kremlin." A few others indignantly consigned him and his books to "a region not nearly as cold as Moscow." Because the details of this survey may have some historic interest as showing the state of business and expert economic opinion in 1959 on what has now come to be called the nation's urban crisis, we have reproduced the breakdown of answers in the Appendix. While this study cannot be regarded as a scientific sample of the

[40] E. Roper, "Whose Affluent Society?", *Saturday Review,* June 6, 1959, p. 39.

Galbraithian technostructure, it is not altogether reassuring with respect to the foresight and economic understanding shown by the businessmen-trustees questioned by Roper. As for the economists, although Galbraith was undoubtedly grateful for the degree to which they shared his views, he was still very critical of them when he wrote *The New Industrial State,* several years after the Roper sampling. In that book he stated very unequivocally that economists are not "the best proponents of the public, aesthetic and intellectual priorities on which the quality and safety of life increasingly depend. They are, in the main, the natural allies of the industrial system."[41]

GALBRAITH AND AMERICA'S
CRISIS OF VALUES

In the last decade Galbraith's ideas about the need for social balance and concern for the quality of life have had wide resonance in the United States and abroad. Regardless of what one may think about the logical validity of the reasoning underlying these themes, their relevance to the search for new values has become increasingly manifest. It is clear too that the turbulence that we have seen in the nation in these years represents a fundamental questioning of the value system of American society.[42] The black protest against racism in all its forms, the student rebellion in the universities, the anguished outcry over Vietnam, and the agitation over environmental pollution reflect this deep disagreement with conventional values. In such a time, an economics such as Galbraith's that concerns itself with social priorities, that raises questions that are beyond the reach of the "hard" version of the discipline, has very wide appeal and interest.

When *The Affluent Society* was published there were those such as Robert Lekachman who thought that it might serve as "a catalyst of discontent." More recently, Irving Kristol has noted the attraction that *The New Industrial State* would have for those interested in social change and reform. Of course, it is difficult to judge the social repercussions of literary works, but it may be significant that some

[41] *The New Industrial State,* p. 384.
[42] S. L. Udall, "Topics: The Value Revolution," *The New York Times,* June 7, 1969, p. 34.

of the Galbraithian rhetoric has become part of the vocabulary of protest in the intervening years.

In noting the relevance of Galbraith's work to the contemporary questioning of the organizational society and its correlate, the gospel of growth, we do not wish to imply that he has presented a social analysis that satisfies all or that he has provided the means for the emancipation of which he writes. As he has stated, his interest was more in telling where the industrial system had arrived. His function has been one of describing the actual or potential domination of man by that system rather than showing how it may be transcended or reformed. He concentrates on what for some is obvious—the manipulation and management of the consumer by the technoculture and the use of the productive machine for destruction and waste. As a liberal, he seems to envision a rational reordering of values and priorities to restore social balance and sanity. He offers a standard of transcendence in terms of emphasizing the aesthetic criterion in life, but he fails to stress the need for a new type of man, a new consciousness that would make such a standard operative and practicable.

When *The New Industrial State* appeared, someone sneered that "it takes a Harvard man to transcend the industrial system." Harvard man or not, Galbraith has perhaps done more to subvert that system by the laughter he has generated at its expense than by his advocacy of beauty as transcendence. If we look at what he suggests will provide the lead in emancipation from the industrial system, we find that he underscores the role of the scientists, humane scholars, teachers, and artists and the community in pressing the issue of the quality of life. There is no mention of youth's role, though he does mention elsewhere that "the young have a reassuring tendency to take a fresh view of life." In another place, he speculates whether youth rebellion is "the natural line of dissent in a society in which the previous lines of conflict [e.g., labor versus capital] have been subsumed." He promises to take this topic up later with other questions, but so far as I can determine, it was never pursued.

In his chapter on education and emancipation in *The New Industrial State,* Galbraith again looks to the mature members of the educational and scientific estate to take the political lead in countervailing the technostructure. In contrast, Charles A. Reich in his *The Greening of America* holds that the new generation is most capable of negating the technosociety. It can break with the hypertrophy of the rational will to make and control, and gain a new capacity for feeling and sensibility, for participation and community because, as Gibson Winter expresses it, it has not yet buried its consciousness in careerism.

In interpreting the nature of the youth rebellion, Reich insists that the revolution must be cultural. "For culture controls the economic and political machine, not vice versa." Power, he says, rests on the control of consciousness. "If the people are freed from false consciousness, no power exists that could prevent them from taking the controls."[43]

In commenting on Reich's book, it is revealing to note that Galbraith states that "the answer [i.e., Reich's] is not to tame and rationalize the bureaucratic purpose but to emancipate ourselves from its compulsions—its standards of achievement, its persuasion and its consumption standards." Galbraith further remarks that he thinks Reich is making a most important point. ". . . I am greatly impressed by his central idea which is that we can reduce the power of his corporate state (I used the milder phrase, industrial system) only by making it less important in our lives. . . ."[44] He then expresses his major reservations about Reich's analysis and prescription. One point is clear from all this— Galbraith admits that characterological change as well as institutional reform is necessary if we are to escape from thralldom to the values of the industrial system.

In the past in the books under review, Galbraith has advocated institutional change much more than psychological transformation. In *American Capitalism* he stressed countervailing power (for disadvantaged groups to get a larger share of the national income); in *The Affluent Society* he proposed higher sales taxes to correct social imbalance; and in *The New Industrial State* he looked to the educational and scientific estate to "tame and rationalize the bureaucratic purpose," as he expressed it in the statement quoted above. But more important than the external institutional changes is the subjective attitude toward economic goods and activities. Nor is the size of our GNP itself to be deplored; it is rather the social compulsions and fixations which prevent us from changing its composition. What America needs, one would think, is not economic asceticism, but autonomy (i.e., psychological freedom) where eco-

[43] C. A. Reich, *The Greening of America* (New York: Random House, 1970), pp. 306, 307.

[44] J. K. Galbraith, "Who Minds the Store?", *The New York Times*, October 26, 1970, p. 37.

nomic matters are concerned. We should have the capacity to consume or not to consume, to conform or not to conform, and so on, rather than be subject to the will of the "hidden persuaders" or the pathological norms of the status strivers. Gibson Winter put it well when he said:

. . . But the rational ordering of things in service to man's productive will is no devil—it is a healthy aspect of man's freedom to shape and order his world. It only becomes demonic when it takes possession of man. When man becomes possessed by the producer-consumer syndrome—the productive will—his existence is impoverished, his sensibilities deadened, and his public world becomes an instrument of further control. When all things become means to further domination, whether in free enterprise systems or in collective states, then man loses his soul; and to lose one's soul is to lose nature, other people and finally one's humanity. So it is the goodness and creativity of man's productive will that now possesses and destroys him. It is against this demonic possession that the new generation is rebelling.[45]

THE GALBRAITHIAN POLITICS OF THE FUTURE

Galbraith has not been inclined to engage extensively in philosophical speculations about the fate of man. He is much more the political activist, concerned with the next step in a realistic program of social action. Recently, he outlined his political outlook in a small book entitled *Who Needs the Democrats and What It Takes to be Needed.*[46] In it he humbly admits that for thirty-odd years he has been "a reasonably active Democrat." He has remained in that Party because he still regards it as a potential instrument for effective social and political change. But he thinks that its present troubles go deeper than the alleged dearth of leadership. The Party has lost its main purposes; "it has become a defender of the status quo, a role in which it is incompetent and cannot possibly compete with the Republicans." He finds its present composition "wildly irrational." In his opinion its recent policies have constituted a politics of anachronism, oriented more to solving the problems of the past rather than those of the urgent present and future. Its political style has

[45] G. Winter, *Being Free, op. cit.,* p. 108.
[46] Garden City, N.Y.: Doubleday and Co., 1970. This and the following half-dozen paragraphs rely heavily on this source.

suffered from too close an association and conformity with the bureaucratic truths of the Pentagon and of the foreign policy establishment. Its rhetoric has tended too much toward "hyperbolic overpromising," such as characterized the speeches of Lyndon Johnson and Hubert Humphrey.

In his view, if the Democratic Party is to offer a real alternative to the Republicans, it must become an aggressive urban party; otherwise, promises of racial equality for the blacks and other minorities of our cities are but empty phrases. A strong urban policy must include large bloc grants of money from the federal government to the cities. And the cities themselves must tax their rich and commuters more heavily to pay for the necessary public services.

The other urgently needed services of the city dwellers— for housing and transportation—must be provided by public ownership, not by "an apologetic half-hearted socialism" of rent controls and dreary public projects. He insists that we need to take on these tasks of urban city ownership as proudly and efficiently as the Dutch, Swiss, and other progressive governments in Europe. "The Democratic Party must henceforth use the word socialism. It describes what is needed. If there is assumed to be something illicit or indecent about public ownership, it won't be done well. . . ."[47] He argues too that effective urban and ex-urban land management requires a greatly increased use of public land ownership.

One idea, says Galbraith, is essential to both foreign and domestic policy: power must be retrieved from the swollen bureaucratic organizations. In foreign affairs, power must be redeemed from the defense establishment, the defense industries, and the foreign policy professionals. Domestically, power must be regained from the civil bureaucracy and the giant corporations. One proposal he advances to accomplish the latter is the establishment of a consolidated regulatory body, beyond the control of any single industry, to rescue the existing agencies from private control.

To curb inflation he reiterates his case for an incomes policy, presumably for governmental review of wage and price decisions in those industries where strong unions bargain with strong corporations. (Galbraith has been such a persistent advocate of such an anti-inflationary policy that the current administration's *volte face of* August 15th and its unfolding plans for the post-freeze period led *Business*

---

[47] *Ibid.,* p. 73.

Week to treat these developments under the title, "The newest Nixon looks Galbraithian."[48]

Paraphrasing *The New Industrial State,* Galbraith insists that there must be a rejection of crude production as the goal of our economic system and emphasis instead on what, for whom, and on what terms we produce. To achieve increased economic equality, he espouses income guarantees, more shared work, and a truly progressive taxation of all forms of enrichment. If we are not to have two conservative parties, he contends, radical solutions such as these must be adopted by the Democrats.

These goals will be thought by some to be altogether impractical or Utopian for the Democratic Party. To Galbraith also they are not attainable without drastic political reform of that organization and of the whole seniority system in Congress. A new coalition of black and white progressives, union workers, youth, and other elements of the educational and scientific estate must be forged. The opportunity to marshall such groups behind a winning ticket lies with the Democrats. Americans for Democratic Action, of which Galbraith is a leader, is currently engaged in a nationwide drive to register college youth for the 1972 elections. Galbraith is as aware as others that the sources of power are changing in American society.[49] The vast influx of new, young voters in the seventies, the increasing enfranchisement of blacks and other minorities, and the growing sensitivity and cultural sophistication of substantial sectors of the present electorate would seem to improve the prospect for radical political and economic change in the nation. These forces, as Frederick G. Dutton expresses it in his recent, insightful book, may provide the support for an Opening to the Future.

THE AGE OF THE ECONOMIST

The outcome of the struggle between private affluence and the antimaterialistic ethic is of great interest to all Americans, and especially to businessmen, because the lat-

[48] *Business Week,* September 25, 1971, p. 37.
[49] See F. G. Dutton, *Changing Sources of Power, American Politics in the Seventies* (New York: McGraw-Hill Book Co., 1971), p. 256. See also "Youths Signing Up for '72," *The New York Times,* September 26, 1971, pp. 1, 72.

ter realize that in the present "age of uncertainty" cultural, social, and political forces are affecting the U.S. economy more than they have during most of the post-1945 period. In a recent assessment of the market for consumer goods, Charles E. Silberman points out that if the prophets such as Galbraith and Reich are at all correct, the consumer market will be totally transformed by the end of the decade.[50] In Silberman's view, there would be major shifts in the pattern of expenditures with a resulting lower level of national income, productivity growth, and industrial capacity. Weighing the probabilities for the next decade or so, he concludes that "a large majority are still devoted to work and consumption, but a new hedonism and an anti-materialistic rhetoric (not always translated into actual life style) do seem to be taking hold among a small and influential minority. . . ." It is too soon, he believes, to judge how these divergent tendencies will balance out.

Similarly, in the world of corporate management some observers report that the intense, new junior executives of this generation are making unprecedented demands on the corporations they work for.[51] They want to "reform the world on company time" and they are critical of the profit motive, especially if it conflicts with personal fulfillment and their involvement with community improvement. If this account has any authenticity, the mature corporations are already beginning to experience the effects of the new values and outlook of the oncoming generation.

In any survey of the social malaise that has accompanied affluence, numerous other signs of discontent and criticism of the production ethic and alarm over environmental deterioration could be cited from the newspapers of the last several years. In April 1971, for example, the president of the Rockefeller Foundation, Dr. J. George Harrar, urged a new environmental ethic on the nation that would transcend most of our traditional values.[52] In such a new ethic, population limitation and a redefinition of economic growth would be primary, according to Dr. Harrar. "More attention," said this scientist, "should be devoted to services and to those areas of life that enrich the quality of human existence: cultural activities, the arts, literature, intellectual

[50] C. E. Silberman, "Identity Crisis in the Consumer Markets," *Fortune,* March 1971, pp. 92 ff.
[51] J. Gooding, "The Accelerated Generation Moves into Management," *Fortune,* March 1971, pp. 101 ff.
[52] "Ecological Ethic Urged on Nation," *The New York Times,* April 12, 1970, p. 40.

and scientific pursuits, aesthetic improvements, and human relationships."

In appraising the prospects of our industrial civilization, some scientists have become very pessimistic indeed. Here is Dr. Bentley Glass in his presidential address to the Association for the Advancement of Science, on December 29, 1970: ". . . Let me suggest, at the risk of grave misunderstanding, that in the future histories of the world the decade of the 1960's may be known not significantly for the miserable Vietnam War but as the time when man, with unbridled lust for power over nature and for a so-called high standard of living measured by the products of an industrial civilization, set in motion the final, speedy, inexorable rush toward the end of progress."[53]

Concern about the human and social costs of economic growth and even advocacy of "zero growth" (recalling the classical economists' concept of a stationary economy) have been heard in the land in recent years. There has been no end of heresies. The President of the United States himself has been drawn into the debate. *Time* magazine in 1970 noted that the President's State of the Union message contained "remarkable echoes of ideas in John Kenneth Galbraith's *The Affluent Society.*" The President stated, "The argument is often made that there is a fundamental contradiction between economic growth and the quality of life, so that to have one we must foresake the other. The answer is not to abandon growth, but to redirect it." Apparently, the President too could not resist the rhetorical appeal of the Galbraithian phrases, for he closed by saying, "The time has come for a new quest not for a greater quantity of what we have but for a new quality of life in America."[54]

Our era has been called "the age of the economist." And, indeed, it is true that the worldly philosophers have dominated the debate over the great social issues and policy determinations in the West in the last two hundred years. Now, however, an economist questions the necessity for the primacy of the economic over the rest of life in all its manifestations. He reminds us of the famous toast that J. M. Keynes gave to economists as "the guardians of the *possibilities* of civilization." He points to the neglected dimensions of life and urges us to move beyond a business civilization toward what humanists have called the fulfill-

[53] B. Glass, "Science: Endless Horizons or Golden Age?", *Science*, January 8, 1971, p. 27.
[54] "Economic Growth: New Doubts about an Old Ideal," *Time*, March 2, 1970, p. 72.

ment, or fulfilling, society—one in which the whole range of human potentialities may have expression.

The discipline of economics is generally thought to have been founded by a Scotch moralist, Adam Smith. There is a certain historical irony, therefore, in the fact that another moralist of indisputable Scotch ancestry should advise us to terminate "the age of the economist." In so doing, John Kenneth Galbraith simply urges his fellows of that venerable profession to return to its great tradition as the study of political economy.

Appendix

The Roper Survey

Concerning *The Affluent Society**

Herewith, in terms of percentage agreements and disagreements from Economists and Businessmen-Trustees, are the responses to Professor Galbraith's views on that major topic:

1. In an affluent society, such as we now enjoy in the U.S., our preoccupation with the continuing high-level production of material goods has become excessive.

	ECONOMISTS	TRUSTEES
Tend to agree	44%	38%
Tend to disagree	54	60
Undecided	2	2

2. The real reason for this country's continuing preoccupation with high production is not so much that we need all of the products themselves but more that we fear the unemployment which reduced production would bring.

	ECONOMISTS	TRUSTEES
Tend to agree	31%	22%
Tend to disagree	60	69
Undecided	9	9

3. With our present mastery of production, a supply of goods wholly adequate to consumer needs can now be produced in the United States at employment levels considerably below "full employment."

	ECONOMISTS	TRUSTEES
Tend to agree	47%	51%
Tend to disagree	47	31
Undecided	6	18

4. The present volume of production is maintained only by

* Reproduced from E. Roper, "Whose Affluent Society?", *Saturday Review*, June 6, 1959, p. 39, with the permission of the publisher. Copyright 1959, Saturday Review, Inc.

225

a "synthesis of desire" whereby consumers are led to consume a volume and variety of privately produced goods which is excessive.

	ECONOMISTS	TRUSTEES
Tend to agree	39%	31%
Tend to disagree	52	58
Undecided	9	11

5. Inflation, actual or threatened, is a constant and unavoidable concomitant of our preoccupation with high production and maintaining strong consumer demand.

	ECONOMISTS	TRUSTEES
Tend to agree	43%	36%
Tend to disagree	47	60
Undecided	10	4

6. Our preoccupation with high production also promotes a continuing social imbalance in American life whereby the private production of goods (automobiles, cosmetics, appliances, etc.) is kept at too high a level at the expense of the public production of services (adequate schools, parks, sanitation, public safety, etc.).

	ECONOMISTS	TRUSTEES
Tend to agree	52%	13%
Tend to disagree	41	78
Undecided	7	9

(This statement is the central thesis in the Galbraith work. It produces a heavy opinion split between the responding groups. A majority of Economists agrees that the imbalance exists, although there is a tendency to ascribe it to "this country's sense of values." A heavy majority of Businessmen-Trustees sees no "social imbalance"; they also oppose any action which would enlarge the sphere of governmental influence.)

7. A much more liberal form of unemployment compensation should be introduced which would provide the worker with a reasonably satisfactory substitute for total dependence on employment in the domain of private production.

	ECONOMISTS	TRUSTEES
Tend to agree	34%	2%
Tend to disagree	55	82
Undecided	11	16

8. Unemployment benefits should be high in times of high unemployment, and low when jobs are plentiful. For example, at an unemployment level of 4,000,000, the unemployed worker might receive a maximum of four-fifths of his last earned wage.

But at "full employment" (unemployment of 2,000,000 or less), the unemployed worker might receive half of his last wage.

	ECONOMISTS	TRUSTEES
Tend to agree	43%	22%
Tend to disagree	39	60
Undecided	18	18

9. A greatly expanded use of the sales tax by cities and states should supplement the present Federal income tax, for the avowed purpose of making private goods more expensive and public services more abundant.

	ECONOMISTS	TRUSTEES
Tend to agree	39%	33%
Tend to disagree	42	56
Undecided	19	11

10. It is the obligation of an affluent society to prevent the self-perpetuation of poverty by spending considerably more money than at present on schools and social services, to assure that no child will be deprived of physical health or full educational opportunity because of the poverty of his parents.

	ECONOMISTS	TRUSTEES
Tend to agree	79%	53%
Tend to disagree	14	31
Undecided	7	16

11. In an affluent society, work that has the connotations of pain, fatigue, boredom or other discomforts can and should be reduced to a minimum. The rapid expansion of a "New Class," to which work offers substantial personal and social rewards in addition to money income, should be a central goal of our society.

	ECONOMISTS	TRUSTEES
Tend to agree	63%	47%
Tend to disagree	16	38
Undecided	21	15

12. America's basic deficiency in facing the future is the inadequate cultivation and education of its human resources. We must therefore place less emphasis on material production and more on developing the applied intelligence and creativeness of our people.

	ECONOMISTS	TRUSTEES
Tend to agree	68%	53%
Tend to disagree	19	33
Undecided	13	14

A Selected

Bibliography

Allen, G. C., *Economic Fact and Fantasy,* Occasional Paper No. 14, 2nd Ed., London: The Institute of Economic Affairs, 1969.

Averitt, R. T., *The Dual Economy,* New York: W. W. Norton, 1968.

Bator, F. M., *The Question of Public Spending,* New York: Harper and Row, 1960.

Bottomore, T. B., *Critics of Society: Radical Thought in America,* New York: Vintage Books, 1969.

Boulding, K. E., *The Organizational Revolution: A Study in the Ethics of Economic Organization,* New York: Harper and Row, 1953.

————, *The Meaning of the Twentieth Century: The Great Transition,* New York: Harper and Row, 1964.

————, *Beyond Economics, Essays on Society, Religion and Economics,* Ann Arbor: University of Michigan Press, 1968.

Clark, J. M., *Competition as a Dynamic Process,* Washington, D.C.: Brookings Institution, 1961.

Downs, R. B., *Books That Changed America,* New York: Macmillan, 1970.

Dutton, F. C., *Changing Sources of Power, American Politics in the 1970's,* New York: McGraw-Hill Book Co., 1971.

Galbraith, J. K., *Economics, Peace and Laughter,* Boston: Houghton Mifflin, 1971. (For other titles by this author, see the text.)

Hansen, A. H., *The American Economy,* New York: McGraw-Hill, 1957.

Harrington, M., *The Other America: Poverty in the United States,* Baltimore, Md.: Penguin Books, 1963.

————, *Toward a Democratic Left,* New York: Macmillan, 1968.

Heilbroner, R. L., *The Limits of Capitalism,* New York: Harper and Row, 1967.

————, *Between Capitalism and Socialism,* New York: Vintage Books, 1970.

Hession, C. H., and H. Sardy, *Ascent to Affluence: A History of American Economic Development,* Boston: Allyn and Bacon, 1969.

Mermelstein, D., Ed., *Economics: Mainstream Readings and Radical Critiques,* New York: Random House, 1970.

Mishan, E. J., *The Costs of Economic Growth*, New York: Frederick A. Praeger, 1967.

Monsen, R. J., Jr., *Modern American Capitalism, Ideologies and Issues*, Boston: Houghton Mifflin, 1963.

Nieburg, H. L., *In the Name of Science*, Chicago: Quadrangle Books, 1970.

Nossiter, B., *The Myth-Makers, An Essay on Power and Wealth*, Boston: Houghton Mifflin, 1964.

Palamountain, J. C., Jr., *The Politics of Distribution*, Cambridge: Harvard University Press, 1955.

Potter, D. N., *People of Plenty, Economic Abundance and the American Character*, Chicago: University of Chicago Press, 1954.

Reich, C. A., *The Greening of America*, New York: Random House, 1970.

Shepherd, W. G., *Market Power and Economic Welfare*, New York: Random House, 1970.

Seeley, J., *The Americanization of the Unconscious*, New York: Science House, 1967.

Sievers, A. M., *Revolution, Evolution and The Economic Order*, Englewood Cliffs, N. J.: Prentice-Hall, 1962.

Weidenbaum, M. L., *The Modern Public Sector, New Ways of Doing the Government's Business*, New York: Basic Books, 1969.

Wilklus, D. H., and C. B. Friday, *The Economists of the New Frontier, An Anthology*, New York: Random House, 1963.

Winter, G., *Being Free, Reflections on America's Cultural Revolution*, New York: Macmillan, 1970.

Yarmolinsky, A., *The Military Establishment, Its Impacts on American Society*, New York: Harper and Row, 1971.

Zebot, C. A., *The Economics of Competitive Coexistence, Convergence through Growth*, New York: Frederick A. Praeger, 1964.

INDEX

Academic envy, Galbraith as victim of, 18

Acquisitive Society, The (Tawney), 199, 212

Adams, Walter, 49, 163–65, 176–80, 190–91

Advertising: demand creation through, 35, 79, 80, 98, 99, 103, 106, 107, 148, 182; historical perspective of role of, in American economy, 100–101; organic role of, in specific demand management, 148–49; critics of Galbraith's position on, 182, 183

Aesthetic criterion and the future, in Galbraithian vision of the economic process, 206–9; ideas on relationship between the industrial system and aesthetic experience, 206; criticism of Galbraith for introducing aesthetic considerations into economies, 207–8; artistic dimension as providing a criterion of order for society, 208–9; analysis of aesthetics and economics cast in sociological terms, 209

Affluent Society, The (Galbraith), 18, 26, 29, 60, 64–81, 148, 158, 168, 171, 183, 196, 200, 211, 218; ideological background against which it was written, 64–68; in its historical context, summary of theses of, 64–87; our legacy of economic despair, 68–74; inequality and insecurity as source of controversy, 74–76; the mystique of production, causes and consequences, 76–77; scarcity, natural and contrived, 77–79; the problems generated by economic attitudes in affluent society, 79–83; artificial creation of demand through advertising and high-pressure salesmanship, 79; inflation as problem of society infatuated with pro-

231

duction, 80–82; social imbalance as problem of the affluent society, 82–83, 97, 213, 218; and disenthralling ourselves about production as central concern of our lives, 83–87; chapter on "The New Position of Poverty," 85–86; labor and leisure in the affluent society, 86; chapter "On Security and Survival," 86–87; as best-seller, 89; semantic consequence of, for word "affluent," 89–90; included in *Books That Changed America*, 90; revised edition (1969), 130–31; and Galbraith's use of terms "affluence" and "affluent," 134; Elmo Roper's opinion poll on, 214–16, 225–27; echoes of ideas from, in the President's 1970 State of the Union message, 223

Affluent Society, The (Galbraith), and the critics, 88–134, 216; first assessments, 88–90; verdict of the popular journals, 90–92; the professionals bear down, 92–94; some foreign views, 94–95; the pros and cons of, 95–98; the dependence effect reconsidered, 98–106; social imbalance and its causes, 106–10; the disputed facts of social imbalance, 110–14; cultural and political context of social imbalance, 115–23; "the tyranny of small decisions," 123–29; treatment of poverty, 129–31; some unanticipated consequences of *The Affluent Society*, 131–34; creation of myth of American affluence, Galbraith accused of, 132–33

Age of the economist, 221–24; Galbraith's plea for termination of, and return of profession to its tradition as the study of political economy; 224

Aggregate demand regulation, in